Pamela Petro

lives in New England and daydreams about Wales. She is a frequent contributor to the *New York Times* Travel Section, and remains an enthusiastic, if slow, Welsh learner.

More from the reviews:

'An image and a mystery have stayed with me from this book. The image is startling. The author, a young woman, is lying on a hotel bed, face down, naked to the waist. She has lain like this ever since the Greek hotel manager breezed into her room early one morning and without so much as a by your leave, proceeded to give her a massage, yanking off her shorts and knickers in the process.

Her room-mate, another woman, looks on but says only 'Just what do you think you're doing to her?' And she, too stunned to say anything, just lies there counting to ten. After that image of Miss Petro's bum in air being manipulated by a total stranger, you might think nothing about her book will surprise you. And of course you could not be more wrong . . . It is wonderful and [written with] genuine Welsh emotion.'   BYRON ROGERS, *Spectator*

'Pamela Petro is the sort of writer you really look forward to meeting. Both entertaining and informative, she writes with such disarming frankness that you feel that you know every intimate quirk about her. She is perceptive and brilliant.'   LEELA DUTT, *Big Issue*

'She sees Welsh words as a series of molecules: 'they can be broken down and recreated, they perpetually change and adapt according to the linguistic environment'. Petro makes mutations in Welsh a central and brilliant theme in the book – "Welsh is like Silly Putty. You can stretch it and twist it and mould it into any number of shapes and it's still Welsh". She has understood the conceptual and political presuppositions behind the language and explains them in fresh and convincing ways. These are insights of which native speakers need to be reminded.'   GWYNETH LEWIS, *Planet*

'What are the defining characters of a nation? How does geographic distance and the use of a language effect one's sense of national identity? To be Welsh, does one have to be hospitable, musical, eloquent and enthusiastic? Perhaps it takes a foreigner to ask the question in the first place, as Pam Petro does in *Travels in an Old Tongue*. She is aptly named for 'pam' means 'why' in Welsh and 'why' is a question that dominates this account of a world tour searching for, and conversing haltingly with Welsh speakers in far flung destinations.

The spirit in which Petro undertakes the journey is very Welsh for one of the indisputable truths reflected in the book is that when Welsh people meet, they invariably seek to establish a connection through family ties or acquaintance. And there usually is one. Pamela Petro applies a global dimension to the task, searching for a way through the language barrier to connect with Welsh speakers who like herself are in self imposed exile. Their observations paint a fascinating portrait of a country, its language and people, viewed from the outside. Petro's journey across continents is imbued with an awareness of the bizarre nature of her quest, and is recounted with self-deprecating humour and honesty. The account is compelling reading as cultures and prejudices clash all over the world. *Travels in an Old Tongue* is suffused with a love of the Welsh language that is infectious.'
FFION JENKINS, *The Times*

'Indomitable Pam Petro... developing a romantic passion for the Welsh language... travels the world... with humour.'
JULIAN CRITCHLEY, *Daily Telegraph*

'Even if you have no comprehension of the language (only 18 per cent of Wales' inhabitants can speak Welsh) it is worth picking up Petro's witty and unique debut book.'
MELANIE TRAIN, *Geographical*

'The account of her global travels, written in a very bright, conversational style, is entertaining.'
South Wales Argus

'A wonderful, crazy travel book'
Chic

PAMELA PETRO

Travels in an Old Tongue

Touring the World Speaking Welsh

Flamingo
An Imprint of HarperCollinsPublishers

Flamingo
An Imprint of HarperCollins *Publishers*
77-85 Fulham Palace Road,
Hammersmith, London W6 8JB

Published by Flamingo 1998
9 8 7 6 5 4 3 2 1

First published in Great Britain by
HarperCollins *Publishers* 1997

ISBN 0 00 655010 X

Set in Bembo by
Rowland Phototypesetting Ltd,
Bury St Edmunds

Printed in England by Clays Ltd, St Ives plc

For my parents,
Patricia and Stephen Petro

The author and publishers of this work would like to express their gratitude to the following:

David Higham Associates for permission to quote 'The Sunset Song' from *Under Milk Wood* by Dylan Thomas; Gwydion Thomas for permission to quote R. S. Thomas' poem 'Something'; J. M. Dent & Sons for permission to quote 'The Small Window' and 'Welsh' from *Collected Poems 1945–1990* by R. S. Thomas; and Gwasg Gomer for permission to quote T. H. Parry-Williams' poem 'Hon' from *Poetry of Wales 1930–1970*; Meic Stephens for permission to quote Harri Webb's poem 'Ode to The Severn Bridge'.

Acknowledgments

I would like to thank everyone whose brainstorming helped to create my itinerary, especially Chris Rees of the Welsh Language Teaching Centre at the University of Wales, David Thorne of the Welsh Department at the University of Wales, Lampeter, Arturo Roberts, editor of *Ninnau*, Arturo Lowndes, John Barnie, editor of *Planet*, Irene Williams, Heulwen James, the Wales Tourist Board, and Cymru a'r Byd. Thanks also to Mark, Ereig, Sian, and the crowd at The Cellar for getting my ear ready.

No group deserves more credit for this book than the Welsh-speakers around the world who had the patience to endure my halting conversation. I'd also like to thank all the gracious people who opened their lives and homes and kitchens to us, with special gratitude to the Imadegawa family of Tokyo for putting up with us with such good humour for so long. Heartfelt thanks to Rebecca Ferguson, Margaret Huws, the Helset family of Norway, Lynn Edwards (for missing his golf game), Iori Roberts, the Mercat family, Boyd Williams, Nesta Pierry, Philip Jonathan, Rhiannon Barrar and Ed Sides, Geoff Poyson, the Harvie family, Heinz Fröehls, Bethan Kilfoil, Eleri and John Roberts, Keith Pritchard, Eirlys and Pat, Liz Shepherd, Kittipat Jeamsripong and his sister, Leonie Vejjajiva, Rose and Masa Iwata, Catherine Nagashima, Laura Lockwood, Alex Mackay-Smith, Lawrence John, Ruth Davies, Takeshi Koike, Valeri Irianni, Rona Davies, Elena Arnold, Luned, Moelona and Tegai Roberts and their families, and Gwilym Roberts. Thanks as well to members of the Welsh societies of Paris, the Netherlands, Belgium, Singapore, Bangkok and Tokyo, and to the members of the Welsh-L on the Internet and the library staff of the University of Wales, Lampeter (especially Kathy Miles), who unselfishly answered all my arcane questions.

On the home front, thanks to Pam Kimel for being one fine travel agent, to Heidi Dix for her heroic physical labours, to my parents and aunt and uncle for their letters and for giving up Cape time for the sake of this book, to my brothers and sisters-in-law for their generosity, to Mary Diaz for showing up in London and Verona, to Beth Sullivan and Martha Evans for the scope of their knowledge, to Dick Newman for all the Welsh arcana over the years, and to Tom Ferguson for his unwaffling hospitality. I'd also like to acknowledge Jody Alesandro, Janet Piorko and Nancy Newhouse of the *New York Times* Travel staff, as well as editors Jackson Mahaney, Anne Diffily and Tom Swick: without their assignments the trip would not have been possible. And to the nuts and bolts people stateside, Bill Rae and Lora Urbanelli, and Paula and Casey Knynenburg: thanks for paying all those bills.

A most important thank you to Philip Gwyn Jones of HarperCollins, not only for subscribing to *Planet* and taking the initiative to contact me, but for his confidence, enthusiasm and patience.

Finally, thanks to Marguerite Harrison, for, among other things, enduring Panjim at 3 a.m. and the Trelew bus station. Without her help I'd still be trying to unlock my backpack in London.

Contents

PROLOGUE

Something to bring back to show
you have been there: a lock of God's
hair, stolen from him while he was
asleep; a photograph of the garden
of the spirit. As has been said,
the point of travelling is not
to arrive, but to return home
laden with pollen you shall work up
into the honey the mind feeds on.

R. S. THOMAS
'Somewhere'

Dechrau ❧ to Begin

'*Pam*, Pam?'

It could be irony or it could be destiny, but either way my name means Why? in Welsh. My full name, Pamela, smacks of tea and foxhounds.

There's an episode of *I Love Lucy* in which Lucy dresses up in riding gear and fakes an English accent to impress Ricky's friends. Her assumed name, of course, is Pamela. *PAHM-ula*, that is, sprung from the mouth with the velocity of a ping-pong ball shot from a toy gun. Now hear a Welsh person speak my name, and the tidy hierarchy of syllables goes right out the window. There's an anarchic pulse to *PAM-eL-A* that I like much better. My name becomes a quick trip over the hills on a sled in winter. It's a less efficient way of calling me, but imagine what that extra syllabic beat does for the musculature of the tongue.

The most efficient way to get my attention is to shout 'Pam!', which is what I've answered to for most of my thirty-five years, but which over the past decade or so has become that nagging 'Why?' question as well. 'Why are you doing this?' I wondered to myself in 1983, when I turned down a job in Washington, DC to go to the smallest university in Britain – the University of Wales, Lampeter – to get a master's degree in something called 'The Word and the Visual Imagination'.

'Just why did you say you're doing this?' my friends wanted to know in 1987, when after two years back in the States I enrolled in a Welsh language class at Harvard.

'But why are you doing this, Pam? Why do you need to spend a summer working on your *Welsh*?' my family asked in 1992, in a tone of supportive desperation that they've become very good at, when I returned to Lampeter to spend two months in a seven-days-a-week intensive Welsh language class in a Portakabin, on the hockey pitch, in the rain.

I don't know. Maybe when I first went to Wales and unwittingly enrolled in an English department, the old Welsh god of Irony vowed to teach me a lesson and made me besotted with the place and its language (I made up the god of Irony, but there really is an old Celtic god of Panic, who comes in handy in cases of both travel and language study). To tell the truth, I really can't say why my desire to continue learning Welsh got so out of hand that I chose to pursue it on a five-month, fourteen-country crusade around the world. Perhaps I had a premonition of what Ursula Imadegawa would tell me in Tokyo. 'Pam,' she said, leaning against her kitchen counter about to hand me a glass of Johnnie Walker Black with pink and purple plastic ice cubes floating in it, 'you only regret what you don't do.'

I suppose the rejoinder to Ursula's wisdom is that I haven't flown a jet or pierced my eyebrows or gotten married yet, and I'm not racing off to do any of those things for fear of potential regret. So it's '*Pam*, Pam?' again: Why travel around the world when I could just as easily – and for a great deal less money – go back to Wales to study Welsh?

There are two answers to this question. One is, simply, that I like to travel and make up shameless excuses to do so. The other is that learning Welsh is like digging a hole in the sand. You make a dent at first, but as you bore deeper you encounter a frustrating snag of nature called the angle of repose; you can only dig so far before new sand spills in from the top, eternally preventing your hole from getting any bigger. All you wind up with is grit under your fingernails. It's the same with me and Welsh: whenever I try to practise Welsh in Wales I get only so far before English comes spilling in from all sides.

The fact of the matter is that the principality of Wales is buried beneath the verbal tonnage of English. Of Wales's nearly three million inhabitants – compared to around five million apiece for Ireland and Scotland, and 48 million for England – only about 18 per cent, or some 540,000 people, speak Welsh. And these folks are fluent in English as well. Now imagine waiting your turn at a post office in rural Wales. Behind you is a line that winds out the front door, peopled with old men in tweed jackets and ties, leaning heavily on identical canes and making preliminary retching sounds in their gullets; redolent farmers with manure-caked Wellingtons; a mother with three uncontrollable children; and at least one old woman struggling beneath the weight of a heavy shipping box. Your turn comes and you approach the window. The clerk raises his eyebrows in efficient expectation of your request. Do you say: 'Um, *bore da.*' Clear your throat. 'Um, *gaf fi*, no, um, *gai*, uh, *bruny stamp*, um, *os gwellwch chi'n dda?*' Or do you say, 'Good morning. May I have a stamp please?'

If you are a worthy and courageous language learner, you do the former, and sweat, and hold people up, and tell yourself it's for a good cause. If you're a coward like me, you backslide on to the easy cushion of English. I imagine that giving in to the majority language is a lot like drowning. The familiar words, like the waves, come as a relief when they finally wash down your windpipe once you've decided to quit the struggle. But you lose big both ways.

Like Basque or Breton or Catalan, Welsh is a minority language, and it takes fierceness and mental blinkers to learn it by pretending that you and the person with whom you're practising really don't share another language – say French or Spanish or English – in which you are both perfectly fluent. The essential wink and nod between you is a fragile conceit, and it usually invites its hangers-on, self-consciousness, the giggles and a sense of unreality, to come and enjoy the struggle.

I'm not saying it's impossible to learn Welsh in Wales; plenty of people do it every day. But because I'm gutless in crowded post offices, because Welsh-speakers tend to be indulgent with

American learners and hold us to lower standards than their fellow countrymen, and because a five-hundred-year-old blanket of English is pinned tightly to the land, I've had a hell of a time. The truth is, I got so infuriated with myself one day in 1992, when after five years of semi-serious study I still couldn't conduct a coherent telephone conversation in Welsh, that a radical thought came to me. I'd heard there was a mother-lode of Welsh-speakers in Argentina whose other tongue was Spanish – a language in which I knew only menu words like guacamole and burrito; but suppose there were Welsh-speakers in other non-English-speaking countries as well? If they existed, they had to be pretty unusual people. That was a plus. If they didn't speak English, I'd have to speak to them in Welsh. That was scary. And even if they turned out to be bilingual Welsh expatriates, they and I might prove less likely to succumb to the high tide of English than we would in Wales, the nearest moon orbiting the planet England, where the gravitational pull of the imperial language is harder to resist. By visiting Welsh-speakers in places such as Norway and France, Germany, Belgium, Holland, Singapore, Thailand, Japan and Argentina, I'd have an unheard-of opportunity to use Welsh as an international language. Even better, I'd get to travel around the world.

The mere thought brought on goosebumps. Could it be, I wondered, that the Old Man of Pencader was wrong? He's the cheeky devil who foresees the future for Henry II of England at the end of Gerald of Wales's twelfth-century travel guide to his native land. Henry asks the Old Man what he thinks of the Welsh army's chances against the English (an impertinent question, even from a king). The Old Man replies with dignity, 'Whatever else may come to pass, I do not think that on the Day of Direst Judgement any race other than the Welsh, or any other language, will give answer to the Supreme Judge of all for this small corner of the earth.'

God give me such self-possession in the face of kings (the irony is that Henry would have asked his question in French – another language that makes me weak at the knees). Now I didn't doubt the Old Man of Pencader's prediction, but, I thought, maybe the Supreme Judge should just get his ear ready to hear accounts of Oslo, Tokyo and Buenos Aires in Welsh as well.

Of course, all this was just pub talk. I never expected any of it to happen, and spent the next three years wallowing like a happy sow in the murk of American English.

Paratoi ✱ to Prepare

Mind you, I didn't quite abandon the idea either. I took to baiting the bio-lines of articles I wrote for the Welsh journal *Planet* with the bare bones of my scheme – more to prove to readers that I had an association with Wales than anything else. Then one day I got a letter from Philip Gwyn Jones, *Planet* subscriber, Welshman and HarperCollins editorial director, who thought it might be a good idea. Six months later he called to say that my travelling the world in search of Welsh-speakers – not to mention questing after the language itself – was officially a good idea and, well, *bon voyage*.

To say I was not prepared is like saying the *Titanic* didn't expect an iceberg that night. Philip had called in January; the earliest I could possibly leave for the world was June, the same time my friend and housemate Marguerite, a bilingual Brazilian-American, was due to finish her doctoral dissertation on Brazilian fiction. By then she'd be PhD'd but jobless. I invited her to come along. You never knew, I pointed out, when we might run into a pack of Welsh-Portuguese speakers, whereupon her presence would be invaluable. She agreed, we drank a bottle of champagne, then we became devotees of the god of Panic.

While Marguerite wrote night and day about fictional Brazilians I hunted the Welsh. My strategy was to find address lists of all the Welsh societies in exotic (that is, non-English-speaking) spots around the world and write to them. Simple enough, but procuring the lists took time. The daffodils were up before I was actually addressing letters to the Mashonaland Cambrian Society in Harare, Zimbabwe and the St David's Society of Singapore, among thirty-four others.

In March I made a brief foray to New York to try to persuade newspaper and magazine editors to assign me enough travel stories to pay for the trip. One night after a long day of wheedling I met my friends Mary and Tom at Tom's office. They'd just hooked up to the World Wide Web and he wanted to show us how cool it was. 'See if it does anything with "Welsh",' I asked. He pressed some keys and in moments had overcome the space–time continuum.

'Here's something.'

The screen held a message from the *Clwb Cymraeg* – the Welsh Club – of the Shimizu Girls' Junior High School in Shimizu City, Japan. They were looking for Welsh-language pen pals.

'Now that's just plain weird,' said Mary. 'But it looks as if you're in business.' I felt like I'd finally made contact with aliens. So they were out there after all. We were high above Central Park late at night and the lights of Manhattan receded from our office tower like a distant galaxy. The three of us were chartreuse with the green glow of the Japanese schoolgirls' message. 'Well *duw, duw,*' I murmured to myself, astonished, in the idiomatic Welsh equivalent of a good slap on the thigh.

The trouble with finding the Shimizu *Clwb Cymraeg* was that I had to write back to its members in Welsh. The Welsh part was the problem. After speaking it poorly but daily in the summer of 1992 I'd returned home to Providence, Rhode Island and my Welsh had gone fallow. Since more people in Rhode Island probably speak Pig Latin than know Welsh exists, practice opportunities were at a minimum.

I dug out my old cassettes and repeated the *ABC of Welsh* in the car. Every night as I made dinner a man correctly guessed 'Ella Fitzgerald' on the Welsh version of *Name That Tune* and

Hurricane Andrew slammed into Florida as people were evacuated from their homes (I'd taped the news in Welsh off Radio Wales three years earlier; consequently at dinnertime in my kitchen it was perpetually 24 August 1992). I was never bored listening. Other things happened that day as well – I think mortgage rates rose and there was a sailing accident off Llandudno – but come May all this was still new to me, since I couldn't quite figure out what the announcer was saying. Surveys have shown that about half of all native Welsh-speakers can't understand the news either, so I didn't despair.

But I did need speaking practice. Tom's computer in New York had also turned up an on-line Welsh course that went out to hundreds of learners around the world. Remarkably, the guy who produced it lived about ten minutes away from me in East Providence. The world was shrinking and I hadn't even found affordable luggage yet. I looked him up in the phone book and we agreed I'd come over on a Thursday evening to speak Welsh.

Mark Nodine is an American computer jockey who visited Wales once on a two-week vacation and decided to learn the language. That seemed excessive even to me. I imagined he could speak rings around me and downed a big glass of wine to lure my vocabulary out of its usual cocoon before appearing on his doorstep with a bunch of supermarket daffodils. Mark was waiting for me. He projected earnestness and clean living. I sucked in my breath after the prerequisite *Noswaith dda* – Good evening – so he wouldn't smell the wine. My stomach ached.

I sat on his sofa and he drew up a chair. He spoke. I tilted my head like a parrot. He spoke again and I tilted again, smiling mightily. I couldn't understand a word he said. His vocabulary seemed arcane and his rhythm – the syncopated, palpitating heart-beat of the Welsh language – fell into a monotone like the pulse of a long-distance runner. I, meanwhile, had rhythm. Sometimes I even had music. But I could ask my Welsh language memory for nothing more than an occasional unconjugated verb followed

9

by an inblown hiss of winy breath. Forty-five unintelligible minutes later I suddenly remembered an important phone call I had to make. On the way out Mark told me he'd learned Welsh from the Bible.

'I didn't understand a word. Do you hear me? Not a single word,' I cried to Marguerite later, clutching the rest of the Merlot.

'But you've been studying all the time.' She looked concerned.

'Get this,' I whimpered, 'he learned Welsh by reading the Bible. Can you believe that? Jeez, the Bible! And now he's creating this mega Welsh vocabulary program on the computer. How does he have time for that? He's got a job. He's got a wife and kids. Man, I hate that.'

'So he probably speaks in Welsh thees and thous and uses verbs like smite. How could you possibly understand him?'

Coulda shoulda woulda, I thought darkly, but time for fear was running out. I painstakingly wrote the Shimizu girls. Marguerite spent Easter weekend summing up her thoughts on Brazilian fiction. Responses from Welsh societies began to trickle in: a Welsh Studies Centre in Germany would be happy to see me, same with the Paris Welsh, and the Dutch. A hearty invitation arrived from the Argentinians. No word from Asia, but for a letter from a very old Japanese Celticist who was in the hospital with pulmonary emphysema. He wrote wishing me luck from his hospital bed. The Mashonaland letter came back from Zimbabwe stamped 'Return to Sender'. The travel agent demanded an audience.

'You can't go below the equator,' she said matter-of-factly.

'Why?'

'It's just a hemisphere thing. Most round-the-world packages don't.'

'That discriminates against Brazil,' said Marguerite.

'You'll have to buy a separate ticket from New York to Buenos Aires, but now you have more immediate concerns. You have to choose your round-the-world route today.'

With less than half the response letters in, selecting an air path was like taking so many shots in the dark. We closed our eyes, drew our travel bow and shot: New York–London–Paris–Frankfurt– Athens–Frankfurt–Bombay–Singapore–Bangkok–Tokyo–Hong Kong–Tokyo–New York, followed by New York–Buenos Aires-Rio-New York. For better or worse, it was done. We were committed.

Then life speeded up. The director of the language course I'd attended in Lampeter sent me names and addresses of all the overseas learners who'd attended the programme in the past two years: it seemed Poles, Germans, Swedes, South Africans and Argentinians have all been flocking to Lampeter. I'd already heard something about Welsh being taught in a high school in Poland, and fired off a letter to Gdańsk. A last-minute invitation arrived from the Oslo Welsh, and I added another leg to the trip. Marguerite defended her dissertation. Hurricane Andrew beat the hell out of Florida every night in the kitchen. Mark called and told me (in English) about the 'Welsh-L', a Welsh-language chat group on the Internet and advised me to get E-mail.

This entailed wrestling a modem into my computer, which brought out a vindictive streak in its software. Over the next week it fought my every attempt to master the art of E-mail, by which I hoped to keep in touch with my editors, my brother, and the over four hundred yakkity Welsh-speakers who monopolized my E-mail box.

In the last, frantic days before we left I began to feel as if I were learning two languages at once: one, the synaptic slang of the twenty-first century, the very cutting edge of computer-speak itself; the other, possibly the oldest language in Europe, a contemporary version of Brythonic, the tongue that had been brought to the island of Great Britain around 600 BC (some argue for an even earlier date, around 2000 BC), and which, along with Basque, is the only language in Western Europe to have been spoken before, during and after the fall of the Roman Empire. It was a sweet, strange moment when I finally managed to unite the two on my computer screen.

This is the gist of one of the first messages I received on the Welsh-L (Welsh, Breton and Cornish are the official languages of the discussion group; English is tolerated, but frowned upon):

> Sir John Morris-Jones, after a series of tests, has ascertained that the proportion of Welshmen who pronounce the double-L on the right side of the tongue, as compared to those who pronounce it on the left, is three to one.

Dychmygu ✿ to Imagine

Unlike most travel narratives this is not a book about place but a book about language. Can a language be said to describe a place, a place the language that is spoken there? Is it possible to travel to many different places and arrive, not back home, but in the terra incognita of a new language? And just where might that be?

I've travelled to Brazil with Marguerite but I don't speak Portuguese. While we were there she read the signs, laughed at the jokes, and got drawn into the *novelas*, or nightly soap operas, that hold the country enrapt. I stared at the outcroppings of abrupt, conical hills that pock Rio de Janeiro and felt I'd slipped into the iconic backdrop of a medieval painting; I was consumed by the tangy tastes and smells of the place. Did my country of the viscera have the same boundaries as hers of the mind? Stumps me.

If these questions were simply knotty in Brazil they're absolutely bound, gagged and tortured in Wales, where 82 per cent of the population does not speak Welsh. Are these English-speaking Welshwomen and -men just tourists in their homeland, as I was a tourist in Brazil, because they can't read the old poets, hold a government teaching post or watch the nightly soap opera *Pobl y Cwm* (*People of the Valley*)? Hardly. And yet ... There is no self-governing political entity on earth that corresponds to Wales: it is not, to use geo-political terms, an historical nation. A leading

Welsh academic, Gwyn A. Williams, wrote a book called *When Was Wales?* Might as well ask *why* is Wales? Because that's where the sheep are? Because that's where it rains all the time? Because that's where Welsh is spoken?

Look at the two names of this twice-spoken-for land. 'Wales' comes from an old Saxon word meaning something like Place of the Romanized Foreigners. It's an audacious etymology: around the fifth century AD Saxon invaders moved into Britain and called the inhabitants foreigners. They subdued most of the southern half of the island, and what they couldn't they called Wales. The word *Cymru* – the Welsh name for Wales – was born around the year 580 in reaction to these events. The unconquered people who spoke Brythonic, the ancestor to Welsh as Anglo-Saxon is to English, called their bit of high, rough, western Britain *Cymru*, or the Home of Fellow Countrymen (the word *Cymry* means Welshmen). As late as the 1180s, Gerald of Wales – ironically writing in Latin – noted, 'To this day our country continues to be called Wales and our people Welsh, but these are barbarous terms.'

Surely *Cymru* and Wales are two different places. They must be, for the languages that contain them, Welsh and English, hold such vastly different memories. In Wales the shorn flanks of the great, catapulting hills and the mottled pasturelands of the valleys are a consolation prize; in *Cymru* they're home. To be a traveller in this place I love, which is all I claim to be – I'm hardly a linguist, I'm not even good at languages – it's not enough to be led by the senses as I was in my tourist guise in Brazil. I want to break through the space–time continuum too, the way Tom did on his computer in New York, and travel into Wales's past, its humour, its spirit, as well as its landscape. The only way I can think to do that, to get beyond Wales into *Cymru*, is to have a command of the Welsh language and the memories it holds within it.

Cue back to the god of Irony. To accomplish this, for me, the language coward, means leaving the geographic country behind in search of its invisible, verbal progeny in Europe, Asia and South America. Only by travelling everywhere but Wales can I hope to find my way to *Cymru*.

Equally ironic, however, is the fact that the Welsh language is in no way mine to have. There simply is no verb meaning 'to have', in the sense of 'to possess', in Welsh. Plane tickets, maps, languages even, are only 'with you', as if by their consent, implying that they, like much of the isle of Britain, are perhaps once and future possessions to be taken away at a moment's notice. To say 'I have language' is to mean, 'There is language with me' – *Mae iaith gyda fi*. This pattern of having things 'with you' seems to me a grammar built on loss and impermanence, the linguistic heritage of the defeated. English, by comparison, is supremely confident in its sense of possession.

Which one will I use, I wonder uneasily, as Marguerite and I hoist our packs and slip on our sensible German walking shoes and begin searching the world for *Cymru*?

PART ONE

Ewrob (Europe)

CYMRU (WALES)

Siarad ✺ to Speak

I have laryngitis. Not the low, burnt-sugar kind that people find so sexy, but the hissy, rasping kind that sounds as if I've been garrotted and just escaped with my life. No one wants to hear me talk for long in any language, which is a blessing.

We've decided to begin the trip in Wales after all, in hopes of tapping the Welsh diaspora at its source, which is doubtless the cause of my illness; any minute now someone's bound to speak to me in Welsh, and since that's precisely the point of this book it would behove me to respond in kind. I blow an inward kiss to my vocal cords.

It happens in the post office.

Tim Evans, the clerk at the far window, spies me and does a slow-motion doubletake. His eyes go as round as his face and blink in mock horror. I bat my lids a few times. This game has been going on since 1984. When my turn comes Tim's window is free, and I steel myself for the inevitable.

'*Wel, wel*' – his voice is clear and sweet as jelly and rippling with amusement – '*sut mae, 'te?*' Relief. He's leading with a simple howdy-do that doubles as a tease and a welcome back.

'*Da iawn, diolch. A sut dych chi?*' I lie that I'm fine and inquire about him, exaggerating the '*chi*' to show that I, too, consider this Welsh exchange a game between old friends. So far the pleasantries are a breeze, though mine sounds like a cat being strangled under a pillow.

Tim launches his eyebrows. '*Laryngitis?*'

I nod and explain in embryonic Welsh that I'm in Lampeter to do research for my book. Before he can reply I switch to English and hiss, 'And to practise Welsh, of course. After my throat gets better. And I need to send these postcards.'

'Psychosomatic, then, is it?' He plays the syllables of 'psychosomatic' like valves on a trumpet: up, down, up, down, up. Tim and I go back to my master's degree days, when I slipped into the unfortunate habit of mailing letters without stamps. That and my American accent earned me a high profile in the post office, as did the fact that I kept coming back. Most students leave Lampeter for good after graduation; not only did I return, I returned often, and from America. That was counted as odd indeed. After each two- or three-year interval I'd walk into the *Swyddfa'r Post*, as it's known in this Welsh-speaking market town, and Tim would greet me with, 'So, back again, are you?' or, louder, playing to the populace, 'Well, if it isn't the crazy American.' But since my intensive Welsh course in the summer of 1992, held across the street at the College, we try to speak in *Cymraeg*. In very short sentences. For very short intervals.

'I want to make you a deal,' I propose.

The eyebrows rise again.

'I'll buy you lunch if you'll speak to me exclusively in Welsh for at least an hour.' This is a bold move, as we've never met outside the post office before.

Tim is a big man, Pavarotti-size at least. And he's a tenor as well, with two albums out on which he sings almost exclusively in Welsh. I figure food is a strong temptation.

'An offer I can't refuse, I see.' He smiles and his features bed down on a cushion of dimples. We agree on a date for next week.

I'm procrastinating, I know, but hey, I'm sick.

Tim Evans is one of only a handful of townspeople I know in Lampeter, which is odd considering I've spent at least twenty-eight months of my life here. By 'here' I mean any one of the three Lampeters: the Town, the College – formerly St David's University College, now the University of Wales, Lampeter – or the

Concept. This last, when referred to with equal parts vexation, perplexity and grudging affection by an inhabitant of either of the former, usually means something like the gulf that exists between them.

Lampeter the town is primarily Welsh-speaking, and therefore officially *Llanbedr Pont Steffan* (six syllables, which together beat out the Church of St Peter at Stephen's Bridge); the College is essentially English-speaking but for the Welsh Department. The town, with its two new traffic lights and three main streets (two of which describe the upper and lower ends of the same trajectory), is a regional hub of around two thousand people. One of the college porters once confessed to me that his wife, a local farm girl now in her sixties, has never gotten over moving to town three years ago. City folk, she claims, just aren't as friendly. The College, meanwhile, thrives like anaerobic bacteria on its sense of deprivation. It was founded in 1823 to keep young Welsh lads bound for the Anglican church out of reach of Oxford's corrupting pleasures. Today, however, most of its staff and students are English expatriates, who gather together as on a deserted island and yearn in maudlin drunkenness for Thai food and foreign films.

These disparities are contained within a simple geography. To the eye Lampeter is plain. The nose is a more reliable guide to its charms: the acrid shiver of coal smoke on damp mornings; an oily stench outside Jones's Butchers that seeps into the pores; the rush of old beer leaking from the pubs; frying oil; the smell of the sea when the wind is from the west; fertilizer; wet wool; incense from the whole-food and hippie shops; fresh baked Welsh cakes; newsprint; cheap cosmetics. The only eye-marker in town is a bald hill behind the College crowned with a tuft of trees at the very top, like a perpetual, green mushroom cloud. From the crest a sheepscape of pastureland ribbons toward the horizon in all directions.

Till now I've spent most of my time here speaking English among the academic crowd, the majority of whom find my smittenness with the Welsh language a little unseemly. Their

Welsh, gleaned over decades of opening the campus's bilingual doors and parking in its bilingual lots, is of the utilitarian or *Dim Parcio* (No Parking) variety. They've all picked up enough to know that Welsh actually has vowels – unlike those who express amazement at my wanting to learn a language composed exclusively of consonants – but that's about as far as their skills go. I forgive them: they've got other things on their minds. No other group of my acquaintance, anywhere in the world, is as prone to divorce, alcoholism, suicide, murder, anorexia, romantic malingering, unwanted pregnancies, nervous breakdowns and hauntings as my pals in this academic, rural idyll.

Today I can't walk across campus without exploding one emotional landmine after another. Coming toward me from the library is an acquaintance whose path since we last met has been crossed by murder, attempted suicide and divorce. I want to sympathize but don't know how, so I duck back into the Canterbury building only to bump into an old friend whose wife, also a close friend, just confessed to me that her nervous breakdown is abating, but she still sees disembodied eyes when she's tired. From him I learn that their marriage is on the rocks. Dinner at the Indian restaurant seems a hazardous idea, but I agree anyway.

In the library the talk is of Mr Ryder, the old librarian, who despite his death last month nevertheless continues to prowl the stacks shelving books.

This may seem callow, but I confess that Lampeter's dark eccentricities have long been what's lured me to the place. Everyone likes to be touched by lunacy now and again, and Lampeter is my source of the stuff. Its fecundity in the department of recklessness and whimsy is legendary: a friend of mine, on his first day on campus, was kidnapped by students in pith helmets and genially held hostage down a manhole. I spent my first week here locked in an old library with eight people I'd never met before, preparing an exhibition of incunabula: it was days before I learned that the word meant nothing more sinister than books printed before 1500. Naked man have been spotted chasing pigs down the main street, rugby players have been seen in make-up, and I, before I became sane, have been known to speed along country roads at night through barricades of mist with my headlights switched off, just for the hell of it.

Over time, however, whimsy has grown a sharp edge. I'm now an occasional visitor from across the sea, and find myself on the threshold of voyeurism. Acquaintances die in car crashes and friends have nervous breakdowns. Now it's language that gives me my fix of loopy thrills. Welsh – a tongue few speak and fewer understand, with vowel sounds so rich I'd swear they have calories – is the grown-up corollary to all that attractive eccentricity and slight touch of peril. (The Welsh word for danger is *perygl*, testimony to the occupation of Wales by one Latinizing army or another – the Romans or the Normans, I forget which, both were liberal with seed vocabulary – and the nature of the words that followed in their wake.)

For me learning Welsh is a way of growing up, though few people may see it that way. I make appointments to meet with members of the Welsh department to discuss my book, grab Marguerite, who's been in the library trying to avoid Mr Ryder, and head home.

Ymarfer ✿ to Practise

'Home' for now means Dolwerdd, my friend Rebecca's bungalow on a sheep farm a mile or so out of town. It's a little cube of a house set amid a wayward grid of vivid green sheep pastures, marked off from one another by dark windbreaks and low, shrubby hedgerows. The air smells of sweet earth and sheep. A hay-swaddling machine is busy in the next field over, snatching up Swiss rolls like a diabolical gift-wrapping device and imprisoning them in black plastic.

'Looks like you got mail.' Marguerite gingerly scoops up several envelopes lying in the hall near the birthing box of Rebecca's cat, Usurper, who's just had kittens.

'Hey, you hit the jackpot. Someone named Ursula – look, she writes in green marking pen – invites you to stay with her in Tokyo. You'd better tell her you're travelling with a friend.'

I nod.

'What's this?' She shows me a letter with a red dragon on it.

'*Cymdeithas Dewi Sant Singapura*,' I rasp, 'the St David's Society of Singapore.'

'. . . will be delighted to meet you. And it seems that a man named Lynn is picking you up at the Oslo airport, but you'll be staying with a woman named Rosemary, who reputedly speaks Welsh "with music in her voice".'

This is good news, but I worry that all the letters are in English. Maybe I won't find Welsh-speakers out there. Then I worry that I will. Then I remember my growing fears about my Welsh comprehension ability. I decide to watch S4C for a while.

S4C is *Sianel Pedwar Cymru*, Channel Four Wales; it is also work. For a learner the Welsh-language television station is about the farthest thing on earth from entertainment. I start to reminisce about watching the strong-man competition back in 1992, a prime-time show in which beefy guys named Davy and Hywel would hold a row of four bricks at arm's length for as long as they could – not much more than a minute, as I recall – before they began to shake, sweat and drop them, but Marguerite shushes me and points at my throat.

On TV a shrill children's programme is in progress. A loud-mouth, shrieking maniac of a host is tossing kids into something that looks like a vat of unformed jelly. Beneath my comprehension, I decide with relief. Alas, *Heno*, a news magazine which means 'Tonight', is not. Most of it goes over my head. It's followed by *Pobl y Cwm*, which has ensnared Marguerite although she understands not a word. From seven to seven-thirty we both stare fixedly at the screen, trying to crack the code. A blonde woman and her husband (?) seem perturbed by a delivery of coal. There's trouble brewing at the hair salon, and someone's in a funk at the estate agent's.

'Are those two supposed to be engaged?'

I have no idea but I don't want to admit it. 'Uh huh. But these people are terrible mumblers, so I can't be sure.' I'm feeling very discouraged.

'What's with that couple and the coal? Is it some kind of conspiracy?'

'Who knows? Maybe somebody's buried in it. Wait! That guy just said, "Come over tomorrow around three." I understood that!'

'See, you're getting it,' she says brightly. I don't know if I'd call one phrase in half an hour cause for celebration, but at least I go to bed with the rhythm of the language pounding in my ears, beating time to the night rain. *Mae'n bwrw hen wraggedd a ffyn.* My brain chugs it out in nine counts, over and over and over. It's raining old women and sticks.

Chwilio ✺ to Search

An odd thing sometimes happens to me when I'm walking in Wales. Without warning a chip breaks off the corner of my mind's eye and goes careening up and away, faster and faster – I can almost feel the rush in the depths of my stomach – until it stops in space and turns back to show me myself as a dot on a tiny bump protruding from an island on the north-western corner of the map of Europe. It seems such a funny place for me to be.

I lose my gravity like this on the way to Irene Williams's house. The sun is shining as if Lampeter were the bloody Caribbean. As ever, I'm the only one in sunglasses (my 'most American' affectation, according to Welsh sources). Wales, this land of tumultuous, messy clouds that bank around the heavens like airborne glaciers, is lazing today under a faultless blue sky. It bothers me.

This morning I've been hard on the trail of far-flung Welsh-speakers, gleaning addresses and telephone numbers. One is Hiroshi Mizutani – who's also known by his bardic name, Hywel Glyndŵr – a former visiting professor at Lampeter who teaches Welsh at the University of Nagoya in Japan. Another is a Dutch woman named Effie Wiltens, a pilot and fellow Welsh nut, described to me for the second time in a month as a 'real character' who's learned to speak Welsh like a native, and whom I 'must meet'. This time, I realize, my unbidden bird's-eye view has a purpose. It's set up the board on which we'll soon start playing global connect-the-dots for real. From what I understand, Irene Williams is what Hollywood would call a 'major player' in the dot game.

Mrs Williams comes recommended as a walking address book of the world's Welsh. Her house is just out of town, past the Cwmann Tavern on the Carmarthen Road ('Cwmann', by the way, isn't a typo; it relies on the perfectly respectable Welsh vowel 'w' to give it the sound 'Coo-man'). Mrs Williams is a lively sprite of a woman in her seventies, wearing striped trousers and a seed necklace. I whisper an apology for my laryngitis as we take seats in her torturously sunny solarium, and tell her I'm hunting foreign Welsh-speakers and expatriates.

'So, dear, you're American. Pardon me for asking, but I've never understood why your country won't forgive Cuba for those old missiles.'

This is unexpected. I explain that I haven't been able to understand it either, but forgo putting my sunglasses on. They suddenly seem way too *American*. Instead I winch my eyes into slits and begin to leak little tears.

Irene's husband is Professor of Theology at Lampeter, and she acts as a kind of godmother to the curious lot of foreign students who show an interest in learning Welsh. Takeshi Koike, a student of Hiroshi Mizutani's, is one of her favourites. She waves his Christmas card at me and I copy the address.

'He was here for ten months and when he left he was fluent

in Welsh. It helped that he played guitar at church. Every Saturday night he'd come over and we'd practise Welsh hymns. He even appeared in all-Welsh theatre productions. Are you all right, dear?'

I think I've groaned involuntarily, remembering Mark Nodine. Irene brings me a piece of spice cake and I thank her in Welsh, which is wilfully reckless, but the Takeshi story nettles me. There's a pause. Will she simply say, *croeso* – you're welcome – or launch into the old tongue in earnest? She takes a middle course which requires a few, simple exclamations on my part before she eases back into English. I don't know how to take this. Is it too painful to hear me croak and struggle for words simultaneously? Am I incomprehensible? God, is she being nice to me?

Irene gives me a number of leads, including one in Poland, which cheers me, as so far nothing has come of my missive to Gdansk. Before I leave we determine that her daughter-in-law, Glesni, is best friends with Rosemary, with whom I'm to stay in Oslo.

'She called Glesni a few days ago asking about you, and here you are!'

An itchy, small-world sensation tweaks me between the shoulder-blades. I have a feeling I could probably write this book if I stayed long enough on Irene Williams's sun porch. Instead I thank her and walk away through a tunnel of hedgerows to the tiny village of Cellan to hire a car.

Ofni 🐾 to Fear

Several years ago Glynne Williams rented a car to me for six weeks. A fortnight into the rental he appeared at my door with an exact clone, another red Fiat Uno. 'Gave you the one without any insurance,' he'd said cheerfully, as we switched keys.

His latest offering is a slovenly white Ford, which gets its first outing en route to the Indian restaurant where we're to meet our troubled friends. As we park Marguerite looks at me solemnly.

'Let's make a vow not to go back to their house after dinner, okay? I'm tired, you're sick . . .'

'Don't worry, it's a done deal. We will not, under any circumstances, go back to their house after dinner.'

On the way back to their house after dinner I pray that the Ford has insurance. It's raining and the roads, wavy and narrow in the best of conditions, are slick as sucked licorice. There's something unsettling about driving in Wales at night; the countryside is so dark that headlights strike me as an imprudent challenge, an invitation to things that shouldn't be seen – things that belong in the dark – to creep forward into the light. Of course this doesn't happen, but I get moods when I fear it will.

Our friends' domestic nightmare is definitely something that belongs in this category. Nonetheless, we've caved in to what was ostensibly a polite request to meet their dog, Peanut, but what we recognized as an urgent plea not to be abandoned. In the middle of dessert – or rather my champagne ice cream, which everyone else watched me eat from a miniature Moët et Chandon bottle – they realized she'd forgotten her pills. We left quickly after that.

When we reach their home in an indeterminately rural area that the postal address calls 'near Lampeter', we pet Peanut, down a quick coffee and desert them an hour later, leaving gifts from New England in our wake: two small, plastic bears filled with honey.

Scant talismans, it occurs to me now as I plough the homeward curves unnecessarily fast, too fast for Marguerite, who complains, against the demons of depression and this ageless Welsh night, too dark even for shadows.

Dringo ✿ to Climb

In the morning it's still raining. I find it troubling that all my indoor memories of Wales are in English – something I've so far done precious little to change. The landscape, however, remains open to translation. I want to be outside with old women and sticks. Indoors we're willing prisoners of these miserable cats and dogs.

We hem, we haw, we hem and haw some more. Finally we decide to brave the inevitable mud and drive to the Brecon Beacons, one of Wales's three national parks, then hike to a well-known beauty spot called Llyn y Fan Fach, or Place of the Little Lake. Beacons – a word I've had to look up in English, which makes a nice change – means 'conspicuous hills', and that's precisely what they are. From our temporary vantage point, with the motor running on the side of a sheep field, the furrows on their bald, grey-brown flanks look like wrinkled elephant skin. By now the sky has cleared and everything in the treeless mid-distance is super-realist with intense sunshine, but the Beacons remain in shadow with fog boiling over their crests. If I were a fanciful person (which I'm not) I could mistake their north-western ridge for the frontier between known lands and the Otherworld.

In 'The Mabinogi', a quadripartite collection of Welsh wondertales distilled from Celtic mythology, first written down around the year 1060, the Otherworld is known as Annwfn. (These four stories are generally combined with other medieval tales in an anthology called *The Mabinogion*.) It's the lot of Mabinogi heroes to journey to Annwfn or to some far-off land, usually in search of a woman or a magic cauldron. My favourite cauldron is a doozy: toss in a dead warrior, brew, and the next day he'll hop out alive, but voiceless.

While Norway and France may not seem very much like

Annwfyn, Argentina, five months, half a globe and the better part of a language away, sure fits the bill. I point out to Marguerite that we are on the brink of just such a journey.

'Sounds like someone already went there and brought you back,' she says archly. Marguerite is getting tired of hearing what sounds like ashes in my voice.

It's late, nearly five, by the time we leave the car at an arguable distance from a *Dim Parcio* sign and begin hiking to Llyn y Fan Fach. A well-trodden footpath slips between rising land that has already lost the tame, parcelled-out look of the pastures around Lampeter. Up ahead an immensity of hills displaces the sky not in craggy peaks but a series of long, oblique planes. As they fold in and out of one another the shadows they cast are the sole interruptions on the landscape: no trees, no shrubs, no bracken, no sheep. A few hikers bound past us on the way down, but we don't bother to ask the distance to the lake.

From over our shoulders the low sun tosses our shadows ahead of us, mine longer and a little more substantial than Marguerite's.

'Did you know that the Etruscans believed their civilization had a beginning and an end?' I ask. 'When they thought the end was near – as it was – artists began to equate the human form with afternoon shadows. Figurative sculpture started out representational, but it got more and more attenuated as the Etruscans approached their social evening. How about that?'

Marguerite gives me a look. I'm famous for this kind of extra-normal information.

'*Mae hi'n oer y bore 'ma*,' she replies instead. This is her only Welsh phrase, which means, 'It's cold this morning.' She can also count to ten.

'Wrong. *Mae'n gynnes y pnawn 'ma*. It's warm this afternoon.'

'Give me a Welsh lesson. Take my mind off my feet.' On my advice Marguerite has worn Wellington boots, which are scant protection from the sharp gravel of the path and are fast turning her feet into well-beaten fillets of beef.

'Do you want to hear about the mutation system or the alphabet?'

'Are you kidding? Alphabet.'

'You sure? No one's really going to believe we talked about the alphabet.'

'Speak!'

'All right. Welsh has two extra vowels, "y" and "w", and no "k", "q", "v" or "z". But "ch", "dd", "ff", "ng", "ll", "ph", "rh" and "th" all count as individual letters, which makes it a big pain to use the dictionary. I always forget and look for "ch" words in with the "c"s, and they're not there, and I have a fit, and rant about the dictionary leaving out a word. Then I find them after the "cy"s. It's weird.'

'If you say so.'

'"Ch" is that throaty, German noise, like a deep whirlpool of spittle.' She grimaces. '"Dd" is easy, like the "th" in the; "ff" is the English "f". One "f" sounds like a "v". Then there's our old friend, the double "l".'

She makes a noise like she's trying to get water out of her nose.

'*Da iawn wir!* Very good indeed! Sort of a "tlch" sound. Put your teeth together and blow it out the sides of your mouth. Since every other town in Wales starts with *llan* – which means something like sacred enclosure – you've got to get it right. Try saying "Llangollen".'

We continue hiking and practising 'Llangollen', sounding like breathless gila-monsters on the prowl. A huge mound of a mountain lies straight ahead. Eventually we can make out vertical rents of red soil on its lower flank, like pleats in the earth. The lake is at its base, about a mile and a half straight up from where we started.

Though it's an unremarkable lake green with the hills' image, Llyn y Fan Fach has been famous longer than there's been a place called Wales. The story goes that one day a shepherd was gazing at the surface, when to his astonishment a beautiful maiden rose out of the water. She teased him and pooh-poohed his offer of gifts, but eventually accepted his marriage proposal. There was, however, a hitch. In one version, if the shepherd struck her three times in the course of their life together, she'd have to return to the lake; in another, older account, the same disaster would befall if he touched her with iron. Naturally this comes to pass, and in a shower of bubbles she disappears beneath the surface of Llyn y Fan Fach with her herd of magic cattle in tow.

The maiden's aversion to iron is the key to this story. Speculation runs that when the Iron Age Celts arrived in what is now Wales, wielding their iron swords and spears, the local Stone Age folk were terrified of the tough new technology. Many took to the desolate places and hid in caves, far up in the hills alongside glacial lakes. To the newcomers, no mean spinners of tales and fables, the native people disappeared as thoroughly as if they'd vanished underwater.

On this sunlit, bronze-coloured evening nothing disturbs the surface of the lake. Two mountain bikers appear trailing a healthy scent of sweat. Far below us, where we've left the car, some hills sharpened by the sun cast a tactile impression of boiled wool; others are already blurry with dusk. It's a long, weary way down.

Colli 🂠 to Lose

Several hours later, as we're watching *Ruthless People* on television, it occurs to me that I am the water maiden's worst nightmare. I may be on her side, but I and my kind come toting verbal iron. What the folktale of Llyn y Fan Fach fails to account for is the fact that in all probability only a small group of European Celts moved into Britain around 600 BC. Despite their numbers they managed in a very short time to convert the indigenous people who didn't hide in caves or underwater to their laws, their stories, their language. By the time the Romans arrived in the first century

AD, Britons had been speaking Brythonic – the predecessor of Welsh – for time out of mind.

This story has a familiar ring to it. After twenty-four hundred years it was only a century ago, in the decade between 1870 and 1880, that more than half the people in what we now call Wales came to speak something other than a form of Welsh. This didn't happen because the English replaced the Welsh in Wales – though since the 1960s the number of English immigrants either retiring to or 'dropping out' in the Welsh countryside has grown exponentially – but because their language, like that of the Celts before them, powerfully eroded its precursor.

Surely this is a case of déjà-vu, in which I and my English friends at college are cast as the New Celts. Maybe it's inevitable. Maybe the linguistic sea change we're heralding is a kind of karma on a national scale, and by learning Welsh I'm throwing the universe out of sync. Maybe I'm just unrepentant about that, even though I can't begin to say why. Maybe I've had too much red wine tonight after too much exercise. And yet . . . I have a nagging conviction that no matter how much Welsh I master, however well I learn to say 'Llangollen', R. S. Thomas's poem 'The Small Window' is a warning written for me.

> In Wales there are jewels
> To gather, but with the eye
> Only. A hill lights up
> Suddenly; a field trembles
> With colour and goes out
> In its turn; in one day
> You can witness the extent
> Of the spectrum and grow rich
>
> With looking. Have a care;
> This wealth is for the few
> And chosen. Those who crowd
> A small window dirty it

With their breathing, though sublime
And inexhaustible the view.

Peanut's owner wakes us in the middle of the night. She's drunk a pint of gin and left her husband. Will we still be her friends, she wants to know, in the morning? I tell her we always will. As the future is a convincing tense in English, she believes me — correctly — and I go back to bed.

Edrych ar y Teledu ✿ to Watch Television

The following day Marguerite discovers back-to-back editions of *Pobl y Cwm* episodes with English subtitles. It turns out that the blonde woman and her husband had been shortchanged on their coal delivery, and were debating whether or not to complain about it. I'm stunned by the dramatic impact of it all. And I sorely regret telling our friend Rebecca, who's just back from London, about my body-in-the-coal theory.

'Why did you say you were learning Welsh?' she snickers. 'It was the quality of the TV programming, right?'

Gweithio ✿ to Work

'So, when shall we begin?'

'Now?'

'Now?' My voice is regrettably on the mend.

'*Pam lai,*' Tim says. Why not.

He's just locked up the post office and I've delayed the inevitable — our all-Welsh lunch — as far as the King's Head Tavern. We remain in public long enough to order a pint of bitter and a curry for me, and a ham steak for Tim, then retire to the large dining room at the back of the pub. It's entirely empty but for an encampment of about fifty tables draped in unaccountably elegant pink cloths. We sit at one, I take a shaky breath — and plunge.

For an hour I feel like I'm holding a live wire between my teeth. Sometimes it slips and jabs my tongue and I spray Tim with *chwech*, the Welsh word for 'six'; sometimes, when I haven't understood what he's just repeated for the third time, very slowly, I feel the heat wave of an electrocution coming on; and once in a while, for a moment or two, that live wire picks up an actual impulse from my brain and I connect and Tim nods and understands and we're speaking to each other. Even better, he insists on paying for lunch.

At two o'clock I look down to discover someone has miraculously eaten my chicken curry. The beer disappeared long ago. I can't remember any of it. I can't even remember what we've said, but whatever it was it was in Welsh. When language evolves into something other than commonplace communication — a badge of identity in foreign lands or, in this case, a gift between friends — the urgency of knowing and making known dissipates and the words slow to a speed at which a learner can catch them. I've wagered a book contract on the hope that it's easier to wield a symbol in Singapore and a gift in an empty back room than a verb in a crowded shop out in the still-unaccustomed sunshine on the High Street. So far, so good. My hour with Tim, I realize, belongs more to the Trip than it does to any of the trinity of Lampeters I've known over the past twelve years. It's time to go.

Gadael ☘ to Leave

The National Express coach slows as all coaches must. I've never crossed the Severn Bridge when it wasn't crippled by road construction. What's that fairytale about some luckless soul's work being perpetually undone in the night, so that for all eternity he has to start over again in the morning? The possibility should be investigated.

The River Severn marks the southern end of the boundary between Wales and England. Small cars have blown off the bridge in fierce side winds, or so I'm told. I remember reading in 1988 about a woman who was stuck in construction traffic so long that she got out of her car, and jumped. Unlike her, I'm not in a rush today because I missed the *Croeso i Gymru* sign on the way into Wales, and I want to see it now. I spin around in my seat, jabbing my ribs into the armrest. There it is. A yellow sign with a red dragon, the symbol of Wales. I'm pushed harder into the armrest as the coach suddenly accelerates toward Heathrow. Welcome to *Cymru*. The 'C' has mutated and become a 'G'. That happens a lot in Welsh.

For a long time I wonder about the woman who jumped back in '88. I sometimes feel that for me, an American with no Welsh ancestry, with no tangible connection to the place, learning Welsh – especially under the circumstances I've chosen – is a lot like jumping off the bridge of common sense. And to make matters worse I'm taking Marguerite with me. Before I fall asleep these thoughts give way, mercifully, to a poem by Harri Webb called 'Ode to the Severn Bridge', which I hum in a made-up singsong:

> Two lands at last connected
> Across the rivers wide
> And all the tolls collected
> On the English side.

NORWY (NORWAY)

Hedfan 🦋 to Fly

I've been bumped to business class, where there are more distractions than in economy to divert my mind from the unassailable knowledge that we'll all die if the plane falls out of the sky. I hate flying. A drawback, considering this is the second of the seventeen flights it will take us to get around the world. Marguerite has gone directly from London to Paris – well, directly being dependent on the vagaries of her round-the-world ticket, which has sent her via Zürich – to visit her sister's family. I'll join her there in about a week.

So for now I'm on my own, half-heartedly attending to the bones in my salmon steak entrée. Somewhere nearby a young American woman is giddy or drunk, I can't tell which. From what I've heard it sounds like she's going to Norway to visit relatives and is unsure of her Norwegian, learned from grandparents. 'I just know I'm gonna forget everything,' she all but hyperventilates. I can see tinsel strands of blonde hair wrapping over the top of her seat by grace of static electricity.

'Listen, sweetheart,' I'd like to say, 'at least you're going to Norway to speak Norwegian. I'm going to Norway to speak Welsh. Now there's a reason to worry.' And I am. Worried.

The truth is I'm really not alone on this flight. I'm with the mysterious stranger who's travelling the world with me: the Welsh language. On my lap is *Y Trip*, 'The Trip', *Nofel Antur i Ddysgwyr* – an adventure novel for learners – that I bought in Aberystwyth. The blurb on the back says it's about Charles, an alluring and arrogant former secret service type who goes bad, starts a drug

35

empire in Liverpool, and enters a sailing race around the Isle of Britain. Or Ynys Prydain, as it was once known, and in some quarters still is.

Not long ago the only marks I would've understood on the page were the periods and quotations. Now Welsh no longer looks like undisciplined gobbledygook. The letters fall into formations that I've come to expect, that don't drive my eyes skittish and shy. The first two sentences of *Y Trip* read, '*Roedd y dyn yn sefyll yn llonydd, yn hollol lonydd. Doedd dim swn o gwbl.*' I say it under my breath, which sounds something like 'Rrroithe uh deen un sevultch un tlchonith, un holtchol lonith. Doithe dim soon o gooble.' This means, 'The man was standing still, totally still. There was no noise at all.'

These sounds are aerobics for the American mouth. I barely have to open up to speak the lazy, slightly slurry English that is my birthright. If I look down, I never see my lips protrude beneath my nose when I'm speaking *Saesneg*, which is the Welsh word for English (*Saeson*, literally 'Saxons', means 'Englishmen'). But when I'm speaking Welsh I constantly catch glimpses of my lips projecting in and out like feeding sea urchins. It takes smiles, frowns, grimaces and active supporting roles from my jaw and neck muscles to get out just one sentence. It's so much work that half an hour of Welsh makes my face quiver. But there's no other way to say a word like *gwbl*. You've got to love a language in which you can make the noise 'gooble' and have it actually mean something (*cwbl* means 'all'; *gwbl* is *cwbl* after it's mutated, but I refuse to clutter my mind with mutations at the moment).

And then there's the rhythm. You can't just speak Welsh, you have to ride its waves. If English is a calm, smooth-as-glass harbour for its nearly four hundred and fifty million native speakers, Welsh is the rough open ocean. It bobs and bounces, I want to say it's a curly language, a curvy language, with the stress in both words and sentences on the penultimate sound. Listen: *Dim o GWB-l*. Da-da-daaa-da. It's incantatory.

Chwarae Golff ♣ to Play Golf

I have kept my word, and worn a bright yellow top and white trousers. My flight is an hour late and my expectations of being met are low, but there, miraculously, in the midst of the arrivals crowd, is a sign that says PAMELA in yellow and blue letters. The man holding it is also fiercely waving a tiny Welsh flag.

'Well met, my lady, well met.' Lynn Edwards is a trim, handsome man in his early sixties, with a tanned face and paler crevices of laugh lines around his eyes. His wiry, greyish hair reminds me of a Brillo pad.

'I can't tell you how glad I am it's you.'

I look surprised.

'You see, I was waiting here watching the women come out thinking, ooh, maybe it's that one. Nooo, maybe it's that one. Oh dear, I hope it's not that one. Then you appeared. I thought you'd be . . . older.' Lynn Edwards doesn't speak Welsh but you could get seasick on his accent anyway. There's very little correlation between the thickness of a Welsh person's accent in English and whether or not he or she actually speaks Welsh.

'So. Let me see if I understand the purpose of your trip. One, you're here to learn to speak Welsh; two, to meet Welsh people and anyone interested in Wales; and three, to see a little of the world. Have I got it right, then?'

He beams me a brilliant smile, rapidly blinking his eyes in what seems to be a slight twitch. This man has just brought clarity to my life.

Lynn Edwards flops backward on to the grassy slope of a sandtrap on a golf course outside Oslo, arms and legs akimbo, demonstrating how he may have lost his wallet here yesterday. I root around on my hands and knees looking for it in the lush grass. Norway is nothing if not green. From the plane I'd spied a scattering of natty, wooded hills that had looked like wild bumps of woolliness amid the paler, cultivated plains. So different from Wales, where the hills have been treeless for most of our millennium. Oslo, too, seemed to have a leafy look about it, clarified by the scrubbed northern air. At least that was my passing impression as we sped by on the freeway and zoomed out the other side.

I have come four thousand miles and straight from Fornebu Airport to watch people I've never met play golf. All in the name of learning Welsh. I seem to be ingesting particles of surrealism today like so many dust mites. Lynn has brought me here because his best friend, Iorwerth Roberts, is playing in a tournament – the same one Lynn would have been in if it hadn't been for me. Iori is from Amlwch on Ynys Môn – Anglesey – and speaks Welsh fluently. We've hiked on to the fairway to intercept him and have a look for Lynn's wallet, which seems to be a goner.

'I'm sorry you couldn't play in the tournament.'

'No matter, my lady, no matter. Here they come now.' Then over to Iori, 'Yo, boy, how many balls you lost, then?'

A foursome appears led by a compact man with a broad, tanned face and silver hair. He grins and pointedly ignores his friend. As Lynn greets the others in Norwegian Iori asks me several quasi-intelligible questions in Welsh. In my heart I wish very, very hard I'd stuck with French, and stammer the two words most beloved by Welsh learners when asked if they speak the language: *tipyn bach*, I say, a little bit. This tends to shut people up.

Because they're only on the third tee and it's a fine, warm day, Lynn and I decide to drive to the seaside village of Drøbak and catch them later. On the way Lynn tells me there are four Welsh members of the golf club, and several Scots.

'Never bothered to count the number of English,' he says, relishing his little bit of wickedness.

Drøbak is about as quaint as it gets in Norway. It was the site of the country's big moment in World War II – the navy sank a German battleship in the fjord here before the rest of the flotilla successfully invaded – but today the town is serene. The vertical clapboards of its old houses are painted gleaming white, mustard yellow, red and green. The air is aggressively fresh. On the fjord-side footpath a Norwegian groom-to-be tries to buy me from Lynn. 'My last beautiful girl,' he shouts in perfect if drunken English, before he's led away by his friends.

Back at the golf club, my heart sinks when we learn that Iori and company have six more holes to go. After what seems like an eternity – the temperature has been dropping fast and there's an old lady in the group who can't hit the ball for beans, which makes their progress painfully slow – they finally finish at nine o'clock, in strong sunshine, at five over par. I've gone from a sleeveless top to a windbreaker and three sweaters; have learned that Lynn came to Norway in 1960 to work for a computer company, married, and has been here ever since. To my amazement, an outdoor barbecue is just getting under way outside the clubhouse. My teeth are chattering so violently I can barely speak English, much less Welsh. No one is speaking Norwegian.

As the club's pro – a tipsy, monolingual American – hands out tournament prizes, a woman leans over with the unsolicited information that few Norwegians eat potato skins. I ask her how it is that the crowd of about fifty or so all understands English.

'Oh, we're a bi- or probably trilingual society,' she explains. I feel a sudden, deep shame for my country's linguistic myopia, and turn suddenly on Lynn, who's also a learner, and comment on the temperature in Welsh. We exchange a few of what Iori notes in passing as 'cat on the mat' sentences, but quickly peter out.

By the time Lynn drops me off at Rosemary's house, where I am to stay while I'm in Norway, it's midnight. Rosemary herself is in Denmark, but her three daughters, ages fourteen through twenty, welcome me with touching formality. They and two friends are sitting around the kitchen table, and when I arrive everyone shifts effortlessly into perfect English. Almost too perfect. Maybe it's creeping exhaustion, but their conversation sounds like the soundtrack from a dubbed film, a half-beat too slow, as if the dubbers were reading the script for the first time.

Liv, the eldest, to Lisa, the middle sister: 'I believe we are going to the same party tomorrow night.'

Lisa: 'Yes, I believe so.'

Liv: 'Shall we go there together?'

Annett, the youngest, to me: 'Would you care for a cup of tea?'

I really need to go to bed. Liv shows me to her room, a little-girl-gone-to-college sanctuary with pink walls, teddy bears, sociology texts, and University of Wales, Cardiff drinking mugs. As I turn out the light I notice that someone has pasted fluorescent stars to the ceiling. Without my contacts, they look like the real thing.

Ailadrodd ♣ to Repeat

My second day in Norway, my second golf course. Lynn, who picked me up early this morning at Rosemary's, points it out – a tiny, green blotch – from our vantage point on the Kongens Utsikt, or King's Viewplace. Somewhere far below Iori is teeing off for the nineteenth time this weekend. I've always considered golf an irredeemably pointless sport: so much lawn, such little holes. Why bother?

I keep these thoughts to myself as Lynn outlines the day. We're to meet Iori, have lunch, see Oslo. It's to be an all-Welsh affair once the golf ends. But for now Lynn and I are perched on a vertiginous, rocky ridge above lake-fronted farmland, just north-west of the city. From the escarpment we can see strands of shocking yellow fields threading through the billiard-table back-drop, red roofs of farmhouses, and a very blue lake splayed into fingers, each one dotted with small, forested islands that look like hunkered-down porcupines. In the far distance are snow-topped mountains. All is bright and faultless and northern.

I tell Lynn a story about gateposts in the Welsh county of Dyfed. Many of the decorative stone balls placed atop Dyfed gateposts are of unequal sizes: one is large, the other small. Legend holds that this tradition is based on a Viking practice of sticking a female head on one side of the entrance to a conquered property, and a male head on the other. All along the Welsh seaboard the English versions of Welsh place names descend from the Scandinavian: Anglesey, Bardsey, Swansea, Fishguard. Apparently I'm not the first to make the trip between Wales and Norway, though the others travelled in the opposite direction, with a somewhat more active intent.

Lynn tells me he started the Cymdeithas Cymry Oslo twelve years ago with Iori, and that they now have about fifty members, mostly expatriates.

'We've got ambassadors, artists, teachers, you name it. A sophisticated crowd, it is. Very different from a lot of people back home. These are the ones who left.'

He adds that a number of Norwegians also belong to the society, including a fifteen-year-old boy who's already gotten a degree in Maths from the University of Oslo and is now going for another in Welsh. More shades of Mark Nodine and his kind. I switch the subject by asking if his Norwegian friends make the distinction between Welsh and English, and Lynn vehemently shakes his head no. Then he looks me in the eyes and squints, perhaps against the strong Scandinavian light, perhaps at the benightedness of his hosts.

'What I tell 'em, my lady, is "Have it your way. You Swedes,"' he says, winking, '"are all alike."'

By eleven o'clock we've tracked down Iori in the midst of the relentlessly scenic golf course. At three we're still there. I divert myself from impending starvation by picking Lynn's wallet, which we found last night in the boot of his car (eventually I give it back). I'm at the point of telling them that golfers who played on Sunday were brutally attacked for breaking the Sabbath in Aberdyfi, Wales in 1927, when Iori saves himself by finally announcing it's time for lunch. He then proclaims an uncompromising ban on English. For two and a half hours, through lasagne, salad, coffee and towering soft icecream cones, I have no problem understanding Iori's soft-spoken Welsh. He teaches English in Oslo, and his measured sentences, slowed to a student's ear, nail their targets in my brain. *Diwylliant*, he tells us, is his favourite word in the language.

'It means culture,' he says, 'but it really means to "un-wild". Isn't that wonderful?'

The word conjures forests and wolves and people tearing meat from bones with their teeth. The hairs on the back of my neck recall some dim, ancestral impulse and flex into attention.

Lynn and I, meanwhile, are handicapped by our one-track vocabularies and find each other mutually incomprehensible. Since neither of us knows enough Welsh to find alternative routes for our thoughts, if we don't comprehend the other's phrasing the first time around we're out of luck.

(Thank you, Vortigern. Had a proto-Welsh king of that name, active *c.* AD 420–50, not seen fit to grant British land to Germanic mercenaries – an incident depicted throughout the ages as ultimately leading to the Britons' loss of the island to the Anglo-Saxons – Wales might never have been 'Englished', Lynn and I might not have been able to communicate at all, and that would have been a terrible shame.)

Surprisingly, Iori is the first to crack and abandon what for him is his first language. Sprawled on the back seat of Lynn's car on the way into Oslo, he interrupts Lynn's painfully faltering monologue and shouts,

'GOOD GOD, EDWARDS, it's like listening to the dog barking.'

Lynn takes this well. As we near Vigeland Park in the city centre, Iori lapses back into Welsh one last time and unexpectedly recites R. Williams Parry's poem 'Ode to the Pylons', dedicated to the high-tension wires that cantilever across the broad, flat sweep of his native Anglesey. I can't understand a word, but sense that the sounds take him to a place a little more *gwyllt* (wild) than this tidy Norwegian highway. To an island that was once a centre of learning for the druids, and even now retains a cool remoteness from the twentieth century, though those pylons carry electricity produced by a nuclear power plant not far from Iori's home town of Amlwch. If you count the druids – and the Romans, who flamboyantly exterminated them there in AD 61, most certainly did – that makes two unholy power sources from one island.

I have requested a tour of Vigeland Park, an outdoor sculpture extravaganza and the *chef d'oeuvre* of the Norwegian artist Gustav Vigeland, and am no longer surprised to find these two golf-mad, former rugby players know it well. In 1921 Vigeland made an extraordinary contract with the city of Oslo: he agreed to give every piece of sculpture in his possession, as well as every piece he would ever make for the rest of his life, to the city in exchange for a studio and living quarters to be built to his specifications, all the materials he would ever need, and *carte blanche* to create what-ever the heck he wanted to with no creative restrictions. Not a bad deal if you ask me.

The result is an immense outdoor studio of figurative works, principally in granite and bronze, its centrepiece a fountain held aloft by burly bronze giants, surrounded by twenty smaller figures collectively known as 'Man and the Tree of Life'. Each of these last depicts a human figure engaged in some muscular way with a tree: young boys climb the tree for a look-out; a girl bursts forth from its trunk, arms extended from her shoulder blades like wings; a man and woman try to separate themselves from each other but the branches entwine them together; an old man feebly clings to the trunk, unwilling to let go.

It's a place to spend some time. Unlike the super-hero icons at Rockefeller Center in New York, Vigeland's bronze and granite women, men and children manage to express the human side of Art Deco. All are naked and caught in momentary poses – a little girl snubbing a little boy from behind her mother's back, an old woman resting against her son – less icons of virtue than aspects of vulnerability. At the other end of the park is the Monolith, a human pillar of twisted, interlaced figures, a veritable granite rocketship of body parts. I point out that it reminds me of a big initial – an 'I' – from the Book of Kells.

Lynn looks away from it. 'All I ever see are the ovens,' he says, casting an unexpected shadow in the bright afternoon.

Bod Rosemary ✿ to Be Rosemary

Dim ond Cymraeg! – Nothing but Welsh! That's what Iori had said when he and Lynn left me at Rosemary's house on the suburban outskirts of Oslo a few days ago. Rosemary was back from Denmark with lots of booze and new suede pumps. Her middle daughter, Lisa, had just auditioned for Holiday on Ice and was waiting to hear if she'd been hired. Since then, Lisa's fate has yet to be resolved and her mother and I have hardly spoken a word of Welsh.

Rosemary is the most enigmatic woman I've ever met who perpetually wears pearls. Lynn was right, she does have music in her voice – her words peal like a clear bell choir up and down the scales of a Welsh accent as thick as his – though until now I've heard her words ring almost exclusively in English. What I've heard mostly is 'PAM-eL-A, where is your glass?' Today she and I have downed enough wine to fill a large birdbath. Miraculously, it seems to have no effect on her. She remains the scrubbed, buffed, pink toe-and-fingernail-polished image of a head-turning widow in her mid forties. Her bright red cheeks and tanned skin damn well glow with good health. Her hair at any given hour can only be described as 'coiffed'. Only Rosemary's laugh, a raucous, high-speed blowout straight from Tregaron, her home town in mid Wales, gives a little tickle to the outer edges of propriety. It's her laugh that makes me inclined to believe the story of Rosemary being dragged out of the Lampeter Post Office in the sixties, following a Cymdeithas yr Iaith (Welsh Language Society) sit-in protesting the absence of bilingual signage (now standard procedure).

In Tregaron she's known as 'Rosemary BBC'. Tregaron is a grey place not far from Lampeter, on the edge of a great bog. On our first evening together we traded stories about the Talbot Hotel in the centre of town: she didn't know there's a circus elephant buried out back, and I didn't know it's haunted by the ghost of Elsa Wilde, a London ballerina who married the publican, tried too hard to stay young, and died pining for the great world she once knew. I hope Rosemary doesn't have plans to move back home. The townspeople listen when she gives reports from Oslo on Radio Cymru, even though they have trouble understanding her.

'I once met a Tregaron woman at the Lampeter Eisteddfod,' she told me. 'We used to call her the chicken lady. And she came right up, wagged her finger under my nose and said sternly' (Rosemary drops into a parody of her own accent), ' "Now you speak so we can all understand you, you hear?" '

Even Rosemary's mother can't make her out. After her latest broadcast, in which she vehemently defended the notion of homosexual marriages, her mother called up and said, 'Well, I couldn't understand what you said, but I know you were talking dirty.'

Herein lies the problem – well, one of the problems – of contemporary Welsh. Because she went to university, Rosemary, like the nation's newscasters, speaks what people in Tregaron call 'posh Welsh', a politically correct strand of the language stripped of its sloppy Anglicisms. It's the difference between *computer* (pronounced 'com-PU-tearrr'), and *cyfrifiadur*, a synthetic Welsh word for the same thing. This rift is a source of no small inferiority complex among the hundreds of thousands of people who speak what's derisively called 'Kitchen Welsh', or the even more adulterated 'Wenglish'. I have acquaintances in Lampeter who won't talk to me for fear of corrupting the 'correct' Welsh I'm learning in books. To me, an American of dubious linguistic breeding, this is ridiculous, but then I also think the French make too much of a fuss. Many in Tregaron consider Rosemary a traitor.

Meddwi ✺ to Get Drunk

The kitchen table is invisible beneath a collection of cartons, tins, platters and plastic containers that seem to provide the raw ingredients for all Norwegian meals. So far I've only been able to tell breakfast apart from lunch and dinner by the absence of wine bottles; otherwise, it's been potato salad, a kind of coleslaw called italiensalad, salamis, cured hams, flat breads and the family favourite, a sweet brown goat's cheese, pretty much round the clock. If you don't put them away there's little point in ever leaving the table, and today we don't.

Rosemary is wearing her pearls with a pert, semi-transparent pink housecoat tied with a bow around the neck. The white wine in her glass is the exact shade of the highlights in her hair.

'Most women are boring, don't you think?'

I don't really think so, but it doesn't matter. Rosemary has a disturbing tendency to listen intently to the first ten seconds of a reply and then drift off, as if she's guessed the rest and lost interest. Perhaps she's hard of hearing.

So far today I've learned the cost of Rosemary's shoes; the saga of her courtship with Bob, a soon-to-be-unmarried English gentleman from Copenhagen; her opinion that people should marry rather than just live together; that women look better in feminine dress; and that Norway has phenomenally stern drunk-driving laws, the consequence of which is that from a young age her daughters have acquired a good knowledge of Oslo's mass transit system.

My wine matches neither my oversize orange T-shirt nor my very short dark hair. I seem calm; I focus on Rosemary's life and decide to buy some Norwegian goat's cheese to bring to Marguerite in France. But there's desperation licking the back of my brain. The only way I can explain my presence in this kitchen on this July afternoon is that I've come to Norway to practise Welsh.

With Welsh I have a purpose; without it my presence here is like a Christmas tree: diverting, but ultimately useless and, to half the world at least, inexplicable.

It's not that I haven't tried to get the *Cymraeg* ball rolling, but without Rosemary's help I find I'm marooned on the flat with no downhill in sight. Unlike Iori, or Tim back in Lampeter, she's shown no interest in the role of language mentor. I can't blame her: I'm still at the stage where speaking Welsh is exercise rather than intercourse, and Rosemary has no stake in doing verbal callisthenics with me. Never mind that's why I'm here . . . Instead I learn that Bob is getting a beer gut, and inwardly berate myself for being the gutless kind of person who needs a language mentor. Every time one of us begins a sentence in English I wince under the twin reflexes of relief and shame.

Rosemary gets up and plucks another wine bottle from the fridge. I foolishly hold out my glass. 'Too bad Aneurin Rhys Hughes, from the embassy, is on holiday. He's very Welsh. But tell me, did you enjoy the party the other evening?'

'Hmmm? You mean tonight?'

'No, Pamela, the Celtic Ladies' party.'

'Oh. Um, yes. Ummm.' Tonight a dozen or so members of *Cymdeithas Cymry Oslo* will shell out fifty kroner a head for the pleasure of meeting me at a wine and cheese hosted by Rosemary. Earlier in the week one of the five women who call themselves the Celtic Ladies – three Welshwomen, a Scot and an Englishwoman married to a Welsh diplomat – had invited us to a 'CL' dinner party. Rosemary was upset that Anne, the hostess, had served plates already fixed with food.

'That's absolutely not done in Norway. I don't know what she was thinking,' Rosemary told me in the pub we'd stopped at on the way home. Indeed, at her daughter's boyfriend's birthday party the next day we passed around a whole cake and each cut our own slices.

'*You're* the Welsh lady writing the book?' Sion, one of the Welshwomen, had asked shortly after Rosemary and I arrived at Anne's apartment near Vigeland Park.

'I'm not really Welsh.'

'I thought you'd be a dumpy little grey-haired lady, about seventy, with glasses and a big handbag.'

'Oh no,' Rosemary countered. 'I thought she'd be another lotus flower. The last woman who stayed with me who was writing a book removed her shoes and sat in a lotus position on my pink velvet settee.'

'She looks Welsh, doesn't she?'

'Oh yes, she looks very Welsh.'

Was my quest really so bizarre that people thought I appeared too normal for the part? The Celtic Ladies all seemed to have picked up Norwegian with ease, which I guess makes travelling the world in search of Welsh a bit radical. To a woman, they were comfortable in Norwegian, but less so in Norway.

'I certainly don't want my ashes scattered over the fjords,' the friendly, gap-toothed Sion had said.

'I'm not ready for a little plot in a Norwegian churchyard either,' echoed another CL. Even Rosemary, who had been married to a Norwegian, who's lived in Norway for years and who considers herself at least in part Scandinavian, hasn't ruled out the possibility of moving back 'home'. For now she makes do with frequent trips to the Royal Welsh Agricultural Show.

It is for expatriates above all, I thought, that Wales glows with its famous once and future sheen. Don't get me wrong: I don't mean that misty, magical, mystical nonsense fed to Wales by PR agencies with the tourism account. That stuff needs to be flushed from the country's bowels, and fast. I mean that expats share a kindred sense of incompleteness with their 'non-historical' home-land. Their experience in Wales is unfinished, yet it is their past and probable future there that give the present boundaries, make it approachable, comprehensible and, above all, impermanent. Wales itself, hijacked by the language of a foreign land, isn't finished with its destiny yet either.

The telephone rings, bringing me back to the kitchen. It's Rosemary's mom, calling from Tregaron. I jealously do the dishes as they jabber in Welsh, until a crash from the living room interrupts their conversation. Rosemary, forgetting my limitations, yells to me in Welsh to investigate. I reply triumphantly, equally forgetful that I'm speaking her language.

'*Beth sy'n bod?*' – 'What's the matter?' I shout. The cats knocking over an ashtray is so far the linguistic zenith of my day.

Siopa 🐞 to Shop

Early evening, hiding in my room with my face buried in Liv's quilted bedspread. I'm trying to coax my voluntary muscles into coming to terms with all the booze I've consumed, when Rosemary's lyrical voice ring-sings down the hall (in Welsh you *canu*, or sing, musical instruments, among which Rosemary's voice must surely be counted). 'PAM-eL-A! Can I get you a gin and tonic?'

At this point I'd rather be exposed to radioactive plutonium.

'*Dim diolch*,' I manage, 'No thank you,' wondering how on earth I'm going to get through the wine and cheese party. I did cope earlier with slipping out to buy some goat cheese at a local shop. Rosemary's neighbourhood has the rolling lawns, the scattered, unregimented houses, the semi-rural feel of parts of northern New Jersey, where I grew up. If it weren't for the architecture – long-profiled, wooden homes that look like the heathen cousins of Lutheran churches – I could forget I'm in Europe.

The convenience store is run by Pakistanis. Liv says that they're the largest minority group in Norway, and are subject to much prejudice. According to Lynn, Pakistanis sound a lot like Welshmen speaking English: both have the same regular bumps in their words, the same cantering accent. Someone explained this by claiming that a high percentage of the Royal Welch Fusiliers were sent to India in the nineteenth century, but I don't believe it.

A woman in a sari greeted me and I asked in English for the sweet goat cheese. Since she spoke only Pakistani she went to fetch her husband, who arrived and addressed me, naturally, in Norwegian. Okay, what the hell. I asked again for goat cheese, this time in Welsh. He tried English, but I'd got the devil in me, and besides, if I closed my eyes I could just persuade myself he came from Cardiganshire.

'*Esgusodwch fi, ond dw i'n chwilio am caws afr. Oes gaws afr dych chi? Dych chi'n siarad Cymraeg? Nag ydych? Dyma dreuni.*'

However this sounds to you is how it must've sounded to the shop owners. I'm repentant now, but then I was on a roll. This was the most Welsh I'd spoken in three days.

Finally, amid a chorus line of hand and foot signals, and a stream of rollicking Welsh from me, we found the cheese. There were six different kinds. I took the red package just for the heck of it, walked directly into the counter, then bid them both a bewildering *pnawn da, a phob hwyl.*

Wedi Meddwi Eto ♣ to Be Drunk Again

I'm no longer drunk. Not scrupulously sober, but not drunk, though I've got a wine glass in my hand again. Rosemary's desk is set up as a bar, but Johan doesn't drink. I'm getting evil-eye looks from Rosemary that I'm spending too much time with him and that, as the evening's human centrepiece, it's time to mingle, but I pretend not to notice.

Johan is an enormously tall Swede with knobbly knees, long, straight hair, and rectangular granny glasses that give him an ardent, scholar-punk look. He's wearing shorts and high-top sneakers, and is the first person in Norway I've recognized as a socio-economic, style-and-age compatriot. He first went to Wales on a mountain climbing trip, then returned to study Welsh in Aberystwyth; now he's getting a PhD from the University of Oslo in Welsh literature.

As far as I can tell, he and I are the only ones speaking Welsh in the house. It was easier when my conversation partner was replying in Pakistani.

Rosemary sweeps by and tops up my glass. 'A lovely boy, but so boring,' she whispers in my ear. 'Come meet Jean, Pamela.'

'*Dwy funud*,' I stall, two minutes.

My mind's eye does its gravity trick again, and I'm treated to a rare view: an American trying to talk to a Swede in Welsh on the outskirts of Oslo. By the time I re-focus on Johan, who can effortlessly switch from Welsh to English like a native, Welsh words are clinking around in my brain like ice cubes, but my tongue is beyond getting a grip on them. I've been topped up about a hundred too many times. It's a relief when the door opens and a Welsh voice shouts in English,

'So, who here is from Verona, New Jersey, then? How about those White Castle hamburgers?'

This literally stuns me. I was beginning to think I actually might be Welsh, and it's a slap in the face to be reminded I'm from New Jersey. The husband of one of the CLs, now a high-up in the British embassy, tells me he went to university near my home town. It's my sad duty to tell him that Verona's White Castle hamburger franchise – the chain was the first with the vision to serve square burgers – has gone out of business.

As the party winds down, Iori, who arrived with Lynn a few hours ago, but whom I haven't spoken to at length, takes me aside and gives me a gift that I won't have to declare at customs.

'I've been wanting to tell you,' he says, 'that I've been thinking about it, and I can't hear your American accent when you speak Welsh. You have a pure *De Cymru* – South Wales – intonation, with a Ceredigion lilt, like Rosemary's. I thought you'd like to know that.'

Like to know that? I'm sure this can't be true, but it's a finer music to my ears than Rosemary singing, 'Where's your glass, Pamela?' I let the wine confuse my brain into a welcome identity crisis. Tonight all the gossip, the references, the Norwegian prices translated for my benefit into pounds, all that I have in common with these people, has been filtered through Wales. When I began a sentence with, 'Well at home we . . . ,' I found my listeners thought I was talking about Lampeter.

'Oh,' interrupted one woman, 'it's probably different in the north.'

As the Trip continues, it is Wales that more and more seems to be the starting point, not the States. The more I use this word 'home', and the farther I get from it (wherever home is), the more I'm beginning to wonder what I mean.

Deffro ✲ to Wake Up

Four a.m. Last night I went to bed with my contacts in. Thank god I'd noticed that Liv's indoor stars looked like bits of fluorescent paper, and wondered why. One night in Wales I put my lenses in a glass on my night-table instead of cleaning them, woke, and drank them in the morning.

Every neuron in my brain feels like it's been on a forced march across the desert. Because of Norway's drunk-driving laws, Rosemary can't take me to the airport (the police, who'd be aware she had a party last night, would almost certainly breathalyze her if she tried to drive anywhere before noon), so I must take a red-eye train to make my seven-thirty-five flight. As I'm creeping out the front door Rosemary appears in her pink housecoat. It's the only time I've seen her without pearls, though her hair is perfect. She gives me a hug, and I feel a sudden respect for her that she hasn't given a damn about having a writer in the house.

Seven o'clock, Fornebu Airport. My digestive system seems unconnected to my head: the one is comatose, the other spinning like a dervish. There will be no *Y Trip* on this flight – or rather these flights, as I have to fly first to London and then Zürich in order to wind up tonight in Paris. A television monitor by the gate asks, 'Have you dressed properly for the occasion?' Rosemary, I think, has found her niche in this country.

FFRAINC (FRANCE)

Dychwelyd ❁ to Return

The Louvre is half-price after 3 p.m. on Sundays. This afternoon
the air in the galleries is thick and still, varnished with a stifling
July heat. People ramble haphazardly in and out of my vantage
point like pieces of curdled cream, surfacing, sinking and resurfac-
ing in a stirred cup of tea. I look into the depths of Leonardo's
dark, seductive 'John the Baptist' but see instead that the humidity
has made my hair curl.

Why do I get goosebumps here? Maybe it's a heat rash; maybe
it's because art, like language, flirts with the impossible. In the
Louvre I can cheat time. I like to think of landscapes as immutable,
but they change – reafforestation programmes have altered parts
of the Welsh countryside, bald for centuries, beyond recognition
– yet I know when I look at Titian's 'Man with a Glove' that
I'm seeing the same young man in the same position in the same
light exactly the same way Titian saw him over three hundred
years ago. It's less a glimpse into the past than a chance to look
through the eyes of the dead.

'Have you noticed that of all the galleries we've been to, only
the French ones have been air-conditioned?' I ask Marguerite,
who frowns.

We move to an open window to catch a feeble breeze. The
air in Norway was so sharp and pure it felt new; continental air,
by comparison, breathes like it has some mileage on it. Rosemary
told me that visitors to Oslo often feel sick at first, they're so
unaccustomed to the freshness. The really telling thing for me was
the shade: one afternoon I sat in a sweater writing on a shady

corner of Rosemary's deck, while two feet away one of her daughters roasted topless in the sun. Here in Paris, where I've been for two days now, even the shadows are suffocating.

'Too bad you didn't get to see more of Norway.'

'I was on golf courses.'

'You were getting drunk in Rosemary's kitchen.'

'. . . and speaking English,' I add, heart-sick.

'You know, that's probably the best thing that could've happened to you. Now guilt will propel you to speak nothing but Welsh for the rest of the trip.'

She's got something there. Marguerite and I met fifteen years ago in Paris, and she knows how receptive I am to language angst. We were both studying French and living with an ancient woman named Mme Peneau, who looked like Samuel Beckett in drag, had a voice like a truck driver, and used to beat us with her cane whenever she caught us speaking English. Mme Peneau watered the wine and vigilantly corrected our genders during dinner; it was under her roof in the elegant seventeenth arrondissement that I learned to fear foreign languages.

Particularly on the telephone. A short time after I'd arrived in Paris I'd fallen into an informal match at the university tennis courts, and my partner had offered to call me to arrange another game. When he'd asked my name I'd thought he said, 'What's that on your finger?' and replied casually, 'A band-aid.' I can still hear Mme Peneau's deep croak when he rang a few days later. '*Vous voulez parler avec qui? Abandaid? Qui est "Abandaid"?*' My subsequent conversation with the tennis player reminded me of Thomas Hobbes's description of life: not nasty, but certainly brutish and short.

So far I've refused to speak Welsh on the phone. A semi-familiar language without visuals – the mimed clues of the hands and face, the dance of the lips – is like a compass without an arrow: there's nothing to point you in the right direction. A few days ago I called Boyd Williams, the president of the Paris Welsh Society, to arrange a meeting. Boyd is a native Welsh-speaker from Abergwam (Fishguard), who wrote to me in English because, he claimed, his written Welsh was 'full of mistakes – mutations, mostly'. I figured someone so sensitive to error would surely understand my fear of speaking Welsh on the phone. He did; unfortunately his secretary did not, and made me speak French, which was worse.

It did my heart good to know that Boyd, too, is stalked by a fear of mutations. Or mutilations, as one of my teachers liked to call them. In a bewildering grabbag of situations – new moon, high tide, to impress singular female nouns – 'c's become 'g's, 'p's become 'b's, and so on. The first letters of words shift their shape like the great magicians of Welsh folklore. But whereas the latter were circumspect about their shapeshifting, the Welsh alphabet is locked in a perpetual game of musical chairs from hell. There are soft mutations (the nicest), aspirate mutations (rarer; forgivable if you miss them), and nasal mutations (horrible). You have to use the latter, for instance, if you live in the capital of Wales. *Rydw i'n byw yng Nghaerdydd*: I live in Cardiff. In this case, all because of a wee preposition, *Caerdydd* mutates to *Nghaerdydd*. A bit of an over-reaction, I'd say. If you were born there you would be *o Gaerdydd*, from Cardiff. Right now I'm not in Paris, I'm *ym Mharis*. Go figure.

Actually, I admire the language's infatuation with the ear. Mutations have no meaning, they're simply built-in riffs and slides, so that even mundane sentences glide together like the blues. *Ym Mharis* is *yn Paris*, slurred like a late-night love song – and grammatically correct, to boot. Welsh isn't alone in this mutation game: its first cousins, Breton and Cornish, and second cousins, Irish Gaelic, Scots Gaelic and Manx – the world's Celtic languages – play too, but by their own rules. The miracle is that all these tongues, even Cornish and Manx, both now extinct, have managed to incorporate flux and change into the heart of themselves and make a fixed system of improvisation. It's almost as if they found the trick of internalizing time, put it on a grammatical wheel instead of a straight line. Speaking Welsh is the poor man's way of flirting with immortality.

Bwyta Caws ❧ to Eat Cheese

The goat cheese sits like a bruiser on Marguerite's sister Nina's cheeseboard, bullying the Camembert and Port Salut. Nina's three kids, all under ten, looked at it when I presented it to the family as if I'd brought the goat instead of the cheese. Their father, Bernard, a Frenchman whom Nina met while also studying in Paris, valiantly tried some, pulled his mouth down, raised his eyebrows and shrugged. He hasn't eaten any since.

When we return from the Louvre Nina is excited.

'You're never going to believe this.'

'What? HarperCollins called and wants to give me more money?'

'No. There's a Welsh movie on TV tonight. Isn't that incredible?'

At ten-thirty I turn on the television, still astonished by this marvel of good timing. Below us on the street are the sounds of migration: laughter, footsteps, the hollow ring of aluminium lawn chairs bumping together. Every evening at this hour half the neighbourhood – Nina and Bernard live in the 'decidedly unchic' nineteenth arrondissement, in north-east Paris – wanders down to the Parc de la Villette, where a series of free films are being shown *en plein air*, beneath a city sky the colour of dark amethyst. Tonight's feature is Elizabeth Taylor in *Cleopatra*. We, however, shut the windows and tune in to *Une Si Jolie Vallée*, 'Such a Pretty Valley', as Nina begins her nightly ironing.

It's the story of a love triangle between Kevin, an unemployed miner (a Welshman but a monoglot English-speaker), his wife Sian (bilingual in English and Welsh) and Nahuel, a dashing, horseback-riding writer from Patagonia who is fluent in Welsh and Spanish, but speaks no English. The dialogue alternates between English and Welsh, with French subtitles. I sit like a pointer spaniel throughout the whole thing, still and tense, with my language brain in hyperdrive. As it is I blurt out French words when I want Welsh ones, and vice versa, but this verbal-visual stew of (for me) half-cooked languages is too much. Thank god Argentina is still four months away. It's a huge relief when Sian decides to stick it out with Kevin (you knew she would), and Nina zaps off the set.

'Is South Wales still so depressed?' she asks, folding up the last of the clothes.

'Actually Cardiff was tops on the list of UK cities last year for economic growth. A lot of high-tech companies, Japanese especially, are moving into the old mining valleys. But coal mining itself is finished. The movie review in *Le Monde* described the valleys today as *vertes comme des choux tendres* – green like tender cabbages. Honestly, the French are too much.'

'Didn't that one mine reopen?' Marguerite asks. 'There was that photo of guys covered in coal dust in the *New York Times*.'

'Oh, that's right. The Tower mine. It was the last working mine in South Wales – four and a half miles straight down – not far from Merthyr Tydfil. After it closed in 1994 the miners pooled their savings and bought it, and they're working it again. But that's just one mine, pulling, I think, around 400,000 tons of coal. In 1920 there were 620 mines operating in Wales. Think about it: Cardiff once exported over 36 million tons of coal and was the largest port on earth.'

At a quarter to one everyone else has gone to sleep, so it's safe for me to plug into the family phone jack and do E-mail (which would otherwise become child's play, literally). The Welsh chat group is in a furore because someone has surmised that Jefferson Davis, the president of the Confederacy, was Welsh, and asks if anyone has noticed the number of professional baseball players with Welsh surnames. One person responds, 'What's your point?'

– that everyone with the name Davis is of Welsh descent, or that Jefferson indirectly fathered a lot of pro baseball players?'

I stay out of it, thinking instead of Welsh coal. That was the real Welsh diaspora. By the late nineteenth century Welsh anthracite had travelled to western France, northern Spain, Italy, Egypt, Brazil, Argentina, India and throughout the Far East. I'll be doing a good job just to keep up.

Cyfarfod ✿ to Meet

It's a warm dusk, and the breeze kicking around Les Halles smells of fresh electricity. A storm is dickering with us tonight; the clouds look bruised and apprehensive.

Emile Zola called Les Halles 'the belly of Paris'. There's a Welsh expression, *llond bola o ofn*, a belly full of fear, which suits the occasion of my imminent meeting with the Paris Welsh at a café nearby. Les Halles means 'the Marketplace'. From 1100 – one hundred and eighty-two years before Wales lost its independence – until the mid 1970s an immense wholesale food market occupied this area. Now there's only a shopping mall, the name Les Halles, and a feeling that something's missing.

I walk past a string of cafés that reputedly specialize in onion soup and pig's feet. Au Chien Qui Fume – The Smoking Dog – sounds nice, but the Welsh are awaiting at Le Comptoir. I spot a table of people all looking past one another expectantly; there's a keen crack of thunder as it occurs to me, good god, it's me they're looking at. Boyd Williams isn't at all what I'd imagined. He's about my age, with shoulder-length, greying hair tied in a pony-tail and a kind of toss-away elegance. With him is Eluned, a violinist *o Gaerdydd*, Arwel from Amlwch, Iori's home town on Anglesey, and Nesta from around Bangor, and older than the rest of us by a good thirty years.

This is the *Cylch Cymraeg*, the Welsh-speaking circle of the

Paris Welsh Society, and they're already doing it. After Nesta tells me that the society has between seventy-five and a hundred members, around thirty of whom speak Welsh, and I give my spiel, which I've nearly memorized by now – *Dw i'n ysgrifennu llyfr am bobl o gwmpas y byd sy'n siarad Cymraeg . . .* I'm writing a book about people around the world who speak Welsh – multiple conversations begin to sprout. It occurs to me that there's a geography of comprehension at work here. I'm sitting between Boyd and Nesta, both of whom I can understand fairly well, but beyond the ashtray in the centre of our round café table, I'm sunk. Eluned and Arwel might as well be speaking Turkish. Physical proximity influences my degree of comprehension! Eureka! Write that down later, I tell myself.

Some of us choose *bière* – beer – when the waitress takes our order, which becomes *cwrw* – beer in its Welsh incarnation – as soon as she sets it on the table. Boyd is explaining how he thinks there are fewer differences between North and South Walian Welsh-speakers of his generation than ever before, because of the influence of television. I want to say how interesting that is. What's the word? Damn, damn, damn. *Intéressant*? No, no, wrong language! Nesta taps my arm because she's finally remembered we've met before, at the Aberystwyth Eisteddfod of 1992, and launches into a story about how she used to fly for free when she worked for a travel agency.

Diddorol. Hell. The Welsh word for interesting finally arrives in my brain, but Boyd is listening to Nesta. I follow his cue as she talks on, and interject *yn wir!* – really! – whenever he and the others seem impressed. Most of what she says is a blur. I'm half aware of a storm of cigarette smoke and French all around us as the café fills up; the waitress eyes us curiously. A few fat raindrops have fallen, but otherwise the thunderstorm is a bust. An hour and a half passes of the best Welsh I've ever spoken.

Suddenly, without warning, my mind shuts down in the middle of someone else's sentence, and the spell breaks. The next words out of my mouth are English ones. Nesta smiles and pats me again, and tells me I did very well. Satisfied for the evening, I let Welsh go without a fight and silently examine Boyd. He has a habit of looking down to think, then up at the person he's talking to, which makes him raise his eyebrows slightly. It gives him a quizzical, amused look, which I find becoming even as I wonder just whom he finds so humorous.

Ten minutes back at Nina's and I burst into tears because I've lost my address book that notes every Welsh-speaker I've been able to locate the world over. When Marguerite returns from brushing her teeth I'm kneeling in the middle of her nephew's bedroom floor looking like the Pietà, with my computer case on my lap.

'That's it. It's all over. *Shit.* We might as well go home.'

It takes her under three minutes to find the missing item stuck inside a notebook in which I've already looked, twice. It takes my heart about forty minutes to stop beating as if it were marching in army boots.

Cynaeafu 🐾 to Harvest

The French have a genius, especially in Paris, most of all on the Ile St Louis, for combining crumbling stone, worn and ingrained with soot and patches of creeping damp (peeling plaster will also do), with freshly washed, gleaming windows, polished brass, massive front doors thick with paint, even discreet touches of neon. The result pulls together some heady disparities – ancient and modern, rough and smooth, dull and vibrant – which for me are the essence of Parisian chic.

The nineteenth arrondissement doesn't really do disparity. Its post-war sprawl of apartment buildings and utilitarian shops is comfortable rather than chic; the people who live here, Africans, Orthodox Jews, Arabs, Eastern Europeans, French, offer more variety than the architecture. That's why it's a shock to come up out of the métro across town at the Charles de Gaulle–Etoile station, at the foot of the Arc de Triomphe, and see only white people.

Nesta Pierry has invited me for icecream at the Häagen-Dazs shop on the Champs Elysées. I haven't seen this street since 1981, and it seems to have grown. It's so wide it's almost obscene, like it's been force-fed with macadam. Tricolour banners – today is the thirteenth of July – snap from the streetlights in a stiff wind.

Something about Nesta reminds me of the American French cuisine queen, Julia Child. Not in looks so much; Nesta has blonde hair and glasses which magnify her pale eyes, though she and Julia have similar, sturdy frames. Perhaps it's her unfazable common sense, her essential, no-nonsense simplicity, in the midst of so many French frills. She and I have just squeezed into the centre of a thicket of sidewalk café tables, when the clouds let loose with torrential rain. What's with the Welsh and rain, anyway? It seems to follow them around the planet.

We find seats inside and begin to steam in the air-conditioning as we wait for our icecream sundaes. My Welsh is halting today, but a group of American children at the next table find us fascinating nonetheless.

'They're speaking something really *weird*, Mom,' one of them shouts, thinking we can't understand. I've lived for this moment.

'You speak well,' Nesta pronounces in Welsh, like a stern yet well-meaning grandmother, 'but your writing is terrible. You must practise. Your letter [I'd written her as well as Boyd] was so simple, like a child's. You do much better in person.'

I don't doubt this – Written or Literary Welsh practically constitutes a different language from spoken Welsh, and is utterly foreign to me – but right now conversation is a struggle too. Remembering Norway, I doggedly stick with it, understanding just over half of Nesta's answers to my prepared questions but cunningly giving an impression of near-total comprehension, or so I imagine. (My trick is to ask the meaning of a word every three minutes or so, which implies that I've understood all the rest of them.) The thing is, I do comprehend most of Nesta's vocabulary, it's just that at this conversational speed recognition often comes without time for comprehension. It's like seeing something in the dark and not quite grasping its outline.

Nesta married a Frenchman and has lived in Paris most of her life. She's the *grande dame* of the BBC Wales 'foreign correspondents' – basically, anyone who can speak Welsh and lives abroad – and was the first to do a live broadcast from the Continent to Wales, around 1960. I ask if she ever thinks about moving home.

She shakes her head and says that the quality of life is far better in Paris. 'Don't need a car here. In Wales you need a car. It's that simple.'

Somehow we get on to the subject of Breton, which began to develop into its own language after Welsh immigrants came to what's now Brittany in the fifth and sixth centuries, fleeing the Anglo-Saxons. Today about twice as many people speak Breton as Welsh, though the latter probably has a more secure lease on life: not only are its speakers younger, but after centuries of harassment it's finally getting a boost from the British government. Breton remains a linguistic thorn in the side of the French.

'Do you know the French word *baragouiner*?' she asks.

I've never heard of it.

'Think about it.'

'*Baragouiner*? *Bara* means bread in Welsh, and *gwin* means wine . . .'

Nesta beams. 'Exactly. Centuries ago, when Breton farmers made the journey to Paris, they'd stop along the way and ask for *bara* and *gwin*. No one had a clue what they were talking about. They thought the Bretons were just speaking gibberish. That's how *baragouiner* came to be a French verb that means 'to speak nonsense'.

It occurs to me that this would be a great code name for my book.

After our icecream Nesta and I walk arm-in-arm down the Champs Elysées, speaking Welsh, by some wicked, unspoken agreement, very loudly. This is sweet Celtic revenge for all those dinners I squirmed through at Mme Peneau's. I'd like to stop a woman who walks by coddling a long, small dog that looks like a badly rolled cigarette and yell, 'Hey, you, Welsh was written down four hundred years before French, so there,' but I just barely refrain.

'You should have seen it, Pamela.' Nesta is gesturing at the avenue. '*Roedd yr holl cae gwenith.*' Huh? Did she just say it was all a wheat field?

'*Pam?*' What?

'It was all a wheat field. One Saturday night a few years ago. I came out and the entire Champs Elysées was covered in wheat. It was a protest to show solidarity with the striking farmers, and by Monday morning there were cars again, but while it lasted it was a wonderful sight.'

For a moment, Paris, that relentlessly better place where I never wear the right shoes and say *le* when I mean *la*, is transformed into Mabinogion country. There's a scene in one of the later Welsh tales called 'Peredur' (subsequently known in France and to the world as Percival), in which a tall tree grows by a river bank. 'From roots to crown one half was aflame and the other green with leaves.' If the Champs Elysées can become a wheat field overnight, then perhaps Peredur's river, for now, can be the Seine.

Cuddio ✿ to Hide

Locked in Nina's bathroom is the only time I get to flip through her stack of *New Yorker* magazines and look at the cartoons in peace. Today I create a furore by staying in long enough to read a story by Robert Olen Butler called 'Jealous Husband Comes

Back as Parrot'. The reincarnated bird intends absurdly more than it can say. It squawks for a cracker and means, why can't you see that even though I have feathers and a beak I'm your husband? I know just how it feels. I sound so skimpy in Welsh, so matter-of-factly shorn of subtlety and, I fear, tact.

Outside the door, Audrey, Marguerite's nine-year-old niece, is about to burst – not her bladder but her patience. She wants to talk about air pockets. We're all travelling tomorrow: Nina, Bernard and the kids to the States for a month, Marguerite and I on a ten-day Eurail trail through Holland, Germany and Luxembourg.

'Pam-Pam, what are you doing in there?' she demands in her precise, French-invigorated English.

'I'll be right out.'

'You said that ten minutes ago. Do you know what air pockets are?'

I'm about to explain but she interrupts. 'They are thief planes. They are like pick-pockets. They are bad planes that steal other airplanes' passengers!' She says this with an appropriate sense of outrage.

'That's not going to happen to you tomorrow,' I call out.

'I hope not,' she says, and leaves me to my parrot.

Darllen ✿ to Read

Gare du Nord: Marguerite and I flip to see who will have to sit backwards on the train from Paris to Rotterdam. I lose.

By the Belgian border things are really steaming up in *Y Trip*, though my progress – about ten minutes on each page – is as laborious as ever. I check my Welsh–English dictionary to make sure I've understood what I just read: *Gorffenodd y ferch ddu ei dawns yn gwisgo'r neidr yn unig.* The black girl finished her dance wearing only the snake. Useful vocabulary, I've no doubt, for chit-chat with the St David's Society of the Netherlands.

Sharing our compartment are Rick and his mom. Rick is from San Francisco; his mom, whose wig is slightly off-kilter, from Truth or Consequences, New Mexico. They are incredulous that we missed the Bastille Day celebrations last night.

'We danced in the streets at a gay ball on the Rive Gauche,' Rick's mom tell us proudly.

'Did you know that a translation of "The Marseillaise" was published in Welsh in 1796?' I ask, diverting attention from the fact that we spent last evening ironing children's clothes.

YR ISELDIROEDD (THE NETHERLANDS)

Cyrraedd ✿ to Arrive

It's been about a five-hour trip from Paris to Delft, with one change in Rotterdam. For the past few weeks a Welshman named Philip Jonathan and I have been E-mailing each other under the heading *Y Barbiciw*, an all-Welsh event which will occur tomorrow afternoon at the home of a woman called Rhiannon, who's also putting us up this weekend.

At the Delft train station I buy a Dutch phone card with a close-up picture of a belly button on it, and call Rhiannon, who appears a few moments later on foot. Tall and big-boned, with cheeks gone ruddy from a day in the sun with her eight-year-old charges (she's a teacher in the English-language school here), Rhiannon has the kind of easy-going, friendly face you hope to see after travelling backwards on a train for five hours. Her Welsh accent conjures hills and high spirits – an accent for outdoors, compared to Rosemary's musical, parlour voice. She leads us down an immaculate canalside street past brick townhouses with brimming flowerboxes. Along the way we discover that she and her husband Ed have lived in Portugal.

'It took a while to pick up Portuguese, but we did it,' Rhiannon says. Marguerite and I give each other a look. I was right: the language gods have provided for us both.

'Go on, you first.' I nudge her, and she and Rhiannon launch into a nostalgic stream of Portuguese.

I an awed by Rhiannon's staircase. Ridiculously tall and narrow, it's like some sheer, vertical rock formation with carpeting. My toes stick over the shallow treads as I perilously climb downstairs to join her, leaving Marguerite to nap in the upstairs guestroom.

'*Hoffech chi gwrw?*'

This question catches me like a deer in headlights. One of the most diabolical things about Welsh is the fact that there is no simple way to say yes and no. There's one set of yes and no answers for the past tense; there's another that matches a particular sentence structure. Most of the time, though, you can't use either one: you have to reconjugate the verb, which is why I usually wind up silently nodding my head. Each simple question in Welsh is like a surprise quiz. *Hoffech chi gwrw?* Would you like a beer? Of course I want a beer, but how to say it? Seconds pass as I shuffle grammatical paradigms in my head. A beer would taste really good right now. Rhiannon waits with the refrigerator door open.

'Umm.' I give my head a vigorous up and down shaking.

'*Hoffwn,*' Rhiannon says kindly. Oh god, *hoffwn*: Yes–I–would–like. Where was that when I needed it?

She puts on a Welsh CD and we take our beers out on to the balcony, which overlooks a well-kept garden and a slew of other balconies. From across the way an old man totters out and stares at us.

'Not much privacy, I'm afraid,' apologizes Rhiannon. 'The Dutch never close their curtains. I've been told it goes back to the war. People figured only collaborators had something to hide, so everyone else kept their curtains open. They still do.'

Our Welsh conversation is porous, with plenty of English running through it. Rhiannon is from the *Rhymni*, one of the narrow fissures – the famous Valleys – that run like curtain folds, up to seventeen miles long by one mile wide, between the Brecon Beacons and the sea in South Wales. By the time she was born there, in the fifties, the Welsh language had been dug out of the locals as thoroughly as the coal had been dug from the ground. English was her first tongue.

'I've been learning Welsh since I was three. It's lurking in me somewhere,' she points nebulously at her chest. 'I went to university in Bangor, where nearly everyone spoke Welsh. But it wasn't until I came to the Netherlands that I really got a grip on it.'

'*Wrth gwrs*,' I say, which is, and sounds like, Of course! 'I knew it was a mistake to go to Wales to learn Welsh. I should've come to Delft.'

Rhiannon snorts. 'I took a correspondence course from Aberystwyth. But now there are so many speakers here that I get a lot of practice. You'll meet quite a few of them tomorrow. Unfortunately Effie can't make it. Have you heard of her?'

Have I heard of her? Effie Wiltens is fast becoming a quest in herself. Her name came up before I'd even left the States; she was mentioned in Lampeter; Boyd told me in Paris that she has 'a strong personality'; now Rhiannon says, 'Effie learned Welsh on the strength of sheer personality alone.' It would do me good to meet this person.

From what I've been able to learn, Effie is a Dutch woman who went to Wales on holiday and never got over it. She's not only become fluent in Welsh – 'speaks like a native North Walian,' Rhiannon claims – but has even learned to fly light aircraft so she can careen between Holland and Wales quicker than I can say *awyren*, Welsh for airplane.

Sylwi ✿ to Notice

Ed has come home, and the four of us are going to an outdoor concert. Rhiannon and . . . Ed. In a tie-dyed shirt and sandals, Rhiannon is convincingly down-to-earth despite being named for the personification of a deity. In the First Branch of 'The Mabinogi', the character Rhiannon – who spawned the name that has taken hold of parents in Wales as completely as the wretched Ashley has in the States – is a powerhouse who still bears traces of magic about her, left over from her former role as a goddess of horses in the prehistoric Celtic pantheon. Rhiannon of Delft is not my idea of a horse goddess, for which I'm grateful, but the name remains hard to pair with 'Ed'.

Ed is a geologist and a quiet, wry mumbler with an Irish accent ('Irish Gaelic lurks in him, too,' they assure us, though it's skulking somewhat deeper than Rhiannon's Welsh). Tonight the two of them lead us out through the fresh, sea-smelling dusk to a canalside café. As in Amsterdam, Delft's city blocks have been turned into an adjoining series of islets by an intricate canal system, begun around 1100. The canal we're sitting next to has a lustre like molten jade, which deepens as the sun sinks, and is threaded with flowering lily pads. A trio – two violinists and a pianist – bob on a flat-bed barge and play until it gets dark. Further down the canal a pack of kayakers sit absolutely still in two-person skiffs, paddles across their laps, rapt.

We talk softly. Rhiannon tells us she would never have been caught dead baking Welsh cakes in Wales, but last year found herself making a ton of them for the Welsh Society, which has about fifty members.

'The things you do when you leave home,' she says, wincing.

'It's *hiraeth*,' adds Ed.

I broach my *hiraeth* theory about Wales and Portugal. One clings to the western edge of an island, the other to the western edge of a peninsula; both are tiny nations hemmed in by the sea and bullied by bigger, wealthier neighbours to the east. And both suffer from the same malaise, which in Wales is called *hiraeth* and in Portugal *saudade*, a kind of longing that is more than simple homesickness, because you can get it at home too. It's a lament not just for what has been lost, but for what should have been but never was; a weary and, so far, an impotent protest that history hasn't played fair.

We all fall silent. In a window above the musicians' barge a woman lights a cigarette, backlit by a pale, incandescent glow. She turns her profile to the flared match and puffs out the window, smudging the blue twilight. I wonder if she's rehearsed this gesture, and then I know, with utmost certainty, that had we been speaking Welsh just now instead of English, I never would have noticed her.

Cymysgu ✹ to Mingle

Dutch toilets, I remark to Marguerite, have a flat ledge rather than a bowl filled with water, so you can examine your waste should you so desire. We try to read significance into this but fail.

This morning we wandered around the town centre looking for Delft tiles. Marguerite, who is a world-class fretter, wanted one like Rhiannon and Ed have next to a Welsh lovespoon in their guest room, which reads, 'Worries are like crumbs in the bed. The more you wriggle, the more they itch,' but she couldn't find any by the time we had to get back for the barbecue.

'Okay,' I drill her, 'what's your mission at this shindig?'

'Remember what everyone tells me in English so I can tell you what you missed in Welsh.' I give her a thumbs up.

'By the way, Pam, isn't this cheating?'

'One woman's cheating is another woman's book,' I reply, pointedly.

Unlike the wine and cheese party in Norway, the Delft barbecue is not a lipstick-imperative affair. Phil Jonathan shows up in gym shorts as does Geoff, an Englishman from Amsterdam who's stuffed a lumberjack shirt into his. Rob and Eryl, both native speakers from Wales, round out the group. I like these people immediately.

Phil and his wife Jana have brought their new baby and their three-year-old daughter Catrin. Perhaps as some unconscious sign of respect for his command of Welsh, I'd assumed Phil was fifty at least; it's a shock to see he's my age, maybe younger. He and Catrin immediately flop on the floor to put together a crossword puzzle. Catrin speaks Czech to her mother, who's from Prague, and Welsh to her father; last year they lived in Houston for a while where she picked up a few words of English, which she's just beginning to learn in earnest now, in Holland. Of all the people in the room, this little girl with the immense eyes and shiny dark bob makes me the most nervous; she is the first person I've encountered on earth with whom I can communicate only in Welsh. It doesn't go well. I try to help with the crossword puzzle but drive her near desperate with frustration.

'She says you're too slow,' Phil relays sympathetically in Welsh, after she whispers something in his ear.

On my way out to the balcony I notice Rhiannon's kitchen calendar: yesterday is circled with a note, 'Welsh woman comes.' Funny, no one here has asked me why I'm bothering to learn Welsh, something that drives Americans nuts. At home my 'Welsh thing' is like an affront to the national cult of utility and pragmatism. Among these people it's taken for granted, and again, as in Norway, my identity seems more a construct of shared passion and individual practice than something I was merely born with.

On the balcony a barbecuing frenzy has seized Ed, who seems bent on crisping every sausage, steak, chicken wing and veggie burger in Delft. When he runs out of these he grabs a banana, which he roasts in its peel and passes around to whomever wants a taste. Geoff, Rob and Eryl are standing downwind of the grill and by the time I join them have begun to look like baby ducklings, each covered in a fine, fuzzy ash. They're discussing Welsh in Welsh.

I haltingly tell Rosemary's story of being yelled at by a woman from Tregaron for speaking high-falutin' Welsh on the radio. Like Catrin, they get the point before I'm through and move on.

'*Cymraeg Byw*, in my opinion,' adds Phil, who's joined the group, 'is whatever Welsh is spoken by living people. If they say *leicio* instead of *hoffwn*, or *ffeindio* if they've just found something. What the hell. It's still Welsh.'

The only word I get for certain is 'hell', which he says in

English, but that's his gist. Both *hoffwn* and *leicio* mean 'to like' (the latter, pronounced 'lickio', has always struck me as vaguely obscene); *Cymraeg Byw* means Living Welsh. It's a made-up language that was invented in the sixties as a way of uniting all the discordant strands of Welsh: the spoken language of the South, the spoken language of the North (each of these have their own brood of variations), and Literary Welsh (itself an artificial creation). Unfortunately, the only people who spoke *Cymraeg Byw* were students, and it turned out that no one else could understand them. The simple fact of the matter is that Welsh is like Silly Putty. You can stretch it and twist it and mould it into any number of shapes and it's still Welsh – which is both a boon and an anxiety for learners. If you're used to the authoritarian dictatorship of English or French, for example – two of the few systems in the universe in which there exists an absolute right and wrong – then the sloppy democracy of Welsh is unnerving. On the other hand, it's pretty hard to sin against grammar in any really grievous way.

(This said, there are, of course, no perfect democracies, and a hierarchy does exist among the language's various incarnations, with Literary or Written Welsh on top, media Welsh next – the formal spoken dialect that Rosemary uses on BBC broadcasts – followed by everyday spoken Welsh, and finally Wenglish, which is spoken Welsh mixed with a liberal sprinkling of English words. Like most dysfunctional families, this group is bound by mutual suspicion and resentment in a fierce love-hate relationship.)

Cymharu Nodiau ✿ to Compare Notes

Immediately after the barbecue Ed and Rhiannon prepare to go to a friend's fiftieth birthday party. It's a Dutch custom, they tell us, to put a scarecrow in someone's yard when the person turns fifty. Tonight their friend is compromising by dressing like one.

They give us a key, and Marguerite and I decide to take a walking tour of Delft.

'So what do you know that I don't know?' I ask her, stepping over the brick mosaic of a fish set in the sidewalk outside a tropical fish store.

'That I want to stay here and live with Rhiannon and Ed. Their friends are great, we can speak Portuguese . . .'

'Forget it.'

'Travelling around the world is tiring, you know?' She sighs and gives in. 'Rob and Phil are in the oil business, Rhiannon and Eryl are teachers. Geoff's a translator. They all said they'd go back and live in Wales in a second, but they can't because their jobs don't exist there. Everyone but Geoff. He's not Welsh.'

I sigh. I'd heard the same thing in Norway. There's a limited apparatus in Wales to support people with specialized educations and high incomes.

Marguerite continues. 'They all agree that living abroad is better than living in England. Here they can be in a safe, mid-size city, drive three hours and wind up in Brussels. In England they'd probably live near London, commute to work, and after a three-hour drive only get to Bristol.'

As she's talking we come upon Market Square, a cobblestoned plaza the size of a football field where the bells of Nieuwe Kerk, or New Church – begun in 1383 – inexplicably begin to play '*Frère Jacques*'. In my pocket I find a nest of grape seeds. Earlier, speaking to Rob and Eryl in Welsh, I'd been explaining our route around the globe when I'd recklessly eaten a grape. Had I been dealing in English I could've discreetly spat my seeds into a napkin, or on to my fork – jeez, I could've blown them into the air and caught them behind my back and still made my point. But because I was concentrating so hard on Welsh all I could manage was to put them in my pocket.

The grape seeds are emblematic of the afternoon. In six weeks I haven't improved in Welsh so much as lost some of my fear of speaking (to all but Catrin); yet while I can understand what's being said at the time, I can't repeat later what we've talked about. It's a strange and particular kind of amnesia. When I'd mentioned this to Rhiannon she'd got a wise look on her face.

'I know what you mean. It goes in your ears, through your brain, but just can't come out your mouth.'

Precisely. I explain to Marguerite that my Welsh brain knew all she'd just said, though I had no corresponding memory of it in English.

'Isn't that the language your book is supposed to be in?' She sighs again.

Shops have begun to close and waiters are hunched down over outdoor blackboards, chalking in the evening's menu. Tight, canalside parking places are filling up with expensive cars, and the brick façades of gable-fronted townhouses, which look to me like rows of ageing, uneven teeth, send the clop-scrape of high heels on cobblestone echoing back to the street. I like the townhouses' immense windows – in these narrow enclaves they're a necessity through which furniture must come and go by means of hoisting hooks that dangle from the upper gables. Tonight the window panes look like oblong ponds spawned from the dark canals below.

There is a cosy taste of wealth in the air, which neither Marguerite nor I can afford. We go back to the house for leftovers and dark yellow Dutch cheese, which Rhiannon told us comes from summer milk, when the cows graze on grass; in winter Dutch cheese is pale yellow, made from the milk of cows who eat hay.

Mwynhau ✿ to Have Fun

Rhiannon and Ed both have hangovers, and I empathize (the word Norway still makes my brain throb). In the middle of my shower this morning, just after I'd shampooed my hair, the water ran to a trickle, then vanished altogether. Marguerite had to wake Ed,

who uncomplainingly performed some voodoo with the kitchen
door and made it flow again.

After breakfast we leave them with reluctance to catch the
hour-long train to Amsterdam. It's bliss to have left most of our
stuff back in Paris; for this ten-day trip we've borrowed two small
bags of Nina's which are a cinch to hoist after our wretched
backpacks. We'd been too clever by half in getting bags that
convert into standard, hand-held suitcases. They were supposed
to be a cagey merger of form and function, but lacking a frame
they ride low on our torsos, converting us into the image of tall
box turtles on holiday, and swing from side to side if we walk
too fast. The swinging action has a dire effect on one's panties,
which tend to roll up in a tight little ball under the buttocks.

No packs today, no Welsh. The Dutch, bless them, speak Eng-
lish. All the Dutch: the Asians and blacks as well as the big blond
people. Unlike Norway, it's a pleasure in Holland to have our
expectations assaulted and thwarted by the diversity of the popu-
lation. The day is warm and our shoulders don't ache, and in this
city where you can get a rush from ready pot as easily as from
Vermeer's lapis lazuli blues and deep golds – probably for the same
price, since the Rijksmuseum costs a fortune – we choose to sit
on the edge of a canal and lick icecream as tourists line up to visit
Anne Frank's house.

Geoff has offered to put us up for the night. He lives in Lelylaan,
which is pronounced Lay-lee-lan and sounds to me like a suitable
home for Winken, Blinken and Nod. That it's really a nondescript
suburb of Amsterdam doesn't change my opinion. Besides, Geoff,
in short white shorts, legs splayed over the side of his chair, head
framed in the crook of a high intensity lamp that gives a lumines-
cent sheen to his cropped hair, has the off-beat appeal of a high-
strung, hospitable elf.

'What can I get you? There's some food. A sandwich? Beer?
Wine? Hashish? Maybe a cuppa tea?' At the barbecue he and I
both clung to Welsh, no matter how halting our tongues; tonight
neither of us makes so much as an attempt.

I choose wine and he sweetly brings me a glass and my own bottle. He seems disappointed that Marguerite – who projects a frail quality when she's tired – wants nothing more than water, and appeals to her throughout the evening to let him in some way provide for her. I sense a crush in the making.

Geoff translates from Dutch to English for a living but has taken up Welsh as a hobby. He recently spent two weeks at Nant Gwrthyrn, a famous language school on the Lleyn Peninsula in North Wales, and has a firmer grip on structure and vocabulary than I do, though there's a nervous tic in his cadence. He puts on a tape he made off *Radio Cymru* of news broadcasts and Welsh rock music, and for a long time there's a sequence of synthesized wails and human screams. Coupled with the white walls and high intensity wattage, it makes for compelling evidence that we've slipped into an innocuous version of Terry Gilliam's *Brazil*.

'Why did you decide to learn Welsh?' Marguerite asks. Geoff perks up.

'I think it sounds really good on women. It's got this earthy, sensual quality, don't you think?'

I idly wonder if there are nine-hundred numbers for Welsh telephone sex. They'd have at least one customer. Geoff interrupts this line of thought to point out Gorky's Zygotic Mynci on his tape.

'The Japanese are crazy about them,' he explains. 'They're a young band out of West Wales. Sing about half their stuff in Welsh.'

I've heard of Gorky's. My E-mail chat group is obsessed with them. I get messages from the Physics and Astronomy department of Edinburgh University and the Computing Centres of Jesus and Magdalen Colleges at Oxford, tracking their gigs. In an article called 'From Trip Hop to Welsh Pop to Vietnamese Show Tunes', the *New York Times* named their album '*Bwyd Time*' – literally, 'Food Time' – one of the ten best of 1995, and called them 'mystical and whimsical . . . smart and graceful . . . [and] criminally obscure'. The cut from *Bwyd Time* on Geoff's tape reminds me of the sort of strung-out, circusy sleep-singing the Beatles achieved in the studio just before they broke up.

'I think,' Marguerite says, 'that the desire to learn Welsh is all about place. I can't imagine wanting to learn Welsh without knowing Wales.'

This yanks me from my Gorky's reverie. She's absolutely right. I studied French on faith long before I ever went to France, on the promise of photos of the Eiffel Tower and the coq au vin served at a restaurant on New York's West Side. By comparison, in America anyway, there isn't the faintest trace of an infrastructure of the imagination on which to build the desire to learn Welsh. (What can you expect when most of the country thinks Wales is a group of large sea mammals or, maybe, a county of England near Cornwall?) Johan, Effie, Geoff and I: in each of our cases it was the landscape that initiated interest, before any of us counted real Welsh people among our friends.

'You're absolutely right,' says Geoff thoughtfully, reaching for my wine bottle. I didn't know we were going to share. 'Wales is still rural. I think it's a draw to the pastoral, to the sense of community that you don't get in a city like Amsterdam. The language gives you entry to a world that's disappearing everywhere else.'

I try to explain how I feel about it. 'I read a book once when I was a kid about a guy who takes this drug that lets him go back in time. In his mind he interacts with all these people from the fourteenth century, then, because he's oblivious to the present, he walks into an oncoming train.'

They look at me uncertainly. 'The point is,' I emphasize dramatically, 'that speaking Welsh does the same thing, and you don't even die from it. I find I look for elbow room in time as well as in space . . . for a way to, I don't know, enhance the present. Not for an option to it, maybe just an antechamber. Before I knew any Welsh, Lampeter meant houses, pubs, a college, a superstore. That was it. Now that I know its *Llanbedr Pont Steffan*, I feel like

I've become farsighted. I can see right out of the visible world to Peter's Church at Stephen's Bridge.'

This is too bizarre for them. 'Look, there ain't no "Moor by the Heathery Glade" in Rhosllannerchrugog either, but the language tells me there used to be. You get two landscapes for the price of one.'

A beat passes and Geoff changes the subject. 'Say, Pam, have you heard of a woman called Effie Wiltens? She's famous around here, and in the Nant, too. She's this cool Dutch woman who learned Welsh. Made a huge impression on the people in the Nant by arriving in her private plane.'

I flash him a tight smile. Effie Wiltens is like Mark Nodine to the hundredth power. I thank god when Marguerite yawns fetchingly, and Geoff abruptly gets up and disappears. Some time later he comes back laboriously dragging a mattress under his arm, which he throws down on the dining-room floor. He looks like an urban hunter-gatherer.

'Your bed, ladies.'

Marguerite is nearly weepy with relief.

'You know,' Geoff says wistfully, backing out of the room, 'I need fun. I just don't get enough fun.'

Teithio ♣ to Travel

I wake up thirsty in the night and in darkness and confusion drink something that is not water. I go back to bed certain I've been poisoned.

When we wake – to my astonishment I'm not dead – Geoff is long gone to work. We raid his fridge and have a daringly frivolous time in Amsterdam, then board the night train to Stuttgart, scheduled to arrive just before 5 a.m., after which we'll catch a commuter connection to Tübingen.

Most of the bleary-eyed kids hanging around the Amsterdam train station are a good fifteen years younger than we are.

'You know, fifteen years ago you said we wouldn't be travelling like this now.'

Marguerite has a point. The train ride is like one of Dante's circles of hell drawn out in a long, straight line. We stretch opposite one another, feet to face, and try to ignore the fact that the train shudders to a halt every ten minutes or so with an ear-splitting screech like it's shaving steel off the rails. By 2 a.m. my hips ache like an old dog's. Marguerite is possessed by the spirit of an evil jumping bean, and thrashes mercilessly. A pleasant, tinny sound like icicles snapping turns out to be driving rain against the window, which pelts in the open crack and soaks my face.

Hysbyddu ✤ to Weary

The man with the newspaper is gone. So is the guy who was smoking, two compartments down. In fact, we are the only two people on the entire train.

It's morning in Tübingen: according to my watch, we've been in the station – sound asleep – for almost half an hour. As soon as I make this discovery we bolt from the compartment as if pursued by demons.

Tübingen is home to the Welsh Studies Centre, paradoxically housed within the Seminar für Englische Philologie at the university here. I'd read about the Centre in the Welsh journal *Planet* and had written to the director, Christopher Harvie, who in turn had issued me a warm invitation to visit him. Because I'd had to be in Delft for *Y Barbiciw* over the weekend, and he's 'going across' to Wales tomorrow, as he put it, our encounter will have to be limited to lunch today at noon.

It's still obscenely early. A young woman writing a dissertation on how nurses deal with stress – how or, better yet, why we pry this intimate detail from her in five minutes' walk I can't say – leads us to the tourist information centre, which is closed. The morning sun acts like scouring powder on the town, which is a great deal cleaner and brighter than we are. If the sound of Lelylaan conjured Winken, Blinken and Nod, the look of Tübingen invokes the Brothers Grimm. Sitting outside the tourism office like the bovine sisters on parade, neither of us rises to the level of speech. Instead images of Welsh towns slouch past my mind's eye, a dingy parade of greys and off-whites, poured concrete and slate, of uniformity and wet pavement; when I look up, the whimsy of Tübingen seems piercingly foreign. Red gabled roofs of lightning-splitter steepness; rows of shutter-flanked windows; colour-saturated stucco in red and ochre; Gothic church spires; lots of geraniums.

When the office opens we learn there is only one hotel in town we can afford, the Hotel Kurner. It is as drab a place as I've ever stayed, and the bathroom smells like fermenting urine, but I'm comforted knowing there is a knee-high statue of Aphrodite just outside our door. We take a self-timed photo squatting on either side of her.

Esbonio to Explain

Chris Harvie is a small man with a small round belly and a small round head, wearing small round glasses. He has a nest of white hair and bright, curious eyes. His tongue-contorting Scottish accent comes as a surprise. He is furiously busy and we have a disjointed conversation in English as he races around his office.

'Everything all right? Find a hotel?'

'Yes, thanks. It's something of a pit, but we're only staying one night.'

'There's a lecture on modern Scottish poetry this afternoon that should interest you,' he calls over his shoulder.

Well, yes. But what about Welsh? In a few minutes it becomes clear that he has no real idea why I'm here. I mention my visits to Norway, France and Holland, and my goal of practising Welsh around the world.

'Ah, yes. You wrote me in Welsh. Couldn't read a word. I don't speak Welsh, you see. I'm a Scot.'

That would explain his confusion.

Harvie, as everyone calls him, has his wife and young daughter
lead us to the restaurant where we're to have lunch. He and his
grad student-assistant, Alice, will join us shortly. En route Mrs
Harvie proclaims herself to be English.

'I grew up in Wales, but I'm not *Welsh*, if you know what I
mean,' she informs us.

I know just what she means, and feel my heart harden a little.
In England to be *Welsh* is a decided shortcoming: a *Welsh* pearl
is a fake, a *Welsh* cricket is a louse, *Welsh* parsley is a noose, a
*Welsh*man's hug is an itch. We wander along a route Marguerite
and I have not taken before and wind up . . . back at the Hotel
Kurner.

'Wonderful Greek restaurant,' announces Mrs Harvie.

That would explain Aphrodite.

Four inches from my mouth I discover a whole baby octopus
dangling from my fork. Harvie, Marguerite and I are sharing a
gigantic Greek platter, and I thought I'd speared a chunk of feta.
Reluctantly, I bite off a leg.

The Welsh Studies Centre is the progeny of a cooperative
agreement between Wales and the German state of Baden-
Württemberg – one of the new regional alliances that are sprouting
throughout Europe, seeking to bypass unwieldy national ventures.
The Centre itself maintains a small library and sponsors a series of
seminars and lectures on Welsh language and culture. None of
the faculty speaks Welsh, but some of the students are learning.
This seems to be getting it backwards, but Alice is enthusiastic.
Her English is so good I hadn't realized she was German.

'There are three who are learning Welsh. The guy with the
beard –'

'The one who's seventeen going on sixty-eight,' Harvie
interrupts.

' – and two women. After the Centre opened we discovered
that a man who teaches at the gymnasium had been giving Welsh
lessons in Tübingen all along. Dr Schwerteck.'

I make a note to get his address, and notice Marguerite discreetly trying to wipe some shiny pink stuff off her fork. She takes a big gulp of Retsina. I'm desperately trying to fend off a wave of sleep-deprivation giggles.

'So what's the draw?' I manage to ask. 'Why do students get hooked on Wales?'

After Harvie has packed his daughter off to her swimming lesson he replies. 'Once our British Studies students get past the Basil Fawlty Belt' – he checks to see if we Americans have understood, and adds, 'southern England – they invariably end up in Scotland, Wales or Ireland. I think it's the great German obsession with creative photography. The Celtic fringe ideally lends itself to that. It's all so darkly *Romantik*.'

I remember a group of Germans who were on an exchange programme while I was at Lampeter. One paid for her staggering film costs by modelling in the nude for a life drawing class I'd started with a friend. She had perfect calves.

'How about you?' I ask Alice.

'My boyfriend's Welsh,' she says.

Lunch ends with Harvie telling Marguerite a classic joke about Welsh confoundedness. A Welshman is shipwrecked on an uninhabited island. After a long while he's rescued, and the rescuers find he's built a pub, a rugby field and two chapels. Why two chapels, they want to know. That's the one I go to, he replies, pointing at one, and that, he says, indicating the other, is the one I don't.

With that Harvie leaves to prepare for his Scottish poetry lecture, and Alice leads us back to the university along Wilhelmstrasse, which she calls 'The Road of the Three Deaths', where at any moment one can be mowed down by a rogue pedestrian, bike or car. She shows us the Welsh resource room which actually boils down to the resource shelf, and invites me to Harvie's lecture. I decline. This is probably bad policy but – and this is a miracle – I'm too tired to be polite. As we're leaving Alice calls to us that the Anglo-Irish theatre group is putting on Beckett's *Endgame* tonight in English.

'Beckett?' mutters Marguerite under her breath. 'How redundant.'

We spend the afternoon zig-zagging aimlessly around Tübingen like sluggish pinballs. Everywhere in Europe this summer the shoes for sale are criminally ugly, with thick, clunky soles. Been there in the seventies, done that. We should visit the church and what my brochure calls 'a fine, half-timbered town hall dating from the fifteenth century', but instead we sit in the shade above the Neckar River, just short of a nice view, too weary to care.

Back in the sixty-watt glow of our room in the Hotel Kurner, I've just read in John Davies's *A History of Wales* that 'It is . . . unlikely that there is any racial distinction of substance between the English and the Welsh.' Why didn't I know this at lunch? To be Welsh or not to be Welsh isn't such a big deal, after all.

Greek restaurant noises are rising through the open window riding a faint scent of lamb. Just as we were saying goodbye to Alice this afternoon we'd run into a German colleague of hers by the name of Ursula. Alice had to leave, but Ursula, Marguerite and I had gone for coffee. (N.B. This posed a huge problem for me, as the subtext to my goal of rounding the world speaking Welsh is rounding the world without drinking caffeine. It makes my heart skip beats, which feels like a quick peek at death whenever it happens. I have a stash of decaffeinated tea bags in my backpack, but those couldn't save me from the merciless vending machines in the university cafeteria. I drank half a cup of regular coffee, which even now makes me feel like I'm jumping rope at high altitude.)

My notes from our conversation with Ursula are short and cryptic: 'German obsession with Celts = politically correct nationalism.'

It takes some hard recollection to decipher this. I remember Ursula saying there's an unwritten rule in Germany that makes pride in a national *German* past essentially *verboten*. It's just not tactful, she'd said, giving me one of those 'of course you under-stand' kind of looks. Lateral pride, however, in a disarmingly collective, pan-European history isn't, perhaps, so bad. Rome smacks too much of the present – all bureaucracy and imperial aggression – but Celtic Europe is another story. Those were the days. A simpler, quieter time. The druids worshipped oak trees and wore mistletoe. So they sacrificed one another now and then, they cared about nature. By god, they were the forerunners of the Green Party!

I ponder this in the dark. Is it really true that Wales and its sister Celtic nations – wet, rainy places all, with sub-average per capita incomes and high unemployment – shore up the self-image of an insecure Europe? I agree with Ursula, but this Celtic infatu-ation doesn't seem peculiar to Germany. Everywhere lately, even in the States, you can find coffee-table books with artists' render-ings of the Celtic gods, retellings of (bowdlerized) Celtic legends, Celtic mythologies, even Celtic bloody cookbooks. All in soft focus with Irish calligraphy.

It's our version of William Morris and the Arts and Crafts movement, real end-of-century stuff. Pre-Romanism instead of Pre-Raphaelism. The Victorians sought their simpler, gentler world of neo-medievalism; since we're looking at the end not just of a century but a millennium, we've lopped another thousand years off our obsession and have found ourselves the prehistoric Celts. All to the better that they're still hazily mirrored on earth today in places like Wales, however dark and distorted the glass may be.

This makes me uneasy. All those green hills, all the sheep and the damp, doughy nights, those 'w's and the double 'l's; I'd never thought of them as an airbag for the impact of the twenty-first century before, and the image doesn't charm me.

We leave Tübingen the way we came, by train, first thing in the morning.

Argraffion ✿ Impressions

A hole punched in our Eurail tickets brings us Celtic torques and amber beads at the Württembergisches Landesmuseum in Stuttgart; children bathing naked in a fountain; an opera diva from Long Island, New York, in Mannheim; the couple with the unicycle. Another hole punched and cows bend gums-to-grass, uninterested in passing trains. We meet American backpackers from Lubbock, Texas, a seventy-two-year-old father and his twenty-year-old Vietnamese daughter, on the road together for two months, the talk of the backpack set. Heinz waits for us in Luxembourg City: an old friend, tall, lopsided, fair, with rolls around the middle that move like shifting sand dunes. The hottest damn day of the year.

A dog faints in the sun and my stiff shoe soles bend like a gymnast's back. Heat is the lead story on evening news shows in three different languages. The night that follows is a furnace, too, but still we eat well. Heinz is a banker. Kir Royale cocktails, lobster mousse, baby duckling, Mosel wine, tiny pastries for dessert.

Wildlife bridges over the Autobahn; a buxom, prissy sphinx with lion claws and a periwig in Trier; hillsides plaited like corn rows into orderly vineyards on the Luxembourg bank of the Mosel. Distant thunder. Heinz says 'it's raining seams' is the German equivalent to cats and dogs and old ladies and sticks. A glass of Auxerrois at a roadside stand in the village of Stadtbredimus, chilled by air temperature fallen forty degrees Fahrenheit since morning. Heinz's jackets come down to our knees. We celebrate Marguerite's birthday in a collapsible mirror tent invented by the Dutch.

Rhedeg Amoc ✾ to Run Amok

Metz, a French city near the German border. We left Heinz in Luxembourg two hours ago and in three more we'll be back in Paris. Marguerite convinces me I have time to buy us lunch during the twenty-minute layover in the station.

Leaving my worldly goods behind while I forage for food touches off a primordial chill along my spinal chord; instinctively I memorize track numbers and landmarks along my route to a sandwich shop across the street, and mentally check them off on my way back. I arrive on the platform just in time to see the rear end of Marguerite's train pulling out of the station a good ten minutes early.

Okay, I say to myself, think. Think! But rational thoughts shred on the hard edge of instinct, and I race like a dog after the last car, which disappears around a bend.

Oh god oh god oh god. I have the tickets, she has the money. Why isn't this platform signposted for Paris? By chance I look up and see that the next one over, across the way, has a sign 'Paris, Gare du Nord.' This is an improvement. I run underground and come up beneath the sign, just as a new train arrives from the opposite direction. Is this the train that's going to Paris? A much more composed line of thought, like an avuncular voiceover, tells me to calm down for god's sake, it's not the end of the world. I ignore it. An SNCF conductor — SNCF is the acronym of the French railway — crosses my path, and I literally grab his uniform.

'Do you speak English?'

'*Non. Pas du tout. Pas d'Anglais.*'

Deep breath. '*D'accord.*' I explain in shards of French that my valise and my friend were going to Paris, and I, too, but I buy lunch, and gone they are, and the train is where?

He is calm. Look for the head of the train, he tells me. You will find your friend.

Encouragement is like a shot of adrenaline. I run up and down the platform shouting – literally shouting, '*Ble? Ble, ble est la tête du train?*' which translates as, 'Wheat? Wheat, wheat is the head of the train?' After about ten seconds it occurs to me that there is no head to the train – the locomotive has disengaged and puttered away. Ah ha. I peer far down the track and from this angle can see that Marguerite's train is hovering just beyond the bend. It's going to come back and hook up with these cars and then we'll all go to Paris together. It is at this moment I realize that, one, I really need a rest, and two, I have been yelling about wheat. In Welsh, *Ble?* means 'Where?' I've crossed my wires in public. No one is standing within six feet of me. Worse yet, instead of staring, everyone looks away. I'm being pitied by the bourgeoisie.

FFRAINC (FRANCE)

Parchu ✿ to Respect

Nina and Bernard's apartment is quiet without them and the children, which is good, because I have just over a week to write four articles that will pay for the horizon and beyond.

Actually, quiet is a relative term. We have to close the windows to speak on the phone; cars and trucks rumble by, Parisian trashmen come daily and make the noise of thunder gods, at night men and children shout on the street. Half an hour in the door, not even unpacked yet, the phone starts ringing.

Nesta Pierry calls while she's drawing a bath to say goodbye, as she's heading to Wales in the morning. Instinctively she speaks in English. She's been busy commentating for Radio Cymru and S4C TV on the rash of bombs that have been exploding all over Paris; she's also been thinking about a question I'd asked her. I'd wanted to know if the French differentiate between Wales and England. When I'd asked Rhiannon about the Dutch she'd rolled her eyes and said, 'You mean "Englandnwales"?'

Nesta has a different response. 'Absolutely. The French respect the Welsh, but they think the English aren't *clen*.'

'They're not clean?'

'No, *clen*. In Welsh it means kind, friendly, you know.' Ah, simpatico. 'The French admire the Welsh for one reason, pure and simple: rugby. Both France and Wales are rugby-playing nations, and for a long time, until recently, Wales was the best in the world.'

Rugby, eh? Because of a mistake at the Residential Life Office, in my first term at Lampeter I was assigned to live with the undergraduate rugby team instead of in post-graduate housing. We took to each other pretty well; in fact, they used to borrow my make-up before matches, hoping that a little eye shadow and some nice lipstick would lull the other team into a false sense of security. I have, however, seen only one rugby match in my life, and that was in the States: Llandrindod Wells vs. Rhode Island. It was like pairing twigs against tree trunks. Rhode Island got shmeared.

Clen isn't in my pocket Welsh–English/English–Welsh diction-ary. I figure it must be northern slang, and for all practical purposes I speak South Walian Welsh. When the phone rings again it's Boyd, confirming a date to meet at Le Comptoir tomorrow night. No one else can come, but he says he's game. I've just found out from Nesta that he's an interior decorator.

In the refrigerator the goat cheese has adopted the sheen and texture of petrified peanut butter. I've got a piece in my mouth when the phone rings yet again. This time it's Jackie, a friend from home, currently houseswapping in Paris.

'I found something for you,' she says, 'called *The Xenophobe's Guide to the Welsh*. Come to lunch tomorrow and it's yours.' As a favour she also asks me to make dinner reservations for her and her husband at a place called Le Kiosk Flottant. 'You speak French, don't you?'

'Umph.' I finally manage to pry my tongue out of a well of goat cheese. 'Ah, sort of,' I hedge. Right now, as the Metz incident has proved, Welsh is in the ascendant in my bi-polar universe of foreign languages.

When I call The Floating Kiosk I produce a miraculous barrage of French until, ringing off, I inadvertently add 'Bye bye.' Home asserts itself when I'm least expecting it.

Cofio ❧ to Remember

When the doors close on the RER, the *rapide* branch of the Paris métro, the squeeze of bodies thrusts my torso around some stranger's bum. Sweat collects behind the backs of my knees and beneath my breasts, runs in tributaries down my back.

I get off at Châtelet-Les Halles, the world's biggest underground zoo (a.k.a. métro station). Since I'm early for my rendezvous with Boyd, I wander across the landscaped vacuum where the market used to be and step into an early dusk inside the church of St Eustache. I've never known what to make of this place. Its entrance is perpendicular to the nave, rather than opposite the altar. The façade is so elaborate, and so huge, it looks to have been spun by giant, stone-secreting spiders around the turn of the seventeenth century. Inside, the virgin and some of the saints need dusting.

My guide book says that St Eustache was a Roman general who converted to Christianity in the second century, whereupon he was roasted alive in a giant bronze bull along with his wife and children. As I'm reading it gradually dawns on me that this empty, cavernous church is filled with the faint sound of clapping, no louder than the echo inside a seashell. But there's no one here. For some reason I find this uniquely disquieting. Maybe, I think, livening up, it's a miracle. The clapping miracle. It's a real letdown to hear over the loudspeakers the electronic squibble marking the end of a cassette tape.

'So, did you meet Effie Wiltens?'

'*Naddo.*' I spit out the Welsh past tense 'no' so fast I surprise even myself. Boyd and I have both ordered short glasses of hot mint tea, intensely sweet, with pine nuts floating on top. The sugar buoys my Welsh for about an hour, during which he generously puts on the brakes in his brain, slowing his thoughts to the speed of my speech. We switch to English for the second hour, and it's in this tongue – foreign to both Wales and France – that I understand the depth of his antipathy toward it and all it represents.

'The first time I really felt Welsh,' he recalls, 'was when I was a little kid in the car with my mother. Someone had spray-painted "*Cofiwch Tryweryn*" – Remember Tryweryn – on a wall. I asked my mum what it meant, and when she told me I remember thinking, "That's so wrong. They can just take from us without asking."'

I go over the Tryweryn case to make sure I've got it right: in the late fifties the Liverpool Corporation received permission from Parliament to flood the Tryweryn valley in Merionnydd, in North Wales, to create a reservoir from which it could pump water to England – the hitch being that historic Welsh-speaking villages would be drowned in the process. Despite the fact that nearly every Welsh MP voted against it, Wales was powerless to stop the bid and Tryweryn has been underwater ever since.

'You see, a free Wales is no longer part of the memory of the isle of Britain.' Boyd speaks softly; the springiness of Lynn's or Rosemary's syncopated syllables has been chiselled out of his accent, though I can detect a muted stress on that penultimate sound. 'Sehhf'un,' he'd said when I'd asked what time he wanted to meet. Tonight there is an intensity under the softness.

'The English have respect for the Scots. The Labour Party has put forth a plan for a Scottish Parliament with taxation powers, but for Wales they're only offering an Assembly that'll have to beg to pay for what it administers. It's the lack of respect that accounts for the difference. That's what hurts.'

I ask him if he feels more or less strongly about these matters in or outside of Wales.

He laughs. 'It was leaving that turned me into a rabid nationalist in the first place. When I was thirteen I was sent to an English public school in Shrewsbury. On St David's Day the matron, who was from Caernarfon, gave me a daffodil. Symbol of solidarity, I guess. When I came back to my room after class I found it dipped in ink and nailed to my desk, where someone had written, "Get out of England you Welsh bastard."'

'That's terrible! I can't believe that! No, wait, what am I saying? I just read that when *Pobl y Cwm* was shown in England, with subtitles, the producers got letters saying things like, "Get the language of the devil off my television set."'

'I'm not surprised,' Boyd says matter-of-factly. 'Later, in the same school, we went on a trip and the head got all excited that we were standing in the same spot the Queen Mum had just stood. I refused to share the thrill, and told him that from my perspective she wasn't my queen mum, and that "Prince of Wales" was a title taken by military conquest. No one spoke to me for two years.'

'Really? Two years? That's extreme.'

'We were teenagers.'

This is the first time on the trip I've tapped into the anger. Frankly, I'd expected it sooner.

Boyd seems drawn to conspiracy theories. Tonight he's suggested that *Meibion Glyndŵr*, the Sons of Glyndŵr – Welsh nationalists who burned down several vacation cottages belonging to English holidaymakers in the early eighties – were actually MI5, hoping to cast the nationalists in a bad light. (The group, if it ever did exist, took its name from Owain Glyndŵr, one of Wales's greatest heroes, who fleetingly united the nation against the English at the turn of the fifteenth century.) Boyd has also implied that the Bosnian Serbs are behind the métro bombings in Paris in retaliation for covert French airstrikes, and that the CIA is responsible for a rash of industrial spying in Europe. And he could be absolutely right. Whether he is or not doesn't matter, what does is Boyd's worldview. It's the Us vs. Them outlook: they're sneaky and unprincipled, and we're the hunchbacks with the weight of history on our shoulders, still trying to prove ourselves to the world.

I say 'we' because I am shamelessly on Boyd's side. I can't claim anything like a reflex aversion towards England – as the saying goes, some of my best friends are English – but I support Wales in all its nationalists seek to achieve.

In many ways I came of age in Lampeter in the early eighties, and like a new-born animal I was imprinted by what was happening around me. It was a radical and reactionary time: my friends were marching for nuclear disarmament; property values in Dyfed were being driven up by English second-homeowners beyond the means of local families, and holiday homes on the coast were going up in flames. Then the miners walked out on strike. I remember images of Welsh miners' wives on hunger marches, of driving to Cardiff past scab-piloted coal trucks protected by police cars, the set of Margaret Thatcher's mouth whenever she discussed the National Union of Mineworkers. It was a highly charged, politicized, polarized time, it was hard to believe that the Welsh were not being screwed, and all of my assumptions about Wales were coloured by these years.

Since then I've come to realize that not all of Welsh history is locked into an Us vs. Them conflict with England, and that the Welsh language has not always been the politicized badge of difference it is today. In fact in the thirteenth century – arguably Wales's finest hour, when the nation was nearly united under the princes of Gwynedd – the language of their court at Aberffraw was probably French, of all things. But times have changed. I learned in Lampeter that speaking Welsh has become a reaffirmation, not just of cooing vowel sounds and consonants that break against the teeth like waves on a shale beach, but of place; of a unique entity about the size of Massachusetts that deserves the right to provide this language a secure future. Welsh, endangered, ridiculed as gibberish, officially outlawed for four hundred and thirty-one years (up until 1967), is what keeps the beat in the heart of the principality. To become a 'learner', I grasped early on, was to take a political stand. If you're Welsh, that is; I'm still not sure what it implies for Americans.

It's dark when we leave Le Comptoir. I've lent Boyd *The Xeno-phobe's Guide to the Welsh*, which I'd picked up earlier at Jackie's; he promises to send it back in a few days. When we get to the métro station it's eerily empty, though a clot of people ring it at a good distance and there's a smell of apprehension in the air.

'Must be another bomb threat,' pronounces Boyd. 'I wouldn't go that way if you paid me.'

'Well, being a stranger in a foreign city is like being a Welsh learner: you only know how to do, or say, things one way, Boyd. This is my stop.'

'Live dangerously then,' he shouts as we split up, 'and *pob hwyl*!' The last I see of him is his pony-tail bobbing toward the Pompidou Centre like a good Welsh lilt.

The next morning I find a poem called 'Reservoirs' in the birthday present I'd bought for myself in Aberystwyth, a copy of R. S. Thomas's *Collected Poems*. It begins,

> There are places in Wales I don't go:
> Reservoirs that are the subconscious
> Of a people, troubled far down
> With gravestones, chapels, villages even . . .

It chills me to remember a friend and fellow Welsh-learner saying that whenever her mind wandered in Welsh class and she had to rein herself in from a daydream, during the few seconds it took her brain to recover it sounded as if the teacher were speaking Greek underwater.

YR WLAD BELG (BELGIUM)

Methu ✿ to Not Be Able To

To Brussels for lunch. I've always wanted to say something like that, though of course it sounds better if you're coming from the States rather than Paris.

At the last minute Marguerite decides to come with me and explore the city while I attempt to hook up with Bethan Kilfoil, a BBC Wales television correspondent whom I've planned to meet at the Brussels train station. Every woman in newscaster's clothes – a suit, heels, tights – is a likely suspect, but after nearly an hour each one I've accosted has recoiled in confusion from the question *Bethan dych chi?*, Are you Bethan? I'm about to give up when another compact young woman in a sleeveless cotton dress with shortish, brown hair hooks my eye with hers as we pass. We might as well be on an invisible rubber band; we get about six feet apart, then snap back to each other like the mirror images we almost are, resolving into one.

Bethan has worked for BBC Wales for nine years. While covering Parliament she'd written a paper recommending that the network should have its own correspondent in Europe who could report in both Welsh and English for the BBC and S4C: the powers-that-be agreed, and she got the job. The Norwegians had thought I'd be old and dumpy; based on her résumé, I thought Bethan would be middle-aged and slick. Thank god we've both been dead wrong.

We go to a place called Rick's for an American brunch. Every now and then, we agree, you just need some chicken salad. Taking a seat in the back courtyard under the shade of a patio umbrella, Bethan meets an English colleague at the next table.

'Doyen of journalists in Brussels,' she whispers to me. Then to him, 'This is an American woman who's interviewing me for a book about the far-flung Welsh.'

His face says, 'What a funny thing,' but his mouth says, 'I heard a preacher by the name of Christmas Williams slip into *hwyl* once – that's a kind of religious fervour, right, like speaking in tongues? Except it's all in Welsh. Same thing, really. Hope you're not planning to do that during brunch. Ha, ha, ha.'

Bethan tells him we'll try to control ourselves. Taking refuge in the menu I attempt to shake the weight of the past week's work off my tongue. Bethan's Welsh is clear and fresh, has none of that molten earnestness so beloved by broadcasters, but her words swerve away from me at the last minute like low-flying pigeons. Not only is my comprehension slow today but my vocabulary seems glued down in my brain. I'd written out a set of questions for her in English along with some pathetic, all-purpose Welsh phrases like *Gallech chi ddweud yr hanes i fi?*, Can you tell me the story?, but all my attempts to steer the conversation their way fail utterly.

'. . . lived in Italy . . . one year at Princeton . . . PhD in American Literature . . . Emily Dickinson . . . craved drizzle . . . big weather in America . . .'

I'm sweating now. My note-taking, usually a mixture of Welsh and English, is congealing not into Wenglish but a patois of neither. I can't even remember how to spell English words. My pen is balking on the page.

'. . . tending bar in Chicago . . . first European woman they'd . . . "Is that near Germany or Jamaica?"'

Bethan seems to be waiting for a response. 'Uh, Wales, right, you told them you were from Wales, and that's what they said? *Tup iawn.*' How dumb.

When the waiter comes I finally manage to speak to him in Welsh. He looks helplessly at Bethan, who translates into French. By the time the food arrives she's playing with the sugar packets and looking past me, as if for help. I sense I'm losing her.

'Look,' I finally break down, 'I think I'm reaching some critical stage of exhaustion. I do speak better than this, honestly I do. But can we switch to English for a while?' I feel like a fool.

This is how I learn for sure that it was Bethan who'd been interviewing Nesta Pierry about the Paris bombings; that I've just missed the president of the Welsh society, Hywel Kerry Jones, a diplomat at the European Commission who's 'very Welsh'; that she and a friend offer Welsh lessons in Brussels – she teaches North Walian dialect, her friend South Walian – to a group of expats and a Belgian named Guido; and that the Labour Party's plan for a Welsh Assembly is based on a similar body in Catalonia.

'When I went to Barcelona to interview a Welsh woman there I found out she was an old friend of my mother's. My Irish boyfriend couldn't believe it. He says that the Welsh can't rest until we've made sure we're all cousins. And he's right. We have to establish a connection, and there usually is one.'

I'm beginning to know what she means: I bear greetings to Bethan from Boyd, a diplomat in Norway, and a friend of hers I'd run into in Wales. The more of the globe I cross the smaller the Welsh world actually becomes.

'Take the word *perthyn*,' Bethan continues. 'It's translated into English as "related", but we use it to mean "belongs to". Where I grew up in North Wales, near Llangollen, everyone on the farms in the area belonged to everyone else.'

'That's nice. It sounds like a more generous sense of kinship.'

She nods. 'Then of course there's the other side of it – the degrees of difference when you don't belong. When I went to England I was aware of being Welsh. In Italy I was aware of being British. In America I was aware of being European. And in the House of Commons,' she pauses a beat, 'I was aware of being female.'

Gyrru ✲ to Drive

Residential Brussels is deserted on a hot, dusty Sunday afternoon. With a Welsh cassette blaring in the car's tape deck and the streets booby-trapped with road construction – 'Very Belgian,' Bethan claims, 'the dig a hole and leave it syndrome' – we get lost on the way back into town, where we were supposed to meet Marguerite half an hour ago.

On the way I try to conjure the image of the Welsh Society of Brussels putting on Dylan Thomas's *Under Milk Wood* with Neil Kinnock, the Commissioner for Transport at the European Parliament, as Nogood Boyo. Bethan says it was a great success, but that it's usually hard to please the whole society. About twenty people attend the monthly meetings, around a third of whom speak Welsh, but for a big event like the St David's Day dinner they can get up to two hundred.

'There are people in the society, *Welsh* people,' she sounds quietly outraged, 'who turn learning Welsh into a utilitarian question: "What are you bothering to learn *that* for?"'

'Boy, is that familiar.'

'So because not everyone speaks Welsh all the events have to be in English. Then you get the long-term expats who latch on to the Eisteddfod and rugby for their quick fix of Welshness.'

Her sentence is clipped by an unannounced traffic barrier, and she fights her wheel mightily to make a three-point turn.

'I'm lucky, I get to go home every few months. It's restful to go back to a place where people are like you.' Then, almost to herself, she adds, 'Though that's not always so true any more . . .'

Rhiannon had expressed similar apprehensions about going home. She'd bought a house near her parents in the *Rhymni* Valley and fixed it up, but is now renting it to the unwed, pregnant daughter of some friends. She thought she'd probably wind up selling it; without children Rhiannon would no doubt feel more out of place there than her tenant. 'The emphasis on family in Wales,' she said, 'can be pretty exclusive.'

Yfed Cwrw ✿ to Drink Beer

Brussels is small enough to have just one central square, aptly named La Grande Place, but big enough for that place to be really, really grand. The tall narrow townhouses with bell-shaped front gables remind me of Amsterdam and Delft, but the scale and intricacy of the public buildings call to mind the spun stone of St Eustache in Paris. Remarkably, in a dense crowd thick with cameras, waist wallets and blue EU shopping bags emblazoned with gold stars, I pick out Marguerite's neon-yellow shirt. At Bethan's suggestion we all decide to go for a *blanche*, a light Belgian beer flavoured with lemon, at a nearby café.

Our *blanches* arrive tall, sweaty and tart, with lemon wedges stuck on the sides like sow's ears. 'It's the colour of milky urine,' Marguerite whispers to me with apprehension, swirling hers at arm's length.

She and Bethan launch into a discussion of the trials of bilingualism, for which I have not an iota of sympathy. Bethan asserts that when you have two languages it's hard to write creatively in either one of them. Unlike most Welsh-speakers, who will tell you unequivocally that Welsh is their *first* language, Bethan grew up bilingual.

'That means you're poised pretty equally between both,' Marguerite tells her. 'That's really rare. I've always tilted toward one or the other. As a child it was Portuguese; now it's English.'

'What about Belgium?' I ask, feeling left out. 'What's the deal with Flemish and French these days?'

Bethan explains that while the French-speaking Walloons have coal mining in common with the Welsh – not to mention the same Germanic root word buried beneath their contemporary names, which they also share with the likes of 'walnut' ('nut of the Roman lands') – it's the Flemish who feel a kinship with the other oppressed groups of Europe. For years Flemish was the kitchen language of Belgium, the one you couldn't use in university or on official documents, though she says it's now in the ascendant.

I've been waiting to bring this up for months. 'Did you know' – out of the corner of my eye I see Marguerite grimace – 'that in 1105 Henry I granted a bunch of Flemings Welsh land in southern Dyfed? Back then Flemish and English were almost interchangeable, and –'

'How do you know that?' Bethan interrupts.

'She's like a magnet for arcane information,' Marguerite informs her in a loud aside.

'I read it somewhere. There was a distinct Flemish colony in South Wales for almost two hundred years. You know, it's funny: the language divide in Wales is such a hot issue right now, but the Welsh have always had to be bilingual, before there even was a Wales. First it was Latin, then Norman French, then a little bit of Flemish, now English. That's probably what "Welsh" originally meant. "Romanized foreigners" were people who spoke Latin as well as their own language.'

As soon as I finish my lecture I notice that nearly everyone within earshot in this Belgian café is speaking *Saesneg*.

Soddi ☙ to Sink

Dinner – a candy bar I'd bought at the station – has melted in my pocket. Our train back to Paris is two hours late. As we speed through the Belgian countryside I gratefully leave all language behind and sink into the view out the window. It is a flat and mild world, soundless, softened by an evening haze. Cows, distant church spires, rows of poplars and fields of leafy vegetables; a red disc of sun like a heavy paperweight with a flat bottom, sinking low near the horizon. Gradually the haze merges the earth with the sky as all colours, greens, golds, browns, are absorbed by the blue-grey patina of a European evening. The scene is timeless and reassuring and known. I bet I'll miss it when we're gone.

FFRAINC (FRANCE)

Adolygu ⚹ to Review

A review in the *New Yorker* of Tom Stoppard's play *Arcadia* asserts that 'chaos is psychologically intolerable, man's need for coherence is greater than his need for truth. Landscape, like ritual, is consoling because it holds the magical promise of permanence.'

Yeah, yeah, yeah. But language travels better. We leave for Greece in two days.

Marguerite finally throws out the goat cheese.

Mail arrives.

From Singapore: the Welsh choir will begin practising while we're there in September. Good.

From Tübingen: Hans Schwerteck writes in simple, Literary Welsh – already out of my league – that he is a teacher of *Saesneg* and *Ffrangeg* (such a wonderfully deflated, earthy word for 'French'), and is an amateur linguist on the side. He's studied Basque – in Welsh *y Fasgeg* – and Breton, and after a summer course in Bangor, curse him, he's now teaching Welsh. The only thing his students have in common, he says, is their cleverness.

From Boyd: *The Xenophobe's Guide*, with a note in Welsh saying he found it funny and for the most part true, but for the section on language. I take a quick look and read,

> THE TAFFIA: It is now taken for granted among English-speakers that there is a conspiracy among the members of the Establishment who run Wales to promote only fellow Welsh-speakers to positions of power in all the important organizations in the country. Of course, a good Welshman

sees conspiracy everywhere. It is part of the 'Us' and 'Them' culture.

I swear I didn't see this before talking to Boyd the other night. I can imagine him fuming, and set the book aside to read later. (A recent study based on the 1991 census seems to confirm the author's fears: Welsh-speakers tend to occupy a higher social and economic rung on the Welsh ladder than monoglot English-speakers born in Wales, though English-speaking immigrants far surpass both.)

From Lampeter: a note from a young Japanese woman who writes in perfect Welsh on tulip-headed stationery printed with the heading, 'Tender Feelings: A Gift of Flower Harmony. Just for You.' I'd missed her when I was in Wales and had left a note pinned to her box in the Porter's Lodge, asking if she knew the whereabouts of the elusive Hiroshi Mizutani, Professor of Welsh at the University of Nagoya and sometime Lecturer in Lampeter. No, she responds, she doesn't, but would I like to be pen pals?

Dilyn ✿ to Pursue

'I would be glad to see a wonder,' said Pwyll. 'I will go and sit on the hill.'

This Pwyll did. As they were sitting they saw a woman dressed in shining gold brocade and riding a great pale horse approaching on the highway which ran past the hill, and any-one who saw the horse would have said it was moving at a slow steady pace as it drew level with the hill. 'Men,' said Pwyll, 'does anyone know that horsewoman?' 'No, lord,' they answered. 'Then let someone go find out who she is.' A man rose, but by the time he reached the highway she had already gone past. He followed on foot as best he could, but the greater his speed the farther away she drew, and when he saw that his pursuit was in vain he returned and told Pwyll, 'Lord,

it is pointless for anyone to follow her on foot.' 'All right,'
said Pwyll, 'go to the court and take the fastest horse and go
after her.' The man fetched the horse and set out . . . but the
more he urged his horse the farther ahead she drew, all the
while going the same pace as before.

From Pwyll, Lord of Dyfed
(The First Branch of 'The Mabinogi')

I know how Pwyll feels. I could use a wonder, too. Since we've
been back in Paris I've made a nightly habit of calling Effie Wiltens,
the Flying Dutchwoman. No answer. I wrote to her once from
the States. No answer. Five separate sources have now told me
that like the lady on horseback, this woman makes an unforgettable
impression. But I'm beginning to wonder if she really exists. It
riles me that I haven't had any more luck catching her than Pwyll
did his lady. I decide to write one more letter, this time in Welsh.
It takes me four hours and three rough drafts; I give her five
American Express addresses throughout Asia at which to write to
me, as well as that of my editor in London. As I struggle Marguerite
is furiously packing our unneeded gear – hiking boots, woollen
sweaters, an antique Dutch light switch I'd bought in Holland to
use as a paperweight – and stuffing it in supermarket boxes to
send home to my parents.

How do you keep up your language skills? How often do you
visit Wales? Would you ever move there? Why did you name
your house *Hanner Ffordd* (Half Way)?

Later I get a Welsh E-mail message from Phil Jonathan, who
writes, 'For all her connections with Wales, Effie has a house in
Hungary and may be there right now, or preparing to go. Who
knows . . . ?' So all is not lost! We could go to Greece for two
weeks, where I have article assignments but no Welsh contacts,
then instead of flying directly to India, travel by train to Budapest
and meet Effie. This is all the more exciting because none of my
leads for Poland ever worked out – you can't reach Poles in
summer, someone told me, they're all out of the country – and
this would give us a chance to visit Eastern Europe. The plan

seizes me like a fever, and I pry open my letter and propose it to her in a postscript.

Though I have no Welsh ancestry whatsoever I am 'half Hungarian', in that curious way Americans have of casting shadow nationalities of places we've never been. Here's a transition to die for: the most famous poem in Hungary is called '*A Walesi Bardok*', 'The Massacre of the Welsh Bards', written by Janos Arany in 1867. In the poem Edward I orders the wholesale slaughter of the bards of Wales following his 1282 conquest of their homeland, in which Llywelyn the Last, the last native and independent Prince of Wales, was killed by English soldiers. The bards are ordered to praise Edward's glorious victory in song, but to a man they choose death by singing instead of the final loss of Welsh independence. That this never really happened is irrelevant; after his victory Edward opted to build castles rather than murder poets, though indeed, Wales was never again a free country. But the theme nonetheless resonates in Hungary, which until recently was another subservient nation, first under the thumb of the Austrian Empire, then that of the former Soviet Union.

Perhaps '*A Walesi Bardok*' accounts for Effie's connection with the place. If so it's fitting, for she's fast approaching the realm of mythology in my book. Even though I can't seem to catch up with her, I cheer myself with the good news that Pwyll managed to snag his horsewoman in the end. She proved, upon inspection, to be none other than that old Celtic good-time goddess, Rhiannon herself.

Drewi ✿ to Stink

Gare de l'Est, 11 p.m. The corners are full of trash and the light is bad, but a current of motion is in the air, of pilgrimages about to be born on the rail lines of Europe. It's early August. For most of this month, unless I find Effie, we'll be in Greece and India, a kind of vacationland limbo between the Welsh-speaking outposts of Paris and Singapore. The hiatus is unavoidable, as I have articles to write on both Greek and Indian travel destinations.

For the first time in either of our lives Marguerite and I have reserved couchettes on a night train. Tonight we are travelling to Frankfurt, then on to Athens tomorrow by plane. Before we even leave the station we have a nasty moment in our darkened compartment, which looks like the back of an ambulance with three racks per side on which to strap prone bodies: we both take off our shoes. The heat in the tight, close cabin is intense. The stench is overwhelming. We're each travelling the world in just one pair of shoes, deliriously comfortable, cloglike German walkers that have only one drawback, in that they smell like high game when you take them off. All the sleeping shelves say *réservée*, which means that people could arrive at any moment. In a panic I grab both pairs and dangle them out the window, narrowly missing a man's head. When our first compartment-mate arrives I tell her it's an old custom in Wales to hang your shoes out the window before you travel, so the wind will be always at your heels.

For a few hours the sensation of being physically comfortable on an overnight train is so exquisite I will myself to stay awake just to enjoy it. A lulling rhythmic rumble and a rural breeze on my face; then after Metz – '*Ble?*' I incant plaintively to Marguerite, who's stretched out a shelf below me, '*ble est la tête du train?*' – we change directions and a chill wind sweeps away sleep. Barrelling through the dark German countryside, I recall something Heinz said about Germans being territorial creatures, that their dialects and their allegiances are regional rather than national in scope. It's the same in Wales, and so different in America, where I feel unanchored, able to move the breadth of a continent without giving away my place of origin through my speech.

In Europe language and place are inbred one into the other; some people bake Welsh cakes in the name of that union, others kill for it. And I take to the railways heading east, farther and farther from Wales, learning its old tongue piecemeal fashion from a northern speaker here, a southern speaker there, even from an Englishman, a Dutchwoman and a Swede. It seems obscene sometimes, like I've got a mad linguist thing going here, trying to re-member Wales without any organic, national memories of my own to build a language on. But then I have no birthright antagonisms either, and that's a plus. Either way, how American can you get, and how ironic? I am most me, most American – enterprising, optimistic, composite – when I'm trying to anchor myself with words in someone else's home, and in motion all the while.

You know, thinking at 4 a.m. is not a good idea. In the end I indulge in another bout of *baragouiner* and hum myself to Frankfurt with a Welsh nonsense rhyme:

> *Mae Jwdi wedi marw*
> *A'i chorff hi yn y bedd*
> *A'i hysbryd yn y wilber*
> *Yn mynd tua Castell Nedd.*

> Judy is dead
> And her body is in the grave
> And her spirit is in a wheelbarrow
> Heading toward Castell Nedd.*

---

* Pronounced 'Nathe'.

INTERLUDE

YR WLAD GROEG (GREECE)

Enwi ❧ to Name

Nancy Banks-Smith, quoting René Cutforth, said that the Welsh were Mediterraneans in the rain. In fact, up until the eighteenth century everybody thought the Welsh were Greek. The story goes that after the Trojan War a man of some foresight named Brutus led the remaining citizens of Troy to a distant island in the west. Brutus named the island for himself, then split it among his three sons: the eldest, Locrinus, got the plum, which he called *Lloegr* (*Lloegr* still means England in Welsh); Albanactus got the top, which he named *Yr Alban* (Scotland); and Camber, the middle son, got the west, which, following the family predilection for naming after oneself, he naturally called *Cambria*, or *Cymru*. According to Gerald of Wales, who repeats this story from earlier sources, the language of *Cymru*, called Cymric, or *Cymraeg*, suggests the meaning 'crooked Greek'.

Maybe my friend was on to something when she said that Welsh sounded like Greek underwater.

'It's a bunch of hooey,' I tell Marguerite, as our train squeezes through a tight pass about an hour north of Athens, encasing us in a long, claustrophobic hallway of living rock. 'But it sure makes a good story.'

She considers this a moment. 'You know, why don't you just try to forget Welsh for a while? I think it'll do you good.'

'*A dweud y gwir, dw i'n cytuno*. To tell you the truth, I agree.' She shakes her head and the train simultaneously rocks on the tracks. The effect seems to give her strange powers.

'You're obsessed, do you know that?'

I smile at her reflection in the window, superimposed over a field of brittle, matted hay the colour of Scandinavian hair. Where industrial-strength sprinklers have sown life into this baked place – so arid otherwise that from a distance the powdery dust looks like a recent snowfall – rows of corn stalks, tomatoes, watermelons and orange trees tick off our six-hour train ride from Athens to Thessaloniki. Ten days in Macedonia and two articles (translated this means two thousand badly needed dollars) lie to the north, where Alexander the Great dreamed as a kid of conquering the whole bloody world.

Brwydro 🦟 to Battle

The Halkidiki is an udder-shaped peninsula that dangles into the Aegean Sea off the coast of Macedonia. The ancient stories say it was the site of a mighty battle between the gods and the giants for supremacy of the earth. Perhaps that's why it's riven into three prongs along its southern extremity: Kassandra to the west, Sithonia in the middle, and Mt. Athos to the east. By edict of the Greek Orthodox church Mt. Athos is a monastic community off-limits to all women and most men.*

Even women whose names mean 'All Honey Rock' in Greek, as, I discover, Pamela Petro does. The EuroDollar Car Rental guy tells me this, and congratulates me on returning to the land of my ancestors. No, I say, I'm Hungarian and German. He looks dubious, but switches into German on my say-so. No, no, I try to stop him, I don't actually *speak* German, but it's too late.

German is the language of the Macedonian summer. It's every-

* This and following excerpts are from the *New York Times*, 'A Sunbaked Peninsula's Many Lures' by Pamela Petro, 4 August 1996.

where: *Zimmer* to let, hand-lettered *Sprechen Deutsch* signs in res-
taurant windows. English, meanwhile, gets as merrily twisted as
Welsh on one of my bad days. Menu selections include 'Tunny
Fish' and 'Fish Toe Salad'; most bed and breakfasts 'Rend' rooms;
the beach town of Sarti is soon to have a 'Sour Whisky Party!';
and all over Macedonia you can buy items of 'Silver and Cold'.

Despite the abundance and creativity of English signage, I
nevertheless find it difficult to impress upon countless hotel clerks
that *I do not speak German*.

'Yes you do.'

'No I don't.'

Perplexity follows, and then a bit of broken English. Macedonia,
we discover, is one of the last places in Europe where it's still
cool to be American. 'Beel Cleenton!' one proprietor says proudly,
and shakes my hand as if I were Hillary. 'Not German? Sure?
Well then, first American ever in hotel!' claims another, and shakes
my hand (I find this hard to believe, though the hotel does look
very new). A café owner makes us an 'American' breakfast to slow
an army – two grilled cheese sandwiches each, four pieces of toast,
marmalade, a wedge of Stilton the size of a new-born baby, and
more, I think – before vigorously shaking our hands. Most cryp-
tically, a hotelier in the village of Vourvourou does a little dance
upon hearing my nationality, saying nothing. Then he comes up
to me and whispers, 'Mary Jo Kopeckne, kaput. Kennedys bad.
Bob Dole, worse. Albanian stock, no good.' Then he shakes my
hand. As I'm leaving he calls after me, 'Oliver North! He will be
your next President!' I leave feeling cursed.

Thessaloniki is the second largest city in Greece, named for
Alexander the Great's step-sister. It has a kind of easy-going
glamour; mimosa trees make shade for a city-wide sprawl of
outdoor cafés, where locals drink iced cappuccinos and cast a
nonchalant eye on a legion of early Byzantine churches (built
between the 5th and 16th centuries), and the city's horde of
Greek treasures. The latter are preserved in the Archaeological
Museum and feature finds from the tomb of Alexander's father,

Philip II, which was excavated in 1979 and ranks as the greatest discovery of the 20th century after that of King Tut.

Thessaloniki is actually two cities in one. The new city that accumulates along the very blue, very empty Aegean front is polished and cosmopolitan, with a craving for shoe stores and cinemas; the old town is a maze of stuccoed homes painted pink, white, ochre and bright blue, jumbled at odd angles like cast-off supermarket boxes, prowled by cats and old women, haunted by the dubbed ghosts of loud TV sets. It's here in the Old City, in the cheapest pension we can find, that I receive a lesson in the relative constructions of public and private.

The pension is run by a young Greek medical student named Abi, who one morning bursts into our room unannounced looking for a Dutch mother and daughter duo whose room is behind ours. I tell him they're getting dressed, more than a little irked that he considers our room part of his house even though we're paying for it, and he tells me I look Greek. Somehow it comes out that my name means All Honey and that I'm a writer.

'Ah, writers,' says Abi, with relish. 'Think too much. Don't care for their bodies. I give you free clinic.'

I'm about to protest but he's tinkering with my vertebrae the way old women pinch melons. It's like pushing the 'Stop' button on an elevator: all my systems go down, and I comply with his order to lie on the bed. Why, I'm wondering idly, do mere words mess with my back like this, when Abi professionally announces, 'These are in the way,' and in one swift move pulls off my shorts, panties and all.

Even with my face buried in the bedspread I hear Marguerite's intake of breath. 'Just what do you think you're doing to her?' she demands.

At that precise moment the younger Dutch woman appears in the doorway.

'Abi, I wanted tooo . . .' She stops in mid-breath, pirouettes on the ball of her foot, and pushes her mother back in their room.

Now I'm torn. On one hand I don't want to make too much

of this, on the other, my bum is stark naked and facing the heavens. It takes an eternity as I count to ten, nonchalantly heave myself upright as I simultaneously grab my shorts, then curtly thank Abi. The phone rings. As he leaves to answer it, I bolt for the door to apologize to the Dutch; the daughter is now stark naked in the middle of their room.

She looks at me serenely. 'Tit for tat,' she says, in perfect English.

> We drove between the first two toes of the Halkidiki, barreling past farm stands that sold speed-blurred patchworks of color – orange tomatoes, green melons and grapes, yellow peaches – and then dipped into the full grandeur of Sithonia. The middle prong of the peninsula takes the tip of Kassandra as a starting point and rises, snakes, and plunges into extremities: the pine copses are thicker, the hills higher, the curves are twistier, the interior vaster and emptier. As we drove down the western shore pine embankments filtered our view of a faultless and calm sea, with only a few boats and the hazy idea of Kassandra riding on the horizon.

The Sunday morning we escape from Abi's we have breakfast at a fast-food chain of sidewalk cafés called Family. Across the street are glamorous shops topped by seven or so storeys of modern apartment buildings, and in front of them, at eye level – from a sitting position – the crooked cupola and red tile roof of what looks like a sunken cuneiform church. Out of the well in which it sits booms the amplified chanting of a Greek Orthodox priest, loud enough to fill the empty streets of the city all the way to the sea.

In a fit of bravado I order an espresso frappé, three sips of which leave me so fidgety I can't sit still. I cross the street for a look and discover a tiny, Early Christian church deep in a hole (one of Paul's progeny, a testament to how riled up the Thessalonians got when he preached here in AD 50). Old women are lined up to kiss a box of relics and receive a handful of grapes – a nice summer twist on communion and a boon for local farmers, I'm sure. I report this to Marguerite, who goes to have a look. Shortly afterward an old, bow-legged woman shuffles past our table on her way home from mass, listing like a ship in rough weather. She stops and addresses us in Greek. We smile and shrug. She shrugs. Then she carefully plucks four purple grapes from their stems and puts two in each of our hands. As she closes our fingers over them I feel an ancient, female bond slip between us that pre-dates Christianity.

> Once again, as on Kassandra, the southern reaches [of the Sithonia peninsula] were the stuff of exhilaration. Hillsides loomed above and below the road; their flanks looked like great swaths of marbled paper, the grey rocks, manilla earth, faded green scrub and rust-colored bushes – the real rust shade of metal corrosion, not the prettified rust that describes sweaters and autumn leaves – all swirling together in the confusion of distance. Perfect beaches and turquoise shallows lay at the bottom of every bend.

I try Effie Wiltens for the third time from the card phone near the harbour of Ormos Panagias: no answer. Damn, I really wanted to go to Hungary. A wind is gusting in off the sea, rocking the cruise boats that take tourists to gape at the coastline of Mt Athos. It flings dust in my contacts and carries an exhilarating chill of danger. A young German woman finishes her call on the phone next to mine and bursts into tears. I touch her shoulder but she waves me away.

> The following morning we reached Ouranopoli, the last 'open' town on Mt. Athos before the road ends and the gates of orthodoxy swing shut. The road initially arched high into pine forests but then emerged upon a limitless vista of empty, sunburnt hills, that looked like the last action they'd seen was when the gods beat the giants here before time began. The road surface was torn to rocky shreds, but its route never ribboned far from the sea, which was a reassurance. The remoteness, the intensity of scale and the color of the sea inspired in us something like reverence, and left us totally unprepared – except in a satiric sort of way – for our arrival in Ouranopoli.

Wantonly travelling the world without a Chicago Bulls T-shirt, a New York Yankees baseball cap, or – what were we thinking? – a Charlotte Hornets beachtowel, we at last have a chance to make up for our lack of professional sports paraphernalia in Ouranopoli. Here in a dusty corner of Greece, only neighbour to a colony of diligently ascetic monks, we have stumbled upon the earthly paradise of souvenir shopping. Trouble is, half the souvenirs are of home – our home, the place we left over two months and several thousand miles ago.

In Greece, more than anywhere else we've been or will travel, we're tourists, grazing with several million of our kind on an imagined land invented for us from our own skewed reflections. It's a sanctuary where the natives speak German, naked Dutch women speak English, ham and cheese sandwiches constitute breakfast, and pro basketball is evidently the national sport. The language gap – how many tourists speak Greek? – has been filled with markers of real or envisioned familiarity, and the occasional communion grape. If language is a yardstick of place, then surely these ball caps, beachtowels and Greek god chess sets take the measurements of Never-Never Land.

Language itself has been locked away like women and children before the barbarian invasion. Whereas English and German are public languages, Greek is private. Like Welsh, it's not one of the tongues of touristic enterprise, which is why most of us can only approach Greece in translation.

Credu ❦ to Believe

The English writer Patrick Leigh Fermor speaks perfect Greek. In *Roumeli*, his book on travels in Northern Greece, he writes about the Sarakatsáns, an ancient, nomadic tribe of fair-haired Greek shepherds, one elder among whom went by the name Uncle Petro. No one can figure out where the Sarakatsáns came from. Walking around the ruins of ancient Pella at dusk, the sunlight dampening and turning dark blond, I work out an answer. They're Trojans, of course, the ones who missed the boat with Brutus. I must be a long-lost cousin, which explains my fascination with Welsh – or, more precisely, crooked Greek.

I nearly run after Marguerite to tell her this joke but stop myself; it's not a joking time of day, and I let her explore the low foundation walls of the capital of ancient Macedon alone. Not much remains of Pella but some slender, almost effete columns and a few dusty mosaics. It's a peaceful place; the vast agricultural plain that surrounds it smells of timelessness, of vegetable life unchanged since Alexander was born here twenty-three hundred years ago. By then, the inhabitants of Britain already had been speaking Brutus's language, Brythonic – pre-historic Welsh – for some three centuries.

As long as the Welsh believed in the Brutus myth the struggle with England had the tone of a sibling rivalry. It didn't so much matter that Edward I had conquered Wales and made it subservient to the English throne, because England was like a big brother: a pain and tyrant, certainly, but still family. Even the Acts of Union of 1536, which effectively abolished legal differences between England and Wales and officially outlawed the Welsh language, were not unwelcomed by the Welsh as steps forward in the family business of empire building. Only after historians smashed Brutus and his sons to smithereens in the eighteenth century did the bickering between Wales and England take on the urgency of a higher struggle, one that dealt in the modern angst of cultural identity and national survival. The Welsh were suddenly on their own and had so much more to lose: Wales wasn't a partner, it was a colony. An Us vs. Them attitude was born.

Down the road from Pella the Motel Fillipos has a vacancy. It looks like a nouveau riche Texas ranch and gives us the creeps. I flop on one of the narrow twin beds, pick up *Roumeli* and read Fermor on the Greeks' search for identity after centuries of occupation by the Turks. He empathizes about how odd it must have seemed after winning independence in the nineteenth century for them to reconnect with an ancient past that had been all but wiped out of the national memory.

> Perhaps the words 'Hellas' and 'Hellene' sounded as awkward and unreal to them . . . as 'Britain' and 'British' still do, after a century or so of Empire and Commonwealth, to the inhabitants of the British Isles: words only used by sovereigns, politicians, passport officials, journalists, Americans and Germans, and no one else; least of all the Welsh and Cornish, the only islanders entitled to them.

The last thing I read before falling asleep is a diatribe by a Greek train conductor whom Fermor has provoked by asking about the ancients. 'They were Greeks and so are we, that's all I know . . . Greece is an idea! That's the thing! That's what keeps us together – that, and the language and the country and the church.'

I make a note in the margin in the language that has kept Wales together all these years: *Cymru am Byth*, Wales Forever.

INDIA (INDIA)

Peryglu ⚓ to Imperil

Marguerite has a bad feeling about India. To get there we must return by train to Athens, backtrack by plane to Frankfurt, then fly to Bombay, where we'll arrive at midnight with no hotel reservations. All of which may explain her apprehension.

We're also reeling from the blow – dealt at Athens airport this morning – that our travel agent has accidentally deleted all of our flight reservations from Bombay onward.

'I will not go to India unless I know I can get out,' Marguerite declares in a take-it-or-leave-it kind of way. We scramble to put the Trip back together again as best we can.

It's a three-movie flight to Bombay. The old Delta 747 bounces in the belly of the monsoon as the end of *Casper* flickers onscreen. Sheets of purple lightning flare dully out the window. Panicked, I declare this to be all Effie Wiltens's fault.

Marguerite has been chatting productively with an Indian businessman named Agnelo about the exorbitant cost of airport hotels; when he invites us to stay with him we accept. En route by taxi to his flat we pass roadside camp fires and dark figures moving through the unlit night; three-wheeled auto rickshaws with dim headlights whirr past us like menacing insects. It's the most sepulchral place I've ever seen; maybe – given the choking heat I consider the possibility – even hell itself.

By morning our slept-in clothes reek of the black mildew that has colonized Agnelo's flat. 'Monsoon season,' he says with a sigh and sweep of his hand, as if targeting weather as the culprit behind the human condition in general. Agnelo is lying on the floor next to our bed where he crept early this morning, seeking air-conditioning.

'By the way,' he says later as we're leaving, 'the police came looking for you around 4 a.m. Suspected you of smuggling drugs. The taxi driver told them I was harbouring foreigners, but I said you were old friends. No need to wake you. Bye, bye.'

'Can we please just get out of here?' begs Marguerite once we're outside, and I know she doesn't mean Agnelo's flat.

We go about this the hard way. Our destination in India is the state of Goa, a beach resort on the Arabian Sea about six hundred kilometres south of Bombay, increasingly beloved by European tour packagers: there I will write another travel article and Marguerite will have the opportunity to speak Portuguese. Goa was colonized by Portugal in the sixteenth century and handed over to India only in 1961; most Goans over fifty still speak the Romance language.

It costs fifty dollars to fly to the capital, Panjim, and takes one hour; it costs seventy-five dollars to be driven there in a mini-van and takes ten hours. We opt to go overland. We want, we tell each other, to see the scenery.

I take notes.

HOUR ONE: 1 p.m. Pass billboard commemorating sale of ten washing machines in greater Bombay. Though promised otherwise, driver speaks no English.

HOUR TWO: Still in Bombay; unleaded exhaust makes sweat black. Trucks say 'Horn OK Please' on rear bumpers; deafening concert of beeps, honks, guzukas. Cows mill around streets humping each other. Children defecate on sidewalks.

HOUR THREE: Shanties replaced by half-flooded rice paddies; lowlands carpeted in lime-green growth, luxuriant, velvety. Women wear saris brighter than parrot plumage, float above roadsides, ethereal; balance copper water jugs on heads.

HOUR FOUR: Everything covered in terracotta mud.

HOUR FIVE: Relentlessly bumpy road, can't sleep. Breasts ache for a bra.

HOUR SIX: Into hills, shuddering, switchbacking above outlandishly green valleys, passing on blind curves. Road full of people carrying black umbrellas.

HOUR SEVEN: Swift darkness. Confess mutual fear of sitting behind driver – certain death in anticipated head-on collision.

HOUR EIGHT: Driver stops for dinner. Aquatic-green room, blue formica tables. After darkness of highway fluorescence looks lurid – perhaps is lurid. No other customers. Men smelling of patchouli assemble to watch us eat. Put piece of chicken masala in mouth, smiling politely; spit it out. Bone. Try again. More bone. Waiter: 'Only bone, no meat. Sorry. Same price.' Check comes in dish of fennel seeds. 'After dinner mints,' says waiter, who sounds like a Welshman on helium. I remember the Pakistanis in Norway; wince.

HOUR NINE: Giggling uncontrollably. Lights come on in roadside huts; wavering orange flames, lemon discs of low-wattage light bulbs.

HOUR TEN: Rash of 'Accident Prone Zones'. Recent crash victim lying on roadside; broken-down trucks outlined Hansel-Gretel fashion in rocks and tree branches.

HOUR ELEVEN: Unsettled by dampness and dark; fearsome, moss-engulfed trees crowd road. Near despair.

HOUR TWELVE: Driver stops for cigarette. Bad sign: didn't know driver smoked.

HOUR THIRTEEN: Driver lost near Goan border; low moon swings in sky. Despair.

HOUR FOURTEEN: 3 a.m. Arrive in Panjim, called Panaji in Hindi. Driver lost. Prowl streets for recommended Panjim Inn; closed. Van's alarm goes off; deafened. Drunk leads us to seedy hotel, we wake manager sleeping in lobby; rubble-strewn hallway, squalid room. To sleep second night in same clothes.

Rhyddau ✿ to Liberate

I am praying with all my might that the Panjim Inn is open. Marguerite is near tears and threatening to go home; I'm shaking from lack of sleep. My perpetual optimism grates on even my nerves. If it's closed, I'm a goner.

With a last burst of energy I run ahead to check. Say hallelujah, sister, it's open. It's not only open, it's a three-hundred-year-old mansion with cool tile floors and massive antique furniture that smells of polish and age. We're shown to a room with a four-poster bed, marble-topped dressers, a majestic armoire, and french doors leading on to a balcony off which is a private bathroom. It costs fourteen dollars a night.

Before sleep, food. At the next table on the second-floor veranda is a red-haired man who introduces himself as Richard. I try not to encourage conversation for fear of betraying our feeble-mindedness and bad scent, but he's enthusiastic. I tell him about my Welsh odyssey.

'I grew up in Cardiff.'

'No.'

'Yes! My family's English, but we lived in Wales.'

'*Dych chi'n siarad Cymraeg?*'

'Huh? Oh, no, sorry. I had the option to take Welsh, but my mother didn't want me to. The *Plaid Cymru* thing was big in our school. I think that was the reason.'

Dadfeilio ✿ to Fall To Ruin

Monsoon season is nearly over, and for the moment the rains are sulking. 'They will return,' locals tell us with grave certainty. 'Two, three days, non-stop rain. Can't see across the street.' We don't doubt them, but for now there's only a damp, menstrual heaviness to the air, as if the clouds are retaining water. It's off-season in Goa, and few other tourists are around.

Like something fungal brought on by the climate, a fondness has crept over me for Panjim. To the eye the city has the ambiguity of an indistinct grave rubbing. Colour was once here: yellow and magenta, aqua, burnt orange and ultramarine, the shades of Portuguese tiles, all ebbing now into crumbling plaster or hidden behind dark patches of mildew. Red tile roofs are repaired with corrugated iron, fancy grillework is eaten by rust. Everything is rotting by slow, picturesque degrees. Billboards enigmatically inform us that 'Goa is hot as hell but icecream is yummy,' and 'Goa! Even in darkness there's something to see.'

Linguistic ghosts haunt the streets. Beneath a crisp 'Dispensing Chemists' hovers the faded '*Drogaria*'; the shop next door hasn't bothered to change its thirty-year-old sign, '*Sapataria Natural*', which Marguerite tells me means 'Natural Shoe Repair'. Though Portuguese is fast fading from public memory, hybrids cling to life. A chapel with red votive candles flickering in its belly is called 'Our Lady of Boa Viagem' (Our Lady of the Good Trip, which my evil mind profanes as a reminder of the sixties and seventies, when Goa was overrun by hippies). A clothing store is advertised as 'O Senhor – Shirts, Trousers, Jeans'. But my favourite is an old white house with a sinking tile roof called '*Casa Lusitania.*' On either side of the door are life-size paintings of turbaned men with Black Watch capes playing the bagpipes, above the words 'Bagpiper Whisky'.

Whether the two old colonial languages mate or fight it out on awnings and buildings and the sides of trucks, few care; people on the street pass oblivious, speaking the local dialect called Konkani. That's the real tongue of Goa, the one in people's mouths; English and its dying partner, Portuguese, are for the eyes only. And perhaps there's a reason for that: for Europeans unused to this thick, gluey climate it's a tight squeeze to inhale, exhale, and speak all at the same time. Our words are nearly suffocated by the air itself.

The tight traffic in my windpipe reminds me of a note I once received from a friend, quoting one W. Richards who wrote in 1682, 'One in our Company . . . having got a Welch Polysyllable into his Throat, was almost choak'd with Consonants.' My friend added, 'Everybody's a joker in 1682.'

In the centre of Panjim I shout 'Llanrhaeadr-ym-Mochnant' to see if I'll survive the lethal combination of climate and Welsh, and I do. Vowels, as I recall, are musical sounds, what people who understand phonetics call 'pure voice'; consonants are basically noises, 'the result of audible friction, the squeezing or stopping of the breath'. Odd that so many people who make a cursory visit to Wales come away proclaiming how musical the language is, but add, 'It's chock-a-block with consonants, of course.' Hmm.

These folks must realize that Welsh has vowels, their ears confirm the fact. It's what their eyes show them that seems to contradict the sounds they've heard. Herein lies the hard lesson for Goa's colonizers: languages are vocal beasts, spawned of the larynx, mouth, teeth, tongue and nose. Like beached sea creatures, from middling ones of Portuguese size to behemoths like English, they die, or are at least sadly misunderstood, beyond the waves of speech.

We don't do much. The heat is enervating. One day on the beach, one day sightseeing in Old Goa. The latter mainly consists of a museum and two immense cathedrals built around the turn of the seventeenth century by the Portuguese, one of which, the Basilica de Bom Jesus, has dibbs on the body of St Francis Xavier. Francis was a scrupulous missionary in the mid-fifteen-hundreds, but didn't become famous until he died and his body miraculously refused to rot. His corpse was said to have such restorative powers that a visiting pilgrim once bit off two of his fingers in a religious frenzy. Now he's protected inside a silver casket, head and shoulders exposed under glass to the curious and devout. (Most Goans retain Portugal's religion even though they no longer speak its language; in fact, fellow travellers we meet at the Panjim Inn cite Catholicism as the guiding spirit behind Goa's liberalism, cleanliness, preponderance of booze ads, and the non-confrontational attitude of its taxi drivers, as compared to the rest of India.)

Small chores unwind across hours, days even. By the time I finally reach someone at the British Commission who can speak English, who puts me on to someone else who knows for sure that there are no Welsh-speaking clubs in Bombay, the scene at the Rocha Secretarial Institute, Beauty School and Public Telephone Office – twenty black braids bent over twenty old Royal typewriters, twenty pairs of elbows sticking out the sides – is as familiar to me as our backpacks.

It takes all morning to get a cash advance. So long, in fact, that we're brought cups of thick, sweet tea while we wait. Marguerite speaks Portuguese to the bank manager, which he calls the kitchen language of Goa.

An entire day passes in the attempt to activate my E-mail at another of Panjim's public phone booths. Finally the manager, who also owns an electric lighting store across town, invites us to meet him there after hours, where I can monopolize his telephone jack in peace. We get lost; an old man leads us to it for three rupees. Tony, the owner, has an old woman bring us more smooth, silky, painfully sweet tea, and my heart goes into overdrive. Floor lamps are everywhere. I'm touched by the kindness of this stranger who's taken on my problem as his own, but the act of unpacking my laptop case in his office – address books, notepads, a nail file spill out – feels like disrobing. It strikes me as such a private thing to do in front of someone I don't know.

We're just about to plug in when the power goes out. This happens several times a day in Panjim, Tony says, and settles back into his chair. We chat awkwardly about his brother who lives in the States. Forty-five minutes later the generator kicks in, my modem clinches its connection, and I discover I'm missing the

India access code. It's a bust. I couldn't get the E-mail working in Greece, either. I miss the Welsh chat group.

Most of the time we sit in our room or on the veranda of the Panjim Inn under brisk ceiling fans and ask one of the inn's 'boys' – five slim young men who smile conspiratorially at the guests behind the owner's back – to bring us something to drink. Reading a Roald Dahl story about a woman who beats her husband to death with a frozen leg of lamb, I choose thin Goan beer (I've selected the Dahl collection from a bookshelf that includes such holiday reading as *Aboriginal Art*, *Africa on a Shoestring* and *Modern Clinical Syphilology*); brushing our teeth we opt for ferociously bubbly soda water; studying Welsh one day on the veranda, secure in the knowledge that I won't choke on consonants, I order coconut Feni, a local moonshine that vaporizes into the memory of roasted macaroons on impact with the throat. The afternoon is quiet, the fan stirs my papers in a low, rhythmic rustle. Panjim is alive in the morning and early evening; in between, a heat lull falls. I speak out loud and there's no one to hear.

Mae syched arna i. There is a thirst on me. Welsh is a profoundly respectful language of inanimate objects and conditions. Fears, longings, sicknesses – they all come on to you or are with you, you never presume to 'have' them. (I've just had to look up 'thirst' in my Welsh–English dictionary, which has absorbed a dark, greasy stain on the inside cover where my thumb habitually rests as I flip through the pages; it's grown perceptibly darker since I wrote the Argentinians a few days ago.)

Mae eisiau bwyd arna i. There is a want of food on me, which means, of course, I'm hungry. (I order a plate of chips.) Consider 'I am hungry': the 'I' is the centre of its universe, it takes its hunger very personally. The Welsh version is so much humbler: 'food' is the subject of this sentence, something that exists independently of the speaker and that she may or may not receive. Hidden, perhaps, in something as dull as syntax is an older worldview, reflecting a time when humans weren't so sure of their mastery over the environment, when food, illnesses and desires held the power of gods. It still amazes me that two such different languages have managed to coexist for so long on such a small island . . . (Contrary to popular belief, Welsh is not at all related to English. It is centuries, if not millennia, older, and belongs to an utterly different branch of the Indo-European language family. The Celtic tongues have far more in common with the Romance languages than either group does with younger, Germanic speech like English.)

Mae hiraeth arna i am fy E-Mail. There is a longing on me for my E-mail.

As I say this the owner of the inn, a big man with a beard who looks like a cross between the Buddha and Al Hirt, appears on the stairs. He politely inquires after my work.

I tell him about the book and wait for the usual blank stare. Instead he goes red in the face.

'It's people like you, you know, who foster international conflicts and wars, and bloody well make a living off it.'

I am wholly unprepared for this. But what about cultural diversity, I stutter. He argues that diversity is a smokescreen for self-serving nationalism. He's Goan but has lived in Ireland, so he knows, he says, shaking a finger at me, that Welsh is dead as a dodo. Why don't I just let it rest in peace? Why do the Irish and Welsh carry on so? Now take the Indians: different languages, different cultures, but you don't see us trying to dismantle our nation, he says. In India all is well.

Something fierce rises in my throat that is not the coconut Feni, but regretfully doesn't find language until he leaves. I go back to our room and wake Marguerite from a sound sleep.

'Don't you think that any language that's spoken anywhere, even badly, even by me on the veranda, is a living language? Of course it is. And don't you think it's better to accustom people to difference through media like travel books – show that linguistic and cultural variety is something to be respected, not feared – rather than pretend the whole world's the same? Jeez!'

'Can you possibly calm down and tell me what you're talking about?'

I explain. Outside the window a woman carrying bananas on her head, Carmen Miranda-style, waits in the universal attitude of exasperation – fists on hips – for someone to open the door of the crumbling Portuguese townhouse across the street. Hours later I lie awake in the dark, half-hypnotized by the ceiling fan, wondering who's right.

Dioddef ☘ to Endure Suffering

Bombay (we fly back).

Half the population of Bombay lives on the streets; the other half lives in the highest priced real estate in the world.

Bombay. Spit-strewn, muddy, jungle-humid, sweltering, wheezing with people, cows, mangy dogs, more people. A few lonely skyscrapers, mouldering Beaux Arts vanities of the British Raj, block upon block of low-storeyed shopfronts caked in a grime I've seen before on Manhattan's Lower East Side. A stench of old waste and fresh sweat, piercing whiffs of trash in a hot climate, a high, acrid scent of roasting corn and peanuts that brings tears to the eyes. The incessant, unspeakable honking of car horns.

There is no salvation here from the insane mass of humanity and its smells, filth and noise unless you fork out over two hundred bucks a night to stay at the Taj Mahal Hotel. We don't. We spend several days with acquaintances of acquaintances, trapped in a nightmarish cycle of kindness and good manners that results in severe stomach cramps, sleeplessness and shattering, feverish confusion. Communication is imperfect; no matter what we say, everyone simply rocks their head from side to side as if an unseen weight were rolling from one ear to the other, and smiles. Somehow we wind up in the empty flat of absent neighbours of a friend of one of the acquaintances. A photo on the wall says 'Lali and Sunita, World's Greatest Couple'.

Our two mornings here seem like grim appendages of the nights before. We can't sleep and we eat little. People come and bow before Marguerite because word's out she's got a PhD. We put our hands together as if we're building little churches and steeples and bow back. One twilight we're led through streets slick with mud to meet more people whose relationship to the acquaintances is never made clear to us. We can't understand more than three words in ten. The English language – our last, selfish sanctuary – turns us away, full up with sounds and exclamations and accents we've never heard before.

During our final night in India impromptu street bands greet every new hour with raucous, tinny bleats and thundering booms as the residents of Bombay prepare to celebrate the festival of Lord Ganesh, the elephant-headed Hindu god of wisdom and, we learn too late to prevent us from taking his name in vain, travellers.

We rise before dawn and take a cab to the airport four hours early. It's a poor sanctuary, but it'll do.

PART TWO

Asia (Asia)

SINGAPOR (SINGAPORE)

Dianc ❀ to Escape

A few words in praise of Singapore airport. It's air-conditioned, it gleams, it smells of expensive air freshener kissed by the faintest, reassuring whiff of disinfectant. It has motorized walkways and an American Express cash dispenser. It's a veritable showroom of lustrous marble, glass and steel. It even has beds you can rent by the hour, and free phones for local calls from the arrivals terminal (these two innovations strike us as evidence of genius). It is, in short, the antithesis of Bombay.

This morning our plane raced down a runway that doubled as someone's front walk – makeshift lean-tos lined the tarmac, so fragile-looking it seemed our exhaust would blow them to shreds; tonight, for all practical purposes, we've landed in a shopping mall, and we're happy about that. Our status as daughters of the first world is secure, and we're too tired to care that it shows.

Cysgu ❀ to Sleep

I tried calling Eleri Roberts, my only contact in Singapore, the night before from Bombay, but I'd reached a Chinese family instead. Later Marguerite discovered I'd written down the wrong number. Now I have to call Eleri cold, from one of the airport's free phones, and pray she asks us to stay with her. It's a tense moment as neither of us can afford Singapore hotel prices.

'Uh, hello . . . Eleri?' I don't even consider trying Welsh.

'Is that Pam? I've been waiting for you. We would've picked you up but we didn't have your flight information. Look, one of the members of the Welsh society is in Wales for a week – a man named Keith Pritchard – and he's lent you his flat. Why don't you take a cab here first, then my husband and I will drive you over there? Okay?'

Her words, rising and falling on the quick tide of a Welsh accent, hit my central nervous system like shots of Prozac, and I feel better before I've even taken in what she's said. When I do, I bound over to Marguerite grinning like a fool, silly with pleasure that I have good news. We seize the first cab in an orderly taxi line.

'I've missed the Welsh,' Marguerite announces, and seems to mean it.

Sundown brings out the essence of Singapore. The island is wired to the hilt, so much so that the darkness looks more like caulking between finely tiled walls of light than the black dome that elsewhere passes for night. It's a shock, especially after Panjim, where at 10 p.m. on a main thoroughfare you couldn't see your hands in front of your face. As we speed down the cross-island expressway I start to tell Marguerite that Singapore's futuristic highrises remind me of the cartoon backdrop on *The Jetsons*, but the cab driver, an elderly Chinese man, interrupts.

'You like me sing you Chinese love song?'

This strikes us as not a bad idea.

'Singing is sign of good, safe driver, you'll see.'

He commences and we do see, until he gets caught up in his lyrics and sails past our exit. This upsets him so much that he scrupulously turns off the meter and is silent until we come to Faber Hill Estates, the leafy, suburban development where Eleri lives. I give him a big tip.

Purposeful, nurturing in a no-nonsense sort of way, thick-waisted, about fifty: the image of the legendary Welsh Mam, and what I'd expected of Eleri, not unlike what the Celtic Ladies in Norway had expected of me. Instead it's an elfin creature who leads us into a spacious living room, introduces us to her husband John, points out a child sleeping on the floor, and sits on her bare feet in a big leather chair.

It turns out we're all exactly the same age. Eleri thought we'd be younger. When she confesses this I realize I must *look* thirty-five tonight, and feel the exhaustion headache that's been lurking at the base of my skull expand until it throbs against my eyes. Eleri is slight with fair skin and freckles and thick, dark, shoulder-length hair, cropped ruler-straight across her forehead. The effect makes her look like a tomboy or, oddly enough, a statue I've seen somewhere of Joan of Arc. She's from the Prescelli Hills in Pembrokeshire, in South-west Wales, where the boulders for Stonehenge were quarried about thirty-five hundred years ago. Her long vowels and roller-coaster consonants have a high, clear pitch, as if they're ringing up out of the earth, tapped from the same deep well as her immense energy and commitment to the Welsh language.

Everything about John, who's from Beddgelert in North Wales, is quieter: a softer accent, a laid-back friendliness that washes like an undertow beneath Eleri's intensity. They want us to eat, drink and talk in the worst way, but my head feels as if there's a big animal imprisoned inside. For the first time on the Trip I turn down free food and alcohol and let Marguerite carry the conversation.

Eleri talks about the difficulties of maintaining a Welsh-speaking household in Singapore. (A big help I am, I think miserably. After nearly a month without practising Welsh the old fear of speaking is back on me full force. 'Tomorrow,' I vow lamely.)

'We try to talk to the children exclusively in Welsh, though it's tough. Sion, the eldest, is nearly bilingual, but he just asked me the other day, "Mummy, why can't you speak like the other mothers?" I felt so guilty.'

'It's not the language of play, you see,' adds John. (I'd been reading about Singapore on the plane: around the turn of the century fifty-four languages were recorded on the little island, a figure that did not, I'm sure, include Welsh; today the government acknowledges four as 'official' – Mandarin Chinese, English, Malay and Tamil. I take it John means English is the children's language of fun.)

'Gethin, the middle one' – Eleri indicates the sleeping child with her foot – 'is four; he understands Welsh but refuses to speak it. And Rhiannon's just a baby, but she'll learn.'

At this point Helen, the family's Filipino maid, comes in and scoops up the deep-breathing lump that is Gethin.

'Helen's learning too,' declares Eleri. Helen smiles shyly. 'She's picked up some useful reprimands. The roll of the Welsh "r" and the latent menace of the "ch" sounds so much more serious than anything in English . . .' I admire the wry way Eleri lets this dangle, eyebrows in a devilish arc, but I've had it.

'I'm sorry, but do you mind if we go now?' I can't stand it any more. By the time we get to Keith Pritchard's flat my headache is volcanic; I feel like brain magma is about to spew forth from my ears any second. I barely notice a fishtank, a cavernous living room, a washing machine, a fridge full of beer, a stocked drinks cabinet, and Marguerite smiling like she found the earthly paradise. Then I crash.

Digwydd ✻ to Happen

Singapore feels more like a verb than a noun, and it's noisily happening around us. Even with the windows closed and the 'coolers' on full blast, we wake to the sounds of construction. The view from the dining-room balcony shows fledgling skyscrapers making their way towards our eleventh-floor flat in a commotion of whirring cranes, clanging I-beams, buzzing rivet drills, and god knows what else. I'm forever in my body's debt that my headache is gone.

The island of Singapore has a distinctive geography: it clings to the southern end of the Malaysian peninsula like a drop of water adhered to the tip of a drippy tap. But nothing in its six hundred and forty square acres – not the pristine streets, the mammoth shopping malls, the near-equatorial heat blasted away by the world's most efficient air-conditioners – describes this place better than its race to distance itself from the past. It's as if Singapore has willed itself to spin faster than the rest of the planet, and in the process of getting to the future first has cast off in a centrifugal fit all vestiges of human sloppiness: trash, poverty, crime, chewing gum, surliness among civil servants, disorganized health care, freedom of the press. In our trajectory around the world, Singapore is the only place we can't get CNN.

I discover this as we rummage through Keith's flat. Bless him for being in Wales.

'Did you see the washing machine?'

I nod. For some reason I can't fathom, Marguerite dearly loves to do laundry. I'm eyeing the phone jack attachment on Keith's fax, thinking of my E-mail. The place is *huge*. Two bedrooms, study, two and a half baths, kitchen, living room, dining room. And ours, all ours for nearly a week! I squat down to investigate the bar.

'No,' says Marguerite firmly, pulling me away.

It is without question the flat of a Welshman. I spot the talons of a red dragon on a folded Welsh flag lying on a bookcase; there's an illustrated poster from *The Mabinogion*, another with the words to '*Fy Nghwlad*', the stirring (and nasally mutated) poem 'My Country', by Gerallt Lloyd Owen, and still another with a poem by T. H. Parry Williams. A video of *Hedd Wynn*, the Academy Award-nominated Welsh film about a poet killed in World War I, lies on the TV.

'Man's a nationalist.'

'He's also insecure. Listen to the titles of these tapes: *Elevate*

Your Self Image, Gaining Confidence with the Opposite Sex . . . oh look, *Discovering Portuguese*. I like him. He's also got *The Best of Bonnie Tyler*. She's Welsh, right?'

'Yup. See? He's a nationalist.'

We spend the entire day revelling in the ability to do simple things simply: brush our teeth with tap water, make decaffeinated tea from an electric kettle, sit – not squat – on the toilet. Stepping into Keith's tub I'm so dirty I leave a black imprint of my foot embedded in the white porcelain which remains even after my bath. This strikes me as some kind of palimpsest of the Trip – a residue of English I can't ever wash away? Something to do with cultural imperialism? Thankfully I recognize this as drivel manufactured for the book, and leave the footprint behind for Marguerite, hoping she'll scrub the tub after she shaves her legs.

After a month of inactivity I'm almost afraid to check my E-mail. Because my three-prong electrical adapter is broken, I have to rig up what looks like a little white jetty made of four different adapter units, each plugged into the other and the last into the wall outlet. The whole contraption is secured by a rubber band and propped aloft by Keith's jade-handed backscratcher, precariously balanced on the parquet floor.

I hold my breath and log on. '*Wel, Bobl Bach!*' – literally this means 'Little People!', but it carries the weight of 'Goodness Gracious!' – it works. I've got a hundred mail messages waiting and lots more that have been turned away. With a deep sigh I begin to sort through them:

ITEM: Several friends and family members think we're dead.
ITEM: Fellow travel writer sends suggestions of things to do in Macedonia.
ITEM: Mark Nodine is the only one of the four-hundred-member Welsh-L group to respond to my question, *Oes Cymry Cymraeg yn yr Wlad Groeg?* (Are there Welsh-speakers in Greece?) He ignores the query but tells me he's been on vacation in French Canada.
ITEM: 'Sian Toronto', one of the chattiest of the chat group, notes

that a new Welsh Spellchecker is available in both Microsoft and WordPerfect versions – she claims it even corrects 'inappropriate mutations' (I make a note to look into this).

ITEM: Our friends in Wales with whom we went to the Indian restaurant send separate messages to say they're alive and that their divorce is proceeding (this is reassuring, since we've been terrified she might've killed herself while we were out of touch); he adds that it's been the hottest and driest summer in Britain since 1652.

ITEM: Buddies back home in Providence post three desperate messages concerning my bank balance.

ITEM: Sian Toronto says that on 30 August 1937 Tommy Farr from Tonypandy fought Joe Louis and lost.

ITEM: A learner, disbelieving her mother who told her 'the Welsh are such a pure race we have no need for foul words', writes seeking bad language, which touches off a lively exchange. Someone notes from the High Energy Physics Lab in Hamburg that the worst thing he can think of is *Iesu Grist* ('*Really* bad,' he says); someone else claims that *Uffach Cols!*, a saying from Pembrokeshire meaning Embers of Hell!, is polite but 'expressive', and that *Twll dy din!*, literally Assholes to you!, is the ultimate insult; a woman offers *cnychu* as 'a translation of the all-powerful F-word' . . . A teacher of mine once told me to shout 'chick peas' at someone in Welsh if I were really riled.*

ITEM: Sian Toronto again, with a sombre reminder that seventy-eight years ago today – 6 September – the Gadair Ddu or Black Chair Ceremony was held at the National Eisteddfod. Ellis Evans (a.k.a. Hedd Wynn, Evans's bardic name, which means 'Blessed Peace', not Head Wind), winner of the highest prize in Wales, the national poetry competition, had been killed on a battlefield in Belgium several weeks earlier. The chair that he would have occupied was instead left empty and draped in black.

Marguerite returns from her bath to find me sitting splay-legged on the dining-room floor with the computer in front of me balanced on a pillow, and my Welsh dictionary by my side. I'm so overwhelmed I'm starting to gibber.

'Did you make that mark in the tub?'

---

* Chick peas in Welsh is *ffa cyw*, pronounced as you'd imagine.

I look penitent, and tell her about Hedd Wynn to change the subject.

Croesi'r Stryd ✾ to Cross the Street

When we finally venture outside we discover that Keith's apartment is just off Orchard Road, Singapore's version of Beverly Hills. It must be the costliest real estate in the city. Our astounding good luck makes us feel like a couple of vagabond Cinderellas. Everything we could possibly desire is price-tagged within a flick of our credit cards, yet we proceed with caution. Marguerite has spooked me with a dramatic reading from our guide book, which warns that in Singapore it's illegal to jaywalk within fifty metres of a crosswalk, to be caught with chewing gum in your possession, smoke in an enclosed public space, not flush a public toilet, spit, litter and to carry a durian – a prehistoric-looking melon that when cut open reputedly stinks more than our shoes – on Singapore's subway, called the MRT.

We gingerly take to the streets, avoiding all fruit.

I'm amused to see T-shirts that say 'Singapore is a Fine City', with crossed-out icons of all the things you can't do here. At least somebody has a sense of humour (and in true Singaporean fashion, is making money off it). We wait with the polite, careful populace, all of whom exhibit crackerjack posture and sport tiny, tailored clothes, to cross with the light. The *Official Guide to Singapore* claims that the Chinese make up three-quarters of the island's population, the Malaysians 15 per cent, and the Indians 6.5 per cent, with mutts and Europeans filling in the cracks. Everyone is beautiful. I stare at a woman whose eyelashes are dyed canary yellow.

Commercial life is encapsulated within acres of glittering malls, from which relentlessly chilled air spills like champagne on to the to-eat-off-of sidewalks. We decide that Singapore must be a police state run by Miss Manners and Mr Clean.

Bwrw Swyn ⚜ to Cast a Spell

I am prepared. I am prepared. *Rydw i'n barod*: I am prepared.

What am I talking about? I'm not prepared. *Dydw i ddim yn barod o gwbl*: I'm not prepared at all. Dear god.

A vicious rainstorm is beating the life out of the plastic roof of the MRT station nearest Eleri's house. The din is tremendous, ear-splitting, overwhelming. It adds rhythm to my anxiety.

Neither of us has any change. I have to borrow ten cents from a guy in a business suit to call Eleri to come pick us up. She's invited us to lunch and to meet her mom, who's just arrived from Wales. 'Someone else to practise with,' she'd said with glee.

There's nothing to see while we wait to take my mind off speaking Welsh; the rain is so heavy it's nearly opaque, like a giant plastic dropcloth thrown over the city. Yesterday I spent a couple of hours reading aloud from *Y Trip* to prepare for today's visit – I've discovered that my ears have picked up the language faster than my eyes, and words I don't recognize in print often slip into comprehension when I speak them aloud – but the story of the evil Charles and his drug-dealing minions has gotten bogged down in stupid sailing vocabulary. If Eleri's mom happens to ask my opinion on trimarans vs. catamarans, I can knowledgeably assert that '*mae dau hwl allanol y trimaran yn tyfu'n fwy bob blwyddyn, er mwyn cael mwy o hynofiant, ac erbyn hyn mae'r hwl yn y canol bron yn ddiwerth*' – the two outer hulls of the trimaran have grown each year, in order to get more buoyancy, so by now the middle hull is almost useless – but if she brings up anything else I'm sunk.

Bewitched is blaring on Eleri's TV. Looks like Samantha's parents, Endora and Maurice, are having a tiff. Gethin is lying on his belly about three feet from the set: with witches and warlocks speaking American English, no wonder he feels he has no need of Welsh.

While Eleri finishes making lunch, her mom, Marguerite and

I grip glasses of white wine in the living room. Eleri's mom chews off the ends of her words in both Welsh and English, filling her mouth with husky noises and making her Welsh exceptionally difficult to understand. But she and I speak it anyway and take turns improvising translations for Marguerite, which for me invokes the terror of a pop quiz: I can't pretend I've understood, I have to prove it. Somehow in the process I learn the word for curtains (*llenni*).

Mrs Harries is talking about having visited Eleri and John when they lived in Bangkok (John's company posted him to the Far East six years ago, first to Singapore, then Thailand, now back to Singapore). She changes the subject and I look stricken. I interrupt Marguerite, who seems to be watching *Bewitched* on the sly, and exclaim, 'Poor Mrs Harries has flown all the way out here although she's just had an accident. She hit her head in a pool!'

'Oh dear, that's terrible.'

Mrs Harries looks confused at this translation. 'I wasn't in a pool, I had hip replacement surgery,' she says.

I feel like I've just lost the prize on a game show.

'*Dewch i'r bwrdd!*' shouts Eleri – Come to the table! – and we all bolt for the dining room.

For an hour and a half food, languages, conversation, stray thoughts, memories and Gethin fly recklessly around the table.

'Do you know the Call for Peace Ceremony?' asks Eleri, just as I push a big piece of vegetarian lasagne into my mouth. I'm not sure about this, and shake my head no.

'It's an integral part of the Eisteddfod. Two men hold the sword of peace half-drawn from its scabbard and cry, "Is there peace?" and the audience replies, "Yes there is!" After that the ceremonies can continue.'

'It's never fully drawn, you see,' adds Mrs Harries.

'I've included it in our annual St David's Day Ball. I felt we needed a stronger Welsh identity. It's not a ceremony to be taken lightly.'

I make a noise of agreement through half a vegetable samosa.

How odd that the cultural arcanum of a country that chews its past like cud, trying to eke out some kind of national nourishment from history and legend, should be transposed to a ball here in calendar-eating Future City. Even odder when the arcanum in question – the Call for Peace – was concocted in the late eighteenth century by a Welsh stonemason named Iolo Morgannwg (*né* Edward Williams), based on his own brilliant, if highly inventive, take on Celtic history. Many of Iolo's innovations have been incorporated into the pageantry of the National Eisteddfod, Wales's annual cultural extravaganza. The Eisteddfod is like a cross between a state fair, held in giant, pavilion-style tents and a sprawl of smaller stalls on a big muddy field – the festival wanders, one year it's held in North Wales, the next in the South – and a kind of cultural Olympics, featuring Welsh-language music and literary competitions. The word Eisteddfod comes from the verb *eistedd*, to sit, referring to the ancient custom of awarding a chair to the winning bard in medieval poetry competitions. The first Eisteddfod on record was held in Cardigan in 1176.

'Eleri's a member of the *Gorsedd*, you know. Ask them if they want seconds, dear.'

Eleri glares at her mother, and passes Marguerite the green salad. '*Yr Orsedd y Beirdd*,' she intones in Welsh – the Assembly of the Bards. 'Anyone with a degree in music, like me, or in Welsh literature can take the membership exam.'

'You mean you're one of those people who gets to dress up like a Druid at the Eisteddfod?' I'm impressed. Despite parading around in long robes in the mud at the National Eisteddfod – members wear green, blue or white depending on their category of importance – contemporary bards include the artistic elite of Welsh-speaking Wales.

Eleri's impatient with the potato salad in her mouth, and fights it down to answer me. 'Um, in a long blue gown. Got to pick a bardic name, too.'

She refuses to tell us what it is. 'My husband was a great one for all that,' says Mrs Harries, remembering.

'Your husband's dead,' announces Gethin. We all politely pretend we didn't hear him. Eleri pours more wine. Then she and I switch back to a conversation we started the other night about the North–South language divide in Wales. Although she's from the South, Eleri has a post-graduate degree in Stage Management and Design from the University of Wales, Bangor, in the North, where she met John.

'I was on Anglesey once and someone asked me if I were *starfio* [pronounced "starvio"]. Do you know what that means?'

'Starving?' I guess.

'Well that's what I assumed. He was asking if I were cold. I think he thought I was daft. He finally said, "Speak in English, girl! I can't understand you." And Welsh is my first language!'

'*Imagine, three hundred daffodils! Flown in fresh for the Ball each year by KLM.*' For a moment I'm sidetracked by what Mrs Harries is telling Marguerite, then I yank myself back.

The geography of Wales is like a natural clause that separates two halves of the same sentence; because the interruption is on a grand scale – the mountains of North Wales are higher than any in England – the thought ends in a different dialect from which it begins. This situation isn't helped by the fact that most roads in Wales, designed either by economic necessity or the British government, run east–west rather than north–south, connecting portions of the principality with England rather than binding them together. Only here in Singapore, in the Roberts household, do the children of North and South Wales share a wholly common vocabulary.

We move on to fruit salad and cream. I ask Eleri what she'd miss most about Singapore if they moved back home. 'The opportunities,' she answers immediately, then elaborates about the chance for her kids to grow up in a diverse environment, to mix with other nationalities and races – not to mention do a little modelling on the side, something apparently 'all the expat kids did' when they lived in Bangkok.

'I'm a big fish in a little pond here,' she adds. 'I wouldn't be nearly so involved at home. I'm President of a hundred-and-fifty-member Welsh Society that meets once a month – the Ball is a huge event – and I'm choir director as well. At home everyone is musical, so the competition is fierce. I'd never be directing a choir back in Pembrokeshire, I'm not that good.'

'*Roger Carruthers . . . stayed with me.*' Whoa. Roger Carruthers? I was just about to probe into Eleri's unexpected insecurity, but her mom's mention of this name derails me. Roger? Oh lord, it's Rod. Mrs Harries knows Rod? How does Mrs Harries, who Eleri told me grew up on a farm and quit school at twelve to take care of her parents, who milked a cow with one hand and held on to a couple of her seven children with the other – how can she know Rod, a big, gay, harp-playing Canadian from Toronto who was in my intensive Welsh language class in Lampeter? I remember him telling me he'd had his face waxed before the course, something I'd found oddly troubling. I feel like I need air. Sometimes I worry that the Welsh world is so tiny and intensely interlaced that one day it will collapse into itself like a dying star, become a Black Hole – one of those mysterious negations of the universe, so dense that not even light can escape – and suck me inside for all eternity.

Just before we leave Eleri pulls out a photo album to show us pictures of Welsh Society members humiliating themselves at last year's *Noson Llawen*, literally 'Joyous Evening', a traditional Welsh musical get-together. We stare at photos of big-bellied guys with pillowcases over their heads and shoulders, and eyes and lips painted on their stomachs, doing a little song and dance.

'They called themselves the *Canu'r Bola*,' laughs Eleri, 'the Tummy Tunes. A Singapore hotel just called asking to book them. They thought the lads were a professional act and I was their manager! Haaa!'

Eleri's laugh blows me right back to Norway: it's the same forward thrust of the head and shoulders, the same great, honking blow-out of pleasure that had escaped from somewhere deep inside

Rosemary. A perfect retort to what I've just read in Davies's *History of Wales*, about the eighteenth-century Calvinist Methodist minister Howel Harris, who once shamefully confessed to his diary, 'I had a temptation to laugh last night.' (Davies notes, 'He resisted it, of course.') Times and meridians, mercifully, have changed.

On the way out of the door Eleri hands me a list she's made of sixteen Welsh-speaking members of the Singapore society, plus their telephone numbers. She ticks off a couple of names and assures me that these folks are 'very Welsh, very Welsh indeed'.

Gorffwys ✾ to Rest

I'm lying spread-eagled on the floor of Keith's flat; Marguerite's on the sofa. On the way in we discovered a wad of chewed gum stuck inside the elevator. Someone in this building is living life on the edge.

'I'm so tired I could weep.'

'You did good. I can't believe you ate, talked in two languages, and took notes at the same time,' mumbles Marguerite, too exhausted to open her mouth.

'You should see my notebook. It looks like a war was fought in there between English and Welsh, and there were no survivors. Was the food good? I didn't have time to taste it.'

'Great.'

We've been back from lunch for ten minutes; John and Eleri are picking us up to go to Pub Night in two hours, where we'll meet even more Welsh speakers. In between we take naps, Marguerite writes our one hundred and ninth postcard of the trip, and I study a list of classes offered by the Singapore School of Continuing Education: 'Good Housekeeping for Maids' (designed for maids new to expatriate households), 'Kitchen Orientation for Maids', 'Perfect Dinner Parties for Amahs' (amahs are live-in maids like Helen) and 'Miracles: A Discussion Group'. I'll come back and take that one should I ever master Welsh.

'Two weeks ago,' says Marguerite wearily, 'we were in the sixth hour of our trip to Panjim. Three weeks ago we were walking around Pella. Hard to believe, huh?'

Chwarae Mah Jong ✣ to Play Mah Jong

'Well, I've just committed a crime,' confesses John cheerfully, as we drive straight across an intersection from a left turn lane. The great thing about Singapore is how easy it is to cultivate the cheap thrill of being an outlaw.

Pub Night is a monthly event held at Sloan Court, a motel and bar that has the dark wood and red vinyl of make-believe English pubs the world over. The enthusiastic air-conditioning even makes me feel like I'm in Lampeter on a cool summer night. Shortly after we arrive Eleri pulls me aside and gives me a second list of Welsh-speaking members of the Singapore society, this time without telephone numbers.

'I thought it best if you use this one tonight,' she whispers. 'Don't want to make anyone uncomfortable.'

This strikes me as at once extremely considerate and evidence that she and the others have been living in Singapore too long. People get very careful here; I can't imagine the Delft group worrying about Rhiannon playing free and easy with their phone numbers. I carefully put the first list away.

Despite the brisk booze consumption – a Welsh trait going back to the 1390s at least, when it was recorded that one household in Caeo went through fifty-five bottles of wine a day – there's something that differentiates this group from any other on a Friday night in a pub in Wales: no one is smoking. 'Singapore gets some things right,' Eleri'd said earlier, referring to the gum ban, and

I've got to agree with her. Smoke makes my contacts itch.

I let John buy me a pint. *The Xenophobe's Guide to the Welsh* makes a point about how in Wales it's not considered good form to be too much of a success or to make too much money. 'Many Welshmen do rise above this prejudice and build successful careers,' admits the author – 'outside Wales.' The Singapore Welsh Society, several members of which haven't lived in Britain for almost thirty years, seems living proof of this truism. These folks inhabit the expatriate world of oil company salaries and live-in maids, served by Singaporeans who take the Continuing Education classes I'd read about earlier. Eleri had told me at lunch about Russ, a Canadian guy who'd dressed up at the *Noson Llawen* in Welsh Lady drag, with a stovepipe hat and shawl, and had sung 'The Power of Love'. 'Distance,' she'd said, 'makes room for humour.' It does the same service, it occurs to me tonight, checking out the seven-dollar-pint prices, for wealth. Like I said, I let John buy.

A woman approaches waving Eleri's flyer exhorting everyone to come to Pub Night. It reads, 'Attention All Society Members!! . . . This is your chance to be mentioned in a book which might sell millions of copies around the world!'

'I've showed up, so your book had better well be a success.'

'I think it needs more sex and violence for that.'

She leans closer and whispers, 'I hear this is a short-term motel, if you know what I mean.' Laughing and dabbing her neck with a tissue, she introduces herself as Mairwen Joseph (check one on Eleri's list). I translate to myself: Mairwen, White Mary. She looks like a jolly, robust young grandmother.

'So, why on earth would you want to travel the globe visiting Welsh people? Someone said you were from Lampeter, but you sound American.' Several others gravitate toward us to hear the answer.

I explain how I'm trying to learn Welsh, and where the effort has already taken us. When I mention Bombay a man named Phil (check two) does the head-rolling thing, and I laugh so hard my beer goes up my nose. Getting a grip, eyes still watering and nose running, I attempt to untangle the *Pam?* question that someone's posed. Why have I chosen to learn this confounded old language?

'I don't know. Maybe it's a link to a place where I was happy,' I grope, 'a way to remember that there are hills when I'm in the city, that there's a town where they know my name in the post office.' This makes me nervous; I'm supposed to be asking the questions here.

'Well, it's not our help you want,' Mairwen informs me. 'Our Welsh is very loose.'

'Loose?'

'Phil and I grew up two villages apart, in *Cwm Tawe* [the Tawe Valley, above Swansea], at different times, mind.'

'And we'd known each other as little girls,' says a woman named Pat, indicating her friend Eirlys (checks three and four), but we hadn't seen each other in nearly forty years until we met again in Singapore.'

'That's amazing.'

'I've spoken more Welsh here in Singapore than in the past twenty years living in England,' admits Eirlys. The others all shake their heads in agreement.

'We used to live in London, and we'd drive forty-five miles to go to a Welsh chapel near Slough every Sunday, just to hear the language,' Mairwen adds.

'But why do you say your Welsh is loose?' I'm concerned about this. I make a timely move into the language itself.

'Oh, we're all from the South,' responds Mairwen in kind. 'We speak *Cwm Tawe Cymraeg*, full of mistakes and English.'

I remember the Goan bank manager who'd helped me get a cash advance in Panjim. He'd told Marguerite that Portuguese was the kitchen language of Goa: Welsh has parlour and kitchen versions of itself.

'You need to practise with Eleri.'

'But she's from South Wales too.'

Not the Valleys, they tell me as one, shaking their heads. She's not from the Valleys. Eleri's Welsh is pure. We'll just fill your head with nonsense.

I drain my beer and chalk up another meaning for that all-purpose French verb, *baragouiner*.

Eirlys, Pat and I make a move on some recently vacated seats at a nearby table. Eirlys, like Eleri, is dark with fair skin, and emanates efficiency if not quite Eleri's sense of mission; Pat has a reddish bob, wistful eyes and a down-to-earth gap between her front teeth. Both have come to Singapore with their husbands' jobs. In a characteristically loose weave of Welsh and English they describe the language hierarchies that shape their lives. To some friends they always speak Welsh, to others English. 'You find you unconsciously separate the two camps,' says Pat, 'and they never get to meet each other. It's like having two identities.'

'We speak to one another in a mixture,' adds Eirlys – 'Mostly English,' Pat reminds her – 'but we always speak Welsh with Eleri.'

'*Everyone* speaks to Eleri in Welsh,' confirms Eirlys. This makes me feel better. No wonder that practising with her is like mainlining caffeine: it, too, makes my heart skip beats. Like David, Wales's patron saint, whose best-known miracle was making the ground rise beneath his feet at Llandewi Brefi – about which John Davies wryly comments, 'In view of the nature of the landscape of Ceredigion, it would be hard to conceive of any miracle more superfluous' – Eleri seems to have the ability to turn whatever bit of earth she's standing on into honorary Welsh soil. Speaking with her, all my fears of using Welsh on home turf – where it's a tool rather than a remedy for a bad case of *hiraeth* – come rushing back in a freefall of stammering confusion. By comparison, Eleri's own insecurities seem all the harder to fathom.

'Both my parents and all my grandparents but one spoke Welsh,' Pat tells me, 'but my one English-speaking grandmother lived with us, and that changed the language balance in the house. I grew up speaking English at home and Welsh only in school. That's one reason I'm so bad at it.'

'But being in Singapore has helped, hasn't it?' asks Eirlys. 'There are so many speakers here. I even spoke Welsh to a Chinese cab driver once.'

'He didn't sing to you, did he?'

'No. He asked where I was from and I said Wales. Then he told me that he'd had a friend seventeen years ago in the Navy who'd been from Anglesey. He said, "You say that long name now, please?" So I said, "You mean Llanfairpwllgwyngyllgog-erychwyrndrobwllllantysiliogogogoch?" He was so happy. He said, "Say again, please? I haven't heard this name in seventeen years." It made both our days.'

I ask them how they like living in Singapore. They smile a bit weakly, and confess there's nothing much to do here for non-working partners (read, wives).

'I've learned to swim,' says Pat.

'We play a lot of Mah Jong.'

Mah Jong. The name works an unexpected miracle on me, and dissolves the red vinyl and fake half-timbering, dissolves the whole clean, well-lit city itself, and glides me back to Wales. It was there, of all places, that I learned what had seemed like a secret, Friday night language that I now only half-remember. Something about the four winds and dragons and flowers, accompanied by the hypnotic click-click of the little Mah Jong tablets as we tapped them against each other. Outside, the hills had pressed hard against Lampeter and made a joke of its few streetlights, granting the darkness a ruthless quality that was almost medieval. Inside, it had seemed so brave that four of us – two Americans, an Irishman and a Frenchwoman – managed to play this ancient Chinese game and listen to Broadway show tunes, breathe our host's sweet pipe smoke and drink French wine, in defiance of the big Welsh night.

What a fine memory of youth, it occurs to me, and what a just come-uppance that I'm honouring it on this bright, electric Singapore evening by speaking the very language that was most at home in the darkness.

Time for another beer. As I get up Eirlys hands me the name of a cousin of her mother's in Argentina. 'I think she may have a B & B; don't hesitate to look her up,' she says. I try to leave again but Mairwen's husband Tal grabs my arm.

'Okay, let's see how good you are. Do you know the most famous toast in Wales?' he asks. 'It's the only thing I can say in Welsh.'

He can't get me on this one. '*Iechyd Da!*' I cry triumphantly, clinking his glass. Good health!

He looks at me with feigned contempt and reaches for my pen and notebook. 'Here,' he says, shoving it back, 'how about this one?'

Tal has written, *Twll dyn pob Sais*, roughly, All Englishmen are manholes, though he's left out the verb. For the second time tonight I nearly choke myself with laughter. Bless my E-mail. He's confused *dyn*, man, with *din*, ass. Spoken aloud it sounds the same, but his written toast has lost a wee bit of its get-off-my-island-you-Saxon-dogs edge.

From the bar I look around to make sure Marguerite hasn't imploded from conversational overload, and spot her sitting next to Mairwen and a beautiful Singaporean woman talking on a cellular phone. (Someone told me tonight that cellular phones are such a status symbol on the island that you can even buy fake ones so people will think you're important.)

Until now the evening has unravelled in a messy stream of Wenglish. Until now. I meet John at the bar and break down and buy him and his friend Ifan a drink (Ifan is my fifth and last check on Eleri's list). We launch into a long, all-Welsh conversation that I'm certain creates new wrinkles on my forehead, so intently am I frowning in the attempt to understand. I manage to say that I often mix up French and Welsh; John, if I'm correct, confuses French and Thai; Ifan has his troubles with German. We all vehemently agree about something to do with Belgium.

Luckily, someone interrupts us with the shout, 'Let's all have a sing-song!' I catch Marguerite's eye: she's signalling desperation.

Eleri takes charge. No sing-song, she says firmly, people are sleeping above us. Not if Mairwen is right, I think, and this is a short-term motel, but I'm not about to point this out. Marguerite looks relieved.

As we're waiting for John to finish his drink Eleri tells me why she opted to take a leading role in *Cymdeithas Dewi Sant Singapore* in the first place. 'It wasn't Welsh enough,' she confides, looking more like Joan of Arc than ever. 'People hate to admit it, but at home there's a narrow corridor of Welsh culture that begins in the Prescellis, veers inland to include Carmarthen, then sweeps up the coast encompassing the Lleyn Peninsula, Anglesey and Colwyn Bay.' What kind of diluted culture the rest of Wales has she doesn't say. The path Eleri's described corresponds, of course, to the traditional strongholds of the Welsh language. If nothing else tonight I've learned there exists a slippery sliding scale of Welshness – whatever that is – and that it can be imported anywhere in the world.

Cadw ♣ to Keep

Animals, as I recall, don't speak languages humans can understand. Not even Welsh. We spend a day at the Singapore Zoo.

An elderly sun bear, her tits sagging like an old woman's, sniffs us on a humid breeze; the lions posture; polar bears swallow whole loaves of bread as if they were Lifesavers; African dogs run in a pack, ears back, maniacal, like escapees from a canine lunatic asylum; the elephants perform tricks and look bored. Singapore is so full of expatriates that some live at the zoo.

We search Chinatown for a jade-handed backscratcher like Keith's, as a present for my father. 'No good,' a man tells me, 'only use as neck scratcher. Jade break off.' But that's why I want it, I say. No luck. Instead I buy a colourful cellophane fish on a string, hanging from the ceiling of a shop with a menagerie of other featherweight creatures: flying horses, pigs, batmobiles, rabbits, roosters. The ceiling is kaleidoscopic with twisting, shifting colours, spinning on heat currents and glimmering like bubbles in a three-year-old's bath. There's an intense aroma of dried fish and citrus fruit. Chinatown is one of the few places in Singapore where business is still done in real, un-conditioned air.

Hunger. Cuppage Road Hawker's Market – regulated like the rest of the city's food stalls by government inspectors, lest the hawkers backslide into the bad old days of salmonella – looks like a concrete parking garage and smells like roasting chicken. We sit under a weak fluorescent light at a round table and drink 'water lychee ice', glasses of what tastes like fresh, slightly perfumed rainwater with lychee fruit floating in the bottom. I feel happy and exotic and glad they're so bloody cheap.

Marguerite is filling me in on Jane, the woman from the Pub Night with the cellular phone who turns out to be Phil's wife. Both her parents came from China. Her grandfather had paid for his wife's and daughter's passages on a ship to Singapore, but hadn't had enough money to buy one for himself. Jane's mother tells how they walked for three days to get to the boat, so they could have a better life.

'Hey, did you happen to notice that John drove to Pub Night and Eleri drove home?' I ask.

'Uh-huh.'

'She said she always drives home. Wasn't it Rhiannon who got so steamed about Welshmen always getting to drink, and Welshwomen always having to be designated drivers?'

'You mean Rhiannon Delft?' Marguerite's getting into Welsh nomenclature. 'I think so.'

It's no coincidence that *din* and *dyn* sound the same, I decide in a sudden snit. Whether the stereotype of the Welsh enjoying a bit of booze is apt or not isn't as important as the fact that in this, as in most things, the phrase 'the Welsh' refers almost exclusively to Welsh*men*. Reading *The Xenophobe's Guide* I discovered this passage under the heading 'Wales's Best Kept Secret': 'Yet no perusal of the behaviour of the Welsh could be complete without a consideration of a Welshman's relationship with the force that controls his life.' Women, it appears, are the communal force that exerts this immense authority. I'm sure Welshwomen appreciate the nod, but the author tips his hand in his equation of 'Welsh' with 'Welshmen'. Welshwomen, it turns out, are a 'secret and sophisticated elite', distinct from the prideful, factious, lyrical lot his book takes sixty-four pages to describe. To my mind this pedestal-setting nonsense is an excuse for being too lazy to look beyond the mirror – and unfortunately, most mirrors in Wales still reflect men far more clearly than women.

Answering a recent questionnaire, women in rural Wales recorded typical eighty-hour work weeks, involving everything from housekeeping and cooking to driving and doctoring sheep, accounting, banking, charity work and service tasks (such as keeping a B & B for tourists). Yet these same women could identify themselves only as 'farmers' wives', mere appendages to the standard-setting male noun, Farmer. In the eyes of the Welsh economy – and perhaps in their own – they rank as invisible assets, like natural gas. A friend of mine from Lampeter, Olive Jones, once won a local literary contest with a poem about life on a sheep farm. She showed it to me and I told her I found it odd she'd written from her husband's perspective. 'Gives it a bit more authority,' she'd said, matter-of-factly.

'You know,' I tell Marguerite later, zapping on Keith's remote-controlled 'cooler' like I'm crushing an ant, 'it's no wonder Eleri and Rosemary have such hearty laughs. They got out.'

'Land of My Fathers,' Dylan Thomas was once reported to have bellowed, stone drunk on a New York City street, 'they can bloody well keep it.' That's probably what some of Wales's expatriate daughters are thinking, too.

Dod Adref 🌸 to Come Home

Keith's home. We find a note on the dining-room table saying he came in at 6 a.m. straight from the airport, took a bath, then left again for work, all while we were sleeping.

'I guess he doesn't mind us still being here,' ventures Marguerite. Our uncertain status as houseguests following Keith's return has been a source of distress, though Eleri has sworn he'll take our presence in his stride. Our game plan is to spend one more day here – if it's okay with him – then catch an overnight train to Kuala Lumpur to visit the Welsh Society there, return to Singapore the following evening, and fly to Bangkok the next day. So far, although Eleri has visited them and Tal Joseph was once their club president, I've had no personal confirmation that the KL Welsh really exist. My letter from the States generated no response, and phone calls have so far been a bust, but I plan to keep trying. In between attempts we do errands.

A visit to the American Express office turns up two letters from my mom but nothing from Effie Wiltens, who's fast passing from reality into the dream-state of myth.

While we're out I realize, with some conviction, that if I don't get a haircut I'll go mad. What started off three months ago short as a sheep-clipped lawn has grown to jungle proportions. In India my locks curled like tendrils in the steamy heat; here in Singapore, where air-conditioning sucks moisture from every molecule, they hang lank as swamp grass. Marguerite's bob, meanwhile, looks like a Paul McCartney 'do circa 1964. We decide to spend the day at the Far East Plaza mall sprucing up: new haircuts, new clothes. I'm devastated to learn that my size – a respectable Medium at home – is considered an Extra Large in Singapore.

Keith Pritchard. He's drawing another bath and looks apologetic when we barge into his living room, as if he's the interloper, not us. Of course we can stay, he assures us; stay as long as we like. It's nice hearing women's voices in the flat. I thank him and apologize for the jerry-rigged adapter jetty still held in place by his backscratcher, and my computer lying in the middle of the dining-room floor.

Like John Roberts, Keith is from Beddgelert in North Wales. He misses the mountains, he misses the spirituality that grows wild in the Welsh countryside. He went to sea when he was young, he's lived briefly in Brazil; he remembers old Welsh sailors from Aberystwyth who'd learned to speak Portuguese from Cape Verdeans. He builds power stations now. He was a founding member of the *Cymdeithas Dewi Sant Abu Dhabi*; he's been divorced twice and has two separate families in Wales. As a kid he played the role of a little Chinese boy in the film *The Inn of the Sixth Happiness*, with Ingrid Bergman, in which the North Walian countryside stood in for China.

Keith speaks in a soft, breathy mumble that's hard to make out. His Welsh sounds more like steam heat coming up on a cold morning than anything resembling words, yet I feel instinctively at ease before his puffy, tired eyes and perpetually inquisitive brows. He doesn't have a bad body for a fifty-year-old. Gellert – with two 'l's – he tells us, before disappearing into his bath, is also a neighbourhood of Budapest.

'Bet that's where *she* lives,' I hiss to Marguerite.

'At least he didn't say her name.'

Canu ♣ to Sing

Despite not having slept for nearly twenty-four hours, Keith drives us to the British Club of Singapore directly after his bath. Napoleon had his reckoning at Waterloo; this is where I have mine.

'Not a place I click with,' Keith confides in the car park, but the Welsh Society Choir is having its first practice of the year here tonight, and he's a member.

Inside we find Eleri bustling with the compact efficiency of a border collie, herding her charges out of the bar and into their seats across the hall in what looks like a hotel conference room. We hide at the back with her mom, lest anyone ask us to sing. Some of the men nudge each other and stare at us when they think we're not looking. Makes me wonder why I've bothered to wear clothes.

Eleri is the only woman I know capable of mastering an unruly situation in a low-backed sundress. When she raises her arms for silence, then snaps her wrists on the first downbeat, and the twenty members of the Singapore Welsh Choir open their mouths in unison, and sing, I'm struck dumb. I have a brief, searing sense of what it must be like for Welsh people who are monoglot English-speakers to be in the presence of the *Cymry Cymraeg*, the Welsh-speaking Welsh. I feel so left out. Music is not a language I know. It requires a kind of fluency I can never aspire to. I look over at Marguerite and see that she, too, is open-mouthed, astonished, awed by the sound.

As Eleri leads the choir through some practice scales, her own voice sailing and swooping like the highest gull in a clear sky, I feel a current of something I can only call Welsh identity racing around the room, born by the voices, passing me by. I can learn *Cymraeg*, and even approximate a Ceredigion accent, but words – Welsh words, English words, any words – suddenly seem like the tip of an ancient, unfathomable Welsh iceberg; far deeper down, in the aqua heart of the ice, is music, anchoring this nation not to a corner of Britain, but together as a people. Music over-comes language and geography and even the damnable east–west bias of the roadways. Tonight I feel like an expatriate too, but from a vastly different country.

The choir has not practised together for six months; of the twenty members present, only three, including Eleri, speak Welsh. Yet it takes them a neat twenty minutes to learn all four parts –

in a language foreign to nearly everyone, which they manage to sing in perfect harmony – to '*Milgi Milgi*', a catchy if inane ditty that means 'Greyhound Greyhound', about a *sgwarnog fach*, a wee rabbit, that escapes from a *milgi*. I see from my copy that the music was arranged by Eleri and John Roberts.

After the rehearsal everyone retires to the smoky bar. I'm cornered by the past president of the society, Lyndon Thomas, who tells me that nosiness is a fine Welsh trait, so as a journalist I shouldn't feel uncomfortable: I have something in common with him and his kind. I'm not sure how to take this. I'm certainly no journalist, and I speak more Welsh than he does. We talk about how around the turn of the century iron and coal masters wiped the Welsh language out of the Valleys, where it was decimated in the wink of a generation.

'It was easy,' he says. 'They made sure education and medical care were only provided in English.' He goes on to tell me that his grandfather wore the infamous 'Welsh Note' – often called the 'Welsh Not' – around his neck as a schoolboy. The 'Welsh Note' was a tag that indicated the wearer had been caught speaking Welsh during school hours; if he or she turned in a friend whom they knew had also spoken Welsh, the collar was passed on to them. Whoever wore it at the end of the day was caned.

Maybe I'm just feeling fragile because I can't sing, but a sudden wave of compassion spills over me for all the schoolchildren whose spirits were dulled by tongue-whipping in a language they couldn't understand, and I actually get tears in my eyes. John Davies writes, 'As late as 1960 it was possible to meet old people who remembered nothing of their schooldays except the learning by rote of a book known to them as "Redimarisi" (*Reading Made Easy*).'

As I take my leave Lyndon calls after me, in what I assume is a brazen attempt to get into print (at least I hope he doesn't talk this way all the time), 'May the emotion of the Welsh heart beat throughout your book!' I join a group of Englishmen at the bar who decide I must be some kind of nut to squander my time and money on a Welsh hunt; they find it particularly amusing that my name means 'Why?' in Welsh. I graciously don't let this stop them buying me another drink. A kind man named Alan Kent tells me that when a Welsh choir hits its stride it makes the hair on the back of his neck stand on end.

Gerald of Wales expressed a similar opinion seven centuries earlier, adding that 'When a choir gathers to sing, as often happens in this country, you will hear as many different parts and voices as there are performers.' Word has it that the finest and biggest Welsh choral group in South-east Asia is the Hong Kong Male Voice Choir, in much demand on the local circuit. Many of its members are Chinese, though they often sing in Welsh. If all goes well we'll be listening to one of their practices in a few weeks.

Eleri says that last year her choir's big number was an old Welsh tearjerker, '*Unwaith Eto'n Nghymru Annwyl*' – 'Once Again in the Dear Old Country'. I wince on the inside: schmaltz in a big way. Practices had been traumatic; people had been scared off by the chock-a-block consonants and unrelenting vowels of the Welsh lyrics. She'd had to write out the words phonetically, so people could memorize the sounds. 'I told them,' she recalls, 'that if you sing this right you'll have the audience in tears.' When they performed it at the St David's Day Ball it was Eleri, of all people, who'd broken down weeping. 'And I don't even like the silly song,' she says.

I'm briefly preoccupied wondering if English-speakers singing phonetically in Welsh – on key but without comprehension – is at all akin to the 'Redimarisi' school of learning, when we're joined by Alan's wife, Brenda. The subject switches from music to another of my shortcomings: math. (I decide, by the way, that it isn't: one is confusion elected, the other was confusion enforced.) Brenda is a Welsh-speaker who confirms – nearly to a word – the remarkable confession Eirlys made at Pub Night, that she's spoken more Welsh in Singapore in the last three months than in England over the past twenty-five years. Brenda tells us that in her school in Wales math was taught in English one day and Welsh the next.

'Bracing! Keeps you sharp that way,' she claims, like a woman who's just gotten out of the Irish Sea on a cloudy day. I shudder to the core of my being. Math, as I recall, was ever a foreign language unto itself. Give me a conjugating preposition – in Welsh even gnat-size words like 'to', 'of' and 'for' assume different endings to match different pronouns – over a square root any day. Eleri's mom looks aghast.

'But how do you do maths in Welsh?' she asks, in Welsh.

On the way home Keith's Japanese sedan glides down Orchard Road past the empty, glittering malls, each protecting its hidden brood of empty, glittering shops. Sometimes to freak myself out I wonder how much cutlery there is in the world.

'How the hell is there public enough to keep on buying?' Keith asks the silence in the car, with more than a touch of venom. Singapore cries out, it really does, for such questions.

Wedi Drysu ✻ to Be Confused

'Maybe we should go to Jakarta. Or Cyprus. I found out last night they've both got Welsh societies.'

'I had the best pineapple juice of my life last night,' comments Marguerite.

'Other people were buying, and you were drinking pineapple juice? Are you crazy?'

'*Milgi Milgi*' plays over and over in my head as I try in vain to make contact with Kuala Lumpur and Bangkok. My schedule has us leaving for KL tonight, but I still haven't reached the Welsh Society there. Finally, mid morning, I get a call back from the current president, someone named Brian McIntyre. No, he says, he can't round anyone up on short notice. Oh, my letter did come months ago, but the secretary forgot to respond. Well, there are only two Welsh-speakers in the society, and neither have paid their dues. 'We like to trot them out for the St David's Day Ball,' he says. He himself might be able to meet us tomorrow. Probably. He can't commit, he has a heavy social schedule. You never know what will come up.

'A day's a long time in Malaysia,' he warns me.

In a sentence Kuala Lumpur disappears from the Trip. Actually, it's a relief to know that not all Welsh people are congenitally nice. It makes me feel better about having been so ornery in Bombay.

Bangkok comes through. We break it to Keith that we're staying until the end of the week, and he seems pleased. Keith has just emerged from his nightly bath and is clutching a rock which in profile looks exactly like a miniature version of one of the mountains near his home in Snowdonia. He tells me it's his meditating rock.

I've been poring over *Y Trip*, and tell Keith it's my Welsh primer. I pass it to him to take a glance at. He snorts. 'Humph. Easy stuff. Real beginner reading. You'll get through this in a few hours.' I'm crushed. I don't dare tell him I've been working at it for three months.

Over the past day or two I've been trying to reconcile the man with the tired eyes and nice torso with the owner of the self-improvement tapes. It's not hard to do. Keith has the insecure, ready-to-please manner of an autodidact, but in his case the self-taught course seems to be on human relations. A conversation with him can be like a grand slam homerun: he covers all the bases in one sentence. Keith, upon being presented with a thank-you gift, a bottle of French wine:

'Thank you; funny that I'm drinking water; you must think I'm parsimonious to be drinking water; I do drink alcohol, I like to drink, I mean, I do sometimes; not all the time; not much, really, though you could drink yourself to death in this apartment if you wanted to.'

Makes my head spin, and I'm sipping decaf tea. But despite Keith's efforts to socialize himself, or perhaps domesticate himself, when he lets his guard down a feral, less equivocal creature seems to be lurking just beneath the surface. I get the unsettling impression that his mild demeanour is not so much instinctive as learned.

Tonight, as Keith spears sushi from a plastic container, the beast stirs a little. He starts blasting the English government for its intractability on the question of Northern Ireland, but I push the conversation over to Wales. Keith says that Welsh is his first language, tossing this statement out like a back-handed slap. Even in an English-and-Chinese-speaking environment like Singapore, he says, he thinks in Welsh, he expresses himself best in Welsh (a shame, since I can't understand his *Cymraeg* worth beans). I'm surprised when Marguerite unexpectedly challenges him. Her experience of growing up with two languages, she claims, was – and still is – like riding a seesaw; circumstances determine which one takes precedence in her brain. As a child living in Brazil it was Portuguese, now as an adult in the States it's English.

Keith nods his head sympathetically but can't agree. No, Welsh is his first language, and that's that.

I draw out of this conversation, beginning to feel a little like I did at choir practice. Wherever they wind up on the map, Welsh-speakers, men *and* women, emphatically use language to assert their nationality. It's their 'first language' because to someone like Keith or Eleri, to lose the precedence of Welsh is to fall out of their difference into the murk of the sprawling, TV-broadcasting, radio-playing, earth-sized Anglo-American abyss. Marguerite is their polar opposite: always feeling like the 'different' kid on the block, American in Brazil, Brazilian in the States, she uses language like a skeleton key, to slip in anywhere and not be unique. Either way, she and Keith both draw on opposition to define themselves. I don't. I'm just American. If Marguerite is the opposite of the Singaporean Welsh, I'm the perfect foil to the whole lot of them. The most distinctive thing about me is Keith's pair of Turkish slippers that I've got on my feet – brutally uncomfortable wooden things with snazzy, Aladdin-like turned-up toes with pom-poms on the tips. To be American, I sometimes feel, is to be blank, without a nationality or language. Is this because America is such a polyglot culture that it contains pieces of everywhere else, or because American culture in the late twentieth century is so monolithic and transcending that it *is* everywhere else?

Or is language the culprit? My native and, until recently, only tongue is spoken as a first or second language by one-third of the earth's population (some two billion people): such universality can't help but corrode the intimate links between language and place. Sometimes I feel we English-speakers are weightless and language is our wings. We circle the globe in a tail-wind of convenience, but from our bird's-eye viewpoints can't tell our destinations from our points of departure.

Goleuo 🎋 to Illuminate

It's dark: a cross between Christmas Eve and Hallowe'en. Climbing heavily out of the horizon the moon is full and hazy, smeared a bit around the edges.

'Forest fires in Indonesia,' says Keith, looking up. 'Always happens this time of year.'

Keith has brought us to the Lantern Festival at the Chinese Gardens in Jurong, a suburb of Singapore city on the island's edge. All around us the ground is glowing in patches of what looks like dense, phosphorescent fog. When I blink to clear my contacts the transformation is astonishing: the fog comes into focus as groups of silken animals lit with tiny white lightbulbs. On the crest of a hill is a pen of life-size pandas; along a footpath are the creatures of the Chinese zodiac (Keith, we learn, is a rooster, though this is the year of the pig); herons fly between tree branches; a lake swims with frogs and carp; turtles bask on rocks; enshrined under a tent is the Merlion, the half-lion, half-fish symbol of Singapore. Lanterns, all of them, sewn from richly coloured silk and glowing from within like beasts in some angelic zoo.

I run off the path to photograph the panda pen. Keith is perturbed, and tells Marguerite that he never walks in the grass in South-east Asia because of snakes. Especially at night. 'I heard on the radio that a twenty-seven-foot python ate a man in Malaysia today,' he announces. 'Swallowed all but the legs by the time they found him.'

I ignore this news. The lantern festival is actually part of the Chinese Mooncake or Autumn Harvest Festival. In traditional Chinese lore the fifteenth day of the eighth lunar month corresponds to the roundest, fullest, most fecund moon of the year. Mooncakes – expensive cookie-size delicacies made with bean or lotus seed paste – are baked to celebrate the season (we've bagged free samples from department stores on Orchard Road). The story goes that in the fourteenth century Chinese peasants passed secret messages hidden in mooncakes to organize a revolt against the Mongols; on the first day of the harvest festival signal lanterns were lit to initiate the fighting, which eventually led to the fall of the Yuan Dynasty.

This memory translates tonight into a carnival that marries free-for-all goofiness with the grace of Asian art. Hawkers sell candy floss and jazzy doo-dads beneath strings of Christmas lights; a Singaporean woman walks past wearing a battery-operated, glow-in-the-dark antennae headband; the herons glow in the trees. I realize with a shock that my cellophane fish has a purpose: it, too, is a lantern – which explains that birthday candle-size wire hole in the middle. Everywhere kids swing similar creatures made of plastic and paper, each precariously lit like a combustible jack-o'-lantern. Singaporeans can't chew gum but once a year they get to risk a fiery death in the Chinese Gardens. Seems fair.

Eventually we get lost and wander out of the fun into the sombre, empty Japanese Gardens, a cool grey-on-grey environment of stones and stunted trees. 'Built by Japanese women sold into prostitution or slavery around the turn of the century,' Keith comments.

This gets me down; actually, I'm beginning to feel a little ragged. '*Dw i'm credu bod annwyd arna i*,' I tell Keith, I think I have a cold.

He looks at me curiously. 'I'd say, "*Dw i'n annwyd.*"' To me this means, 'I am a cold.' Welsh is a heartily twisted language. Later, back in the flat – which Keith divulges is worth roughly two million dollars – he gives me a glass of Glenfiddich for my throat.

'Singapore's a breeding ground,' he says by way of comfort. 'Caught a cold here in 1976 that lasted a year and a half.'

I realize that for the past week I've been sleeping four feet away from his highly effective air-conditioner. When I wake in the morning I can't make a sound. Welcome to my second world-class case of laryngitis of the Trip.

Dyfalbarhau 🐾 to Persevere

Not having a voice doesn't stop '*Milgi Milgi*' from going round and round in my head. Surely insanity can't be far off.

> *Milgi milgi, milgi milgi,*
> *Rowch fwy o fwyd i'r milgi . . .**

* 'Greyhound greyhound, greyhound greyhound,/Give more food to the greyhound . . .'

Tonight we're supposed to go to the Stage Club with Keith, Eleri and John. I'm feeling mildly miserable and toying with cancelling, but I figure watching a rehearsal of expatriate amateur theatre is a fairly passive activity, so I let the plans ride. This afternoon I persevered in meeting Eirlys and Pat for lunch at an American burger joint in the Tanglin Mall. I'd called them after Pub Night to offer them the Tim deal: food in exchange for an hour of Welsh (any correlation between language anxiety and voice loss is, of course, purely coincidental). They'd instantly agreed.

I arrived at the restaurant with the words 'Take malaria pill' scrawled in blue ink across my palm: I tend to forget these things. I could barely speak and Eirlys knocked over her icecream soda, but we pretty much clung to Welsh. I was thrilled to hear that they can't understand Keith's *Cymraeg* either. I taught them the word for chips in Welsh – *sglodion* – and Pat told a story about her uncle, *Jim y Gas* – Jim the Gas – who once dressed up in feathers and skins and presented himself at the Eisteddfod as a Welsh-speaking Native American. Everyone believed him until a TV reporter recognized Jim as his gas meter reader. (An apocryphal story surfaces now and then about the Manadan Indians of North Dakota, who were fair-skinned and supposedly spoke some variant of Welsh before they were wiped out by a smallpox epidemic in 1838; proof, Welshophiles claimed, of the even older apocryphal story that America had been discovered by a Welsh prince, Madog, who sailed into Mobile Bay, Alabama, around 1170.)

'*Tipyn o gymeiriad*,' Eirlys said, meaning that Jim was quite a character. I made a mental note of the fact that *camgymeiriad* means 'mistake'.

Like Tim, they paid. Before we said goodbye they both reminded me, in English, of their inadequacy as Welsh-speakers, again citing Eleri's superiority. I spent the rest of the afternoon trying to imagine an English or, heaven help us, a French speaker feeling insecure in her own language. 'Oh yes, I speak English, but not as well as *she* does.' No, can't buy it. The apparatus for comparison, at least in America, doesn't even exist.

Actio 🐜 to Act

Eleri can't make it to the Stage Club, but we'll see John there in an hour. We're leaving Singapore tomorrow so, with real *hiraeth* on us, we say goodbye to Eleri by phone. I think my last words to her are 'bye bye', in English.

How could we have known? The Stage Club *is* an amateur theatre society but its primary function is to provide expats with the cheapest booze in Singapore at its Thursday night open bar. Marguerite and I keep waiting for a rehearsal to begin – posters advertise an upcoming performance of Edward Albee's *The Ballad of the Sad Café* – but after about forty-five minutes it dawns on us that drinking and jawing are ends in themselves. I see a dull desperation, which usually induces silence, fall over Marguerite. I can't breathe and my throat feels like I've swallowed scythe blades; only a faint, hoarse whisper comes out of my mouth. The clapboard bungalow that houses the Stage Club has no air-conditioning, and through the open windows I can just make out exotic insect noises over the din of English voices. The bar is so smoky that the ceiling fan actually cuts patterns in the air, which reminds me of water going down a drain in slow, slow motion. If there was ever a time to drink Scotch and sodas, this is it.

We grab four stools by the bar. Conversation weaves between Welsh and English. I can understand everything John says but nothing Keith says, and they're both from the same town. I feel like I'm being switched on and off – on off on off on off – depending on who's speaking, like a light switch in the hands of a desperately bored child. Drinks come and go. John makes the revelation that 'penguin' is a Welsh word. Of course: *pen*, head, *gwyn*, white. That penguins have black heads is beside the point. Bad jokes about bestiality are a stretch, but they follow the penguins (the Welsh are obsessed with sheep lust, real and imagined). John swears that he knew a man by the name of *Tal y Defaid* – Tal the Sheep – who, caught in a compromising position with one of his livestock, actually swore in court that he was peeing in a field when a sheep backed up on to his penis.

After this the topic shifts and gets serious. Keith's eyes narrow in a dangerous way when he says that England is economically prejudiced against Wales. 'Still,' he says, 'we'll have home rule in ten years, mark my words.'

Both men believe that a home rule motion will pass under a Labour government – even though the last time the subject of an Assembly for Wales was raised, in 1979, Welsh voters rejected the idea by five to one (more English voters were actually in favour of home rule for Wales than Welsh).

An independent research economist in London recently found Wales to be the least democratic country in Western Europe, so little were its elected representatives – predominantly members of the Labour Party – able to influence the Conservative government's policy towards the principality. Its level of democratic representation was instead noted to be on a par with that of Nigeria. 'If the Welsh were the French,' the author had said, 'they would be on the streets.'

I'd love to hear Keith's reaction to this, but John is already talking about having been at university at the time of the Meibion Glyndŵr holiday home fires.

'When my class learned the passive voice in Welsh we did this exercise,' – I can barely get this out, but the Scotch helps – '*Cafodd y tŷ ei godi, Cafodd y tŷ ei brynu, Cafodd y tŷ ei werthu, Cafodd y tŷ ei losgi.*' They laugh. Neither of them has a problem understanding me, though they have to lean close to hear. I translate for Marguerite, 'The house had its building, the house had its buying, the house had its selling, the house had its burning.'

John tells us that because he was a member of the Welsh student union his phone was bugged. 'And I was the bloody entertainment officer,' he shouts, half laughing, half still outraged. One night two big guys in raincoats had come to his door. He repeats his conversation with them.

'You John Roberts, aye?'

'Yes sir.'

'Studying biochemistry, is that right, aye?'

'Yes sir.'

'I suppose you might, aye, know how to make a bomb, then?'

'No sir.'

'What do the words "incendiary device" mean to you, aye?'

'Oh, you mean a match?'

John and Keith roar with laughter. 'You know,' says Keith, sotto voce, 'it was really MI5 all along.'

Marguerite, the only truly sober member of our party, is allergic to cigarette smoke and is itching to leave. I give her a nod that means, 'I'll try to get us out of here,' and start to say something, but I'm choked by a fierce burning in my throat. I swear I'm sweating louder than I'm speaking.

'You need another drink,' declares Keith authoritatively.

At this moment a man with a memorable Roman nose and shirt unbuttoned to his navel addresses me in a language I can't understand. I give Welsh a shot and he looks blank, but Marguerite jerks her head around in unexpected understanding.

They launch into Portuguese. Someone at the Stage Club has obviously been discussing us.

The unbuttoned one is Roland Jones, a Welshman who's lived in Brazil and speaks Portuguese and English but no Welsh.

'Come on, Roland,' urges John, 'give us a bit of *Under Milk Wood*. Do "The Sunset Song"! This lady's writing a book and maybe she'll put you in it.' Then to us, 'He's got a real Richard Burton voice when he's projecting.'

Keith asks if I know that Llaregyb, the town in *Under Milk Wood*, is essentially Bugger All backwards? I disappoint him by telling him I already know this.

My head is spinning and my throat is blazing. Roland stands so close he pins my back against the bar; I can smell the whisky and Coca-Cola on his breath. Directly above his head, like a pinwheel halo, the ceiling fan cuts cigarette smoke to ribbons. He clears his throat:

'"The Sunset Song", as uttered by the Rev. Eli Jenkins:

> 'Every morning when I wake
> Dear Lord, a little prayer I make,
> O please to keep thy lovely eye
> On all poor creatures born to die.

> 'And every evening at sun-down
> I ask a blessing on the town,
> For whether we last the night or no
> I'm sure is always touch-and-go.

> 'We are not wholly bad or good
> Who live our lives under Milk Wood,
> And thou, I know, wilt be the first
> To see our best side, not our worst.

> 'O let us see another day!
> Bless us this night, I pray,
> And to the sun we all will bow
> And say, good-bye – but just for now!'

John is glowing with sweat and pride. Keith looks undone by beer. Before bed we each give him a fond, damp kiss on the cheek. I go to sleep knowing that in the morning I'll fly to Bangkok, the tenth country of the travelling Welsh language crusade, the way I began: without a voice.

GWLAD Y TAI (THAILAND)

Gallu ✻ to Be Able To

Despite being sick and silent, I'm pretty pleased with myself. I spoke a lot of Welsh in Singapore; I mutated on demand, I didn't get sloppy and forget to roll my 'r's or wimp out on my double 'l's; I put my verbs first and made a small but noble effort to think about genders. I admit to avoiding the future tense like the plague – the suffixes are unappealing to me: I find *gweliff hi*, she will see, not nearly as nice as *gwelodd hi*, she saw – but overall I regained the confidence I'd lost over the past month. Welsh became familiar again. It must be said I couldn't understand a word uttered by Keith or Eleri's mom, but then I had some trouble with their English, too. I'm feeling cocky. I'm ready for the Welsh of Bangkok.

Rhwbio ✻ to Rub

After a few minor misadventures we find Kittipat at the Bangkok International Airport. Kittipat, not Kitticat. I've been forbidden to call him that, though I want to very badly.

Kittipat is a former English-as-a-Second-Language student of Marguerite's, who got his MBA in the States. He's twenty-four, slight and good-looking, a juggler of first impressions who manages to project smooth competence and youthful innocence in equal measure. When we last met, in Providence, Rhode Island, I'd given him a big goodbye hug, which now makes me cringe with embarrassment. On the plane I'd read in *Let's Go Thailand* that casual physical contact is distasteful to Thais; the absolute worst thing you can do is rub someone on the head (to my knowledge I've never so much as mussed Kittipat's hair, so I'm safe on this count), or point your foot at a person or a religious image. Never shout, never, ever lick postage stamps with pictures of the King. These instructions leave me in a state as to how to greet Kittipat, but at the last moment I remember my cold, and use germs as an excuse to keep my distance.

When we first met, several years ago, Kittipat was having real trouble with English. It was as if he felt sorry for the closed, cramped Germanic consonants and curt diphthongs and wanted to set them free. His mouth just couldn't keep an 'l' or an 'r' imprisoned inside, he always had to open up and let them fly off as 'owls' and 'aahhs'.

But he's gotten a lot stricter with English. He's also got a grip on the devil's favourite invention in South-east Asia, a cellular phone. I point at a row of banking machines and croak that I need to get some *bhat* (Thai for cash). Alas, the spiteful things spit both my credit cards, American Express and MasterCard, back at me like pieces of spoiled meat. Above us a giant MasterCard billboard illuminates its international slogan, 'You've Got the Whole World in Your Hands'. I comment to Marguerite in a surly whisper that the only phrase I've seen more often on this trip is 'Entry Failure: Try Again Later'.

Kittipat's sister is a travel agent who's booked us into the Royal River Hotel in Bangkok, where for the first time since Athens, when a mistake by a tourist official got us a room in a three-star hotel for half-price, we brush up against the international tourist trade. Doormen bow; porters seize our packs; the lobby looks like the Singapore Airport and smells of fresh orchids. We stay at the front desk long enough to hear the Muzak versions of 'Raindrops Keep Falling on My Head' and 'Moon River'.

From Room 937 – complete with mini bar, cable TV and coupon for two free drinks – we have a view of the choppy, milk chocolate-coloured Chaophraya River, above which the sky is heavily veined with bruised-bottom rain clouds, far bluer than the water below. I'm busy collecting sample shampoo bottles in the bathroom when Marguerite finds the hotel's rate card and gasps.

'Pam, this room costs over a hundred dollars a night. A hundred dollars a night! What are we going to do?'

'I thought you wrote Kittipat from Paris and told him no more than forty.'

'I did, I swear I did.'

If this is true, I think, I'm going to rub his head. Not only are the ATMs contemptuous of my credit cards, but we're staying in a hotel we can't afford. After reading in *Let's Go* about the Thais' abhorrence of confrontation, we're at a loss as to how to mention this dilemma. Kittipat's sister has paid for us in advance and is sending an invoice tomorrow; we decide to just sweat it out and wait.

A more immediate hurdle is that I have to call Liz Shepherd, who works at the British Embassy here and is my contact among the fifty-member St David's Society of Bangkok, but have no voice with which to do it. Marguerite, who hates to talk on the telephone, especially with strangers, is reluctantly elected my second. While the phone rings I hear her nervously humming the insidious '*Milgi Milgi*' (it does my heart good to know I wasn't its only victim); when Liz answers she conveys the problem, confirms that I'm speechless, not dead, and they set up a rendezvous for tomorrow night at the British Club.

Around sunset we pile into Kittipat's Toyota and drive a half-mile to dinner at a restaurant called Kanabham, which means Along the River in Thai. I'm about to ask why we don't just walk there, when the answer becomes apparent: the street adjacent to the hotel is flooded with foot-high brown water. This seems to unnerve Marguerite. Her anxieties usually translate into dreams about rising water, so it's a good bet she doesn't like this one bit.

The restaurant spills out of an enclosed dining room on to a riverside deck, to which Kittipat leads us after stepping over a litter of newborn puppies by the front door. As it grows dark the constant lap-lap of water against the deck becomes more of a vigorous slosh-slosh. People begin to move away from the tables nearest the river.

Kittipat orders strange and wondrous foodstuffs, which bear no resemblance to the fare that passes for Thai food at home. Sweet chicken baked in woven packets of thick-bladed grass; a prawn soup redolent of cilantro and ginger that smells of early morning, and comes bubbling in an earthenware crock that looks like it's on loan from the National Museum; salty, sticky things that have no name in English; strong, cold Thai beer that sweats against its bottle. Soon after the soup course a waiter runs over and motions wildly at my foot. I'm seized with fear that I've been pointing it at someone when he lifts the tablecloth to reveal a pot of mosquito repellent smouldering on the floor. I try to recall what I know about dengue fever.

'Set feet on fire,' says Kittipat. 'Not a good idea.'

Soon a young Thai woman in a miniskirt plugs in an amp connected to karaoke equipment and begins to sing. 'Yahthaday,' she croons, 'ah mah tubhes seem so fah awayh . . .'

Kittipat leans across the table and says conspiratorially, 'I don't think she speaks English. Just memorize the lyrics.' I've got to agree: she's giving the words strange, random tugs and twists on their vowels. She's also giving the river more than a few nervous glances, as are the waiters. Surely their fear is a bad sign. It occurs to me that the singer's version of 'Love Will Keep Us Together' (where are the Captain and Tennille when you need them?) probably sounds as tangled and attenuated to me as Eleri's choir – singing in Welsh at an early rehearsal – would to a native Welsh-speaker. Still, you can get away with so much more in song than in speech. Would that I could sing.

Without concern I watch a tendril of water curl its way toward us. I'm tired; a lingering motion hangover from the flight, plus about fifteen cough drops, the insect repellent, the beer, the reckless threat of drowning, and the vibration of the amp's bass all conspire to lull my conscious mind into something approximating heedless abandon. The temporary respite from Welsh probably helps too. Someone else's bloody vowels are on the line tonight. From the taut cords in Marguerite's neck I can tell that she's in a different mood entirely.

On the way back to the hotel the water is up to the Toyota's doors. 'Bad floods in the north,' Kittipat tells us. 'Supposed to reach Bangkok in a few days.'

Gawn Ni Ddawnsio? ✤ Shall We Dance?

In the morning the flooding is gone and no one mentions it: I secretly worry that I've been hallucinating. My first impression of Bangkok is that it's ruled by an exceptionally benevolent dictator, a smiling old lady in glasses and a military-style jacket that accentuates the curvature of her spine. Her image is plastered to enormous, vertical billboards all over the city. 'King Mother,' says Kittipat. 'Dead.' He explains that when a member of the royal family dies it's traditional to observe one hundred days of mourning by wearing black, a rule most conspicuously followed by old women, though he's advised us – despite the intense heat – to dress sombrely to visit the Grand Palace. This is the fifty-third day of darkness for the King Mother.

Bangkok traffic is as bad as everyone says it is. So much leaded exhaust spews out of so many tailpipes that the cops and highly efficient street sweepers have to wear respirators. Inconceivably, in this city of almost ten million people there is no mass transportation. 'They are building a, um,' Kittipat searches for the word, 'oh yes, a subway, but above ground. I see it and believe it.' I ask when it will be finished. Kittipat is vague. 'Ten years, maybe more. In the meantime, four thousand new cars in Bangkok every day.'

I pray he means every month. It takes us an hour and fifteen minutes to drive about two miles, plenty of time for him to remember to give us the bill from his sister. Enormous relief: she's gotten us a half-price rate at the Royal River, though we have to pretend we're tourists with a group called Magister Tours. I don't have a problem with that.

Bangkok is a newish city. Its foundations were laid in the eighteenth century, after the previous capital of what was then Siam had been sacked and burned by the Thais' traditional enemies, the Burmese. It seems surprisingly familiar − even more so than Singapore, which was too clean to remind me of home, and never would have tolerated Bangkok's unaesthetic profusion of Dunkin Donuts and Radio Shacks, Seven-Elevens and Toys-R-Us's − yet it has pockets of traditional Thai architecture that set my heart racing. The Grand Palace, actually a complex of royal residences, government offices and temples ensconced in the city centre, puts the light meter on my camera to the test: every inch of the thirty-three-building compound is encrusted with a razzle-dazzle of gold leaf, mirrors, glass and tilework. It's like a kind of Asian rococo, executed by a team of wealthy surrealists. Resplendent, gilded demons with red, aqua and purple faces hold foundations on their backs, knees bent in perpetual pliés; subtle, horned corner mouldings rise from rooftips like slender stalagmites; mythological creatures, half human, half rooster, guard the temple that houses Thailand's most sacred treasure, a jade sculpture known as the Emerald Buddha.

Outside the temple Kittipat dumps a lotus flower-full of holy water on each of our heads. Inside a sign admonishes visitors, 'When Seated Do Not Extend Foot in Direction of Emerald Buddha'.

The baptism backfires: throughout the day something I've eaten − or maybe it's the malaria pills left over from India − flexes its muscles in my intestines every twenty minutes or so, sparking a paroxysm of dull, hot pain and a craving for the nearest loo. I slip at the Marble Temple while crossing a footbridge arched sharp as a cat's back (Marguerite and Kittipat use a nearby stairway, thus avoiding damage), and smash my camera beyond repair. Guards at the Palace take one look at our infamous German walking shoes and pull us out of the crowd passing through the front gate. It seems our straps, always a bit too big, have slipped below our heels, essentially turning the shoes into backless clogs.

A guard with a helmet and machine gun shakes his head. 'He says naked heels are disrespectful,' explains Kittipat. I point out a blonde woman who walks by unaccosted, wearing flip-flops. Still, the guard won't let us go until we both ram our feet backward into the straps; to keep them high against our heels we have to walk around the Palace like bent-kneed ducks. My worst faux pas, however, occurs at the National Museum, when Kittipat mentions a perennial thorn in Thailand's side: *Anna and the King of Siam*, better known as the Rodgers and Hammerstein musical, *The King and I*. Yul Brynner. 'Shall We Dance?' 'Getting to Know You'. The Thais loathe all of it.

'This book is still banned in Thailand,' Kittipat tells me. 'It is all lies. That Anna woman made everything up.'

That Anna woman was really Margaret Landon, who describes herself on shipboard in the first chapter as 'an Englishwoman . . . slender and graceful . . . a light breeze ruffling her full skirts'. She later amends this picture, speaking of herself, as always, in the third person: 'She was born in Carnarvon [*sic*] in Wales on November 5, 1834.' Margaret Landon was Welsh.

I'm stunned. The Thais' greatest enemy is not the Burmese but a Welshwoman. Remember Yul Brynner's rapid-fire finger snapping and imperious 'Et cetera, et cetera, et cetera'? Landon portrayed King Rama IV as petulant and mercurial at best, and Thailand never forgave her. The only nation in South-east Asia not to have been colonized by the West was instead humiliated by a female member of the first colony of the greatest empire of the modern world.

I don't know if I should be pleased or humbled by this revelation. Despite calling herself an Englishwoman, Margaret Landon writes with feeling about her homeland, proud that though Wales had been conquered it never lost face. 'But the Romans had not stamped the love of freedom out of Welsh hearts,' she declares, 'nor could the English do that in the centuries that followed.' She goes on to tell how 'Anna's' parents left for India when she was a baby. Anna/Margaret grew up in North Wales, and at fifteen sailed for Bombay to join her mother and stepfather (her real father had died serving the empire). Being a member of the gentry – a much-Anglicized group long divorced from the Welsh-speaking *gwerin* or common folk – she'd never learned to speak Welsh. While still in her teens Anna/Margaret escaped from both Bombay and her despised stepfather by marrying a man doomed to a short life, forsaking her fortune in the process. When her husband died she was left with no money and three children, whereupon she answered an ad to become governess to the off-spring of the King of Siam. The rest, as they say, is musical history.

The devil gets into Marguerite. 'Pam's book is about the Welsh, Kittipat. You remember that, right?' she asks, poking me.

Kittipat takes off his mirrored sunglasses and gives me a potent, old-fashioned evil eye that's too winsome to be effective. Or so I hope.

Amau ♣ to Doubt

Capitalizing on a ride from Kittipat, we arrive at the British Club forty-five minutes early and are shown to the Churchill Bar. Because we're not members we can't order anything, and since we've been advised against it, we don't drink the ice water that a waiter brings to our table. I consider licking the condensation off the outside of the glass, but remember my manners.

Well, it's almost show time, I think, silently running through some Welsh introductions. *Fi sy Pamela, honna ydy Marguerite.*

Mae'n dda da fi gwrdd â chi – I'm Pamela, this is Marguerite. It's good to meet you. This afternoon at the Temple of Dawn, a veritable man-made mountain affixed with bits of mirrors and Chinese porcelain, we'd been gently accosted by a group of shy Thai schoolgirls asking in English if we spoke French. I'd nodded and managed a hoarse '*Oui*' (laryngitis still has an impressive stranglehold on my voice). Their French teacher had given them the assignment of interviewing tourists with questions like, How are we enjoying Bangkok? What have we eaten here? As they read through the list comprehension became like a kind of verbal, archaeological dig: I had to unearth the French sounds under layer upon layer of thick Thai accents before I could recognize them. Is this what Welsh speakers go through with me and my flat vowels, my masticated American 'r'? The mere thought makes me want to run home screaming to the cushy Royal River Hotel.

The appointed hour comes and goes. A crowd is accruing in a corner of the bar, but no one approaches us. I can't pick up any Welsh accents – they're all speaking English – and, unhelpfully, none of them bursts into song. Can't be the Welsh, I decide rashly, happy with the momentary respite.

After about half an hour a middle-aged woman comes up to us; she's wearing an emerald green blouse with matching rhinestone earrings, and her ash blonde hair is swept into an elegant bun.

'Pamela and Margareta?'

I was wrong. The woman in green is Liz Shepherd, who escorts us back to her table where about fifteen people have now gathered. It's decided I should sit in the middle, to give the folks at either end a fighting chance of hearing me, though that seems unlikely. If I strain hard enough I can make just about as much noise as if I were filing my nails.

'So,' I whisper brightly, '*pwy sy'n siarad Cymraeg?*' Who speaks Welsh?

Everyone looks blank for a moment, then carries on ordering drinks.

'Doesn't anyone here speak Welsh?'

'Nope,' says the man to my right. 'No speakers here. So, what's this you're doing? Travelling the world looking for Welsh people, eh?' Scepticism weighs heavily on his words, though most everyone quiets to hear my answer.

I explain my goals of the Trip: to practise Welsh in outposts where I'm less likely to backslide into English, to meet others who are keeping up not just the language, but the traditions of Wales; to find out what people remember about their home, and if there are other foreigners, like me, who are drawn to the place. As I'm speaking the eye-contact attrition is enormous; halfway through my spiel I realize I've lost most of them. The few who politely continue to pay attention look incredulous.

'But why?' asks a woman named Pat, who's an agent for travelling rock groups and the bard, or president, of the St David's Society of Bangkok. 'How can you feel such passion for Wales? We all couldn't wait to get out.'

Several people nod. When I correct the impression that it's not a 'searching for her roots thing', there's even more consternation. A redhead named Carol cuts to the chase. 'Pardon me for being blunt, but does your publisher really think there's a market for this book?'

Things are not going well. I defend the honour of Harper-Collins's editors until someone asks the question I've been expecting: whyever did I decide to learn Welsh in the first place?

I squirm in my seat and tell them a little story about Lampeter. I'd been living there for months, I say, when someone mentioned a place called *Llanbedr Pont Steffan*; I was humiliated that I didn't know where it was. It was then that I realized I was only aware of half the world around me, and I'd better darn well begin to investigate the other side of it.

This meets a few bland smiles, then nothing. Finally the question-asker mutters, in a tone that's the conversational equivalent to putting on one's coat, 'Yes, you're right, Llansteffan is near Lampeter.' A few people agree and the subject switches to how unfortunate it is that I've missed Gwyn Morgan, yet another diplomat from Wales whom everyone claims is a hoot and very, very Welsh.

For an instant I feel like a character in a horror movie who realizes that maybe, just maybe, she isn't alone in the house. Except in this case the situation is reversed: I'm most definitely on my own here. These people grew up in Wales, their grandparents, at the very least, spoke Welsh, yet they have no idea that Llanbedr Pont Steffan and Lampeter are one and the same place. Without knowing this fact my neat little morality tale makes no sense. I'm beginning to doubt myself again: am I in the right place? Were there really floods last night? Is there really a Welsh Society of Bangkok?

Liz rises and announces it's time to move into another room for dinner. Eleven of us jockey for seats at one long table; I wind up next to Marguerite and a girl of about twenty, the daughter of one of the society's founding members. Liz had mentioned that the young woman was raised in Bangkok and is bilingual in Thai and English. I inquire about this – which is she more comfortable speaking, which does she use more often? – but the effort of opening her lips seems too weighty a prospect, and after a few moist, mumbled replies they clamp shut altogether.

Okay. I try another source and meet Carol's eye. She wants to know if I'll speak to Mel Gibson when I get home and ask him if he'll make another battle epic like *Braveheart*, but with a Welsh subject. I try to explain that I don't know Mel Gibson, but she isn't having it.

'Just try,' she insists.

Roger Daniel is sitting opposite me. He seems guarded at first, but by the time our entrées arrive I get the impression I've passed some sort of test, and he warms a bit to his heritage.

'You should've met my father,' he says, 'he was very Welsh. Swore up until the day he died that he always thought in Welsh, even dreamt in Welsh, though he only spoke to us in English.'

Roger adds a little later that Cliff Richard's real name is Harry Webb, like the Welsh poet who wrote about the Severn Bridge.

Pat leans across Marguerite and hands me the programme of last year's St David's Day Ball. I see they funded a performance by the Hong Kong Male Voice Choir: very classy of them. Included in the programme notes are the words in Welsh and English to the Welsh National Anthem, '*Hen Wlad Fy Nhadau*' – 'Land of My Fathers' – as well as to the Call for Peace Ceremony. The phrase '*Y Gwir yn erbyn y Byd*' is translated as 'The Man Against the World'; close, but it should read 'The Truth against the World' (there the Welsh go again, with that Us vs. Them attitude). I don't mean to be picky, but man and truth are not yet synonymous, even here in Buddhist Bangkok.

Before we leave I'm introduced to Leighton Fowles, father of the close-lipped one and a founder of the society back in the late seventies. He seems a pleasant man and has been in Thailand for thirty-eight years – began his own insurance company here – yet I wonder why he selected Welshness, of all things, as the rallying point of an additional expatriate club. He already belonged to the St George's Society, he tells me, and he believes that the differences between Welsh and English lose meaning once you leave the cosy pale of the European continent. Sounds like something Margaret Landon might have said.

So, he asks heartily, did I know that Liz was *the* original Welsh Lady? I don't get it. I'm still trying to figure out what's so Welsh about the Welsh Society of Bangkok, when Liz herself joins us and explains. A friend of hers had visited Epcot Center at Disney World in Florida, and was appalled that the Welsh Lady outfit wasn't among the slew of national costumes on display there. He raised such a ruckus that Epcot complied; the prototype from which they produced a costume was a photo of Liz decked out in Welsh Lady gear.

That's it. Some kind of weird karma is afoot tonight. The Welsh Lady get-up was invented in the nineteenth century by Lady

Llanover: the wife, states Jan Morris in *The Matter of Wales*, of the Benjamin for whom Big Ben was named. Lady Llanover's Welsh, like mine, was shaky, but she hired Welsh-speaking servants to help her practise (now why didn't I think of that?), brought them to her estate near Abergavenny, and dressed the women in tall black hats that look like stretch top-hats or sawn-off witches' hats, lace caps that tie under the chin in a big bow, woven shawls and white aprons. The look caught on. It was intended as an exercise in reconstructive anthropology, and Lady Llanover did give Wales a recognizable image – today the Welsh Lady is a stock character on the Wales Tourist Board stage – I just wish it weren't so puritanically silly looking.

I recall Rhiannon Delft telling me it had infuriated her to meet an Englishwoman decked out in Welsh Lady garb at a tea shop on the Lleyn Peninsula. I see her point, but the costume does have an iffy pedigree. Liz Shepherd is a kind woman and I appreciate her gathering so many people together on short notice ('You know us,' she'd said, 'any excuse for a booze-up'), not to mention treating us to dinner, but she's more akin to Lady Llanover – a well-to-do English speaker trying to infuse a non-Welsh environment with a little *Cymreictod* or Welshness – than to the maids who would've worn the outfit. Maybe it's fitting that she was the model for a display at Disney World, my country's ultimate tribute to the land of pleasant unreality.

Leaving the British Club I see that Pat has changed out of her red dragon T-shirt. 'Going to another party,' she says by way of explanation. Liz and her husband Tony offer us a ride to a main thoroughfare where we'll be able to catch a cab. There's a tremendous thunder and lightning storm bashing the sky over Bangkok, accompanied by a fierce rain. According to Thai mythology, the commotion is all the fault of a beautiful goddess named Mekhala, who now and then taunts the bad-tempered demi-god Ramasura by flashing a jewel in his eyes; he responds by pitching his axe at her, which clatters through the sky making an ear-splitting roar.

I'd love to know who came up with this explanation: it's so much more aristocratic than the pedestrian bowling-ball theory I got as a kid.

Back on earth in Liz and Tony's car, Liz gives us each little gifts, which we find touching; then Tony abruptly pulls over, lets us out in front of a Holiday Inn, and zooms off in a furious backsplash.

'Guess we didn't make a good impression,' comments Marguerite through her teeth.

When we finally get a cab I accidentally send the driver barrelling off to the Royal City Hotel rather than the Royal River Hotel (the desk clerk gave us a card with 'Royal River' written in Thai to show taxi drivers, plus a picture of the place in case they couldn't read). Unfortunately, I've presented our driver with the wrong side of the card, which bears a photo of the Royal City Hotel. It's not until we've crept halfway across town in the wrong direction that I realize my mistake. The driver takes it personally and slaps himself in the forehead, but doesn't stop the meter. When we reach the right hotel, around midnight, I note with two parts relief to one part alarm that the floodwaters have returned.

Cymharu ☘ to Compare

I have always known, deep down, that I'm a carnivore. I don't cook meat myself, mainly because I don't enjoy it that much, but breakfast at the Royal River brings out the beast in me. Guests have the option to choose from the Asian Breakfast buffet, with fish, noodles, rice and other steaming sundries in big silver bins, warmed by sterno burners below, or the Western Breakfast buffet, with slightly congealed eggs, pancakes and crispy bacon stacked so high it looks like a pile of fireplace kindling. Each morning the 'while in Rome' adage needles me with a second or two of indecision, then I dive into the bacon. Worse yet, I pass up decaffeinated coffee for real tea, and have *two cups*. I write off this enigmatic behaviour as preparation for Japan, where I anticipate drinking herbal tea and losing weight (I despise sushi and fear most fish).

Marguerite tells me that the people she talked to the other night at the British Club seemed to enjoy living in Thailand. They find it more interesting than Singapore – which many of them bad-mouthed – but for the traffic problem. 'Someone told me that Bangkok is a difficult place to live,' recalls Marguerite, 'but said it's always interesting. Singapore, on the other hand, is an easy place to live but it's dull.'

'I heard something similar. I think it was Roger who said that there are always things going on in Bangkok, but you can never do any of them because by the time you get there they're over.'

South-east Asia's worst traffic snafus are not our problem today. Kittipat is busy, it's almost a relief to bed down in Room 937, reading and writing for a change. I've bought one of those Thai baseball caps sewn all over with beadwork and sequin elephants, and wear it throughout the day instead of washing my hair. My elephants' trunks are facing up, which is supposed to bring me luck (trunks down brings money, which I need too, but I went with the aesthetic appeal of luck).

The elephants do their thing immediately. I flick on the TV and conjure up a pre-season American football game, the very emblem, to me, of early autumn and the dwindling of the year. I love football. I associate it with the vivid vegetable colours of falling leaves – pumpkin orange, squash yellow, russet potato red – with the smell of moth balls (the first sweaters plucked from summer storage), with bad band music, with wood fires, with early twilight, with *home*. Nine floors below us the Chaophraya River is bringing typhoon season to the bamboo huts next to the hotel, turning their yards into wavy rectangles of brown water; here in the room, Star TV is beaming autumn to me by satellite. Green Bay leads Detroit thirteen–ten.

Though I may seem inexhaustibly American, I admit the other night to having felt more Welsh than most of the assembled throng, British passport holders all. Hey, in Singapore Pat said I looked Welsh – 'like Eleri', she'd told me, as if looking like Eleri were proof that by travelling the world practising this old tongue I'm earning myself a degree of Welshness, much the same way I'm picking up frequent flyer miles. There seems to be a consensus among the Singaporeans that Eleri is just a little 'more Welsh' than everyone else on the island. This idea of nationality by degrees, the very concept of a sliding scale on which people rank as more or less Welsh, is beginning to trouble me. If I've heard the phrase, Oh, he or she – usually he – is 'very Welsh' once on this trip I've heard it a thousand times.

I can't imagine a more foreign notion. I would never think to call myself more or less American than anyone else I know. The state of being 'very American' is usually reserved for inanimate objects, like big cars and cheeseburgers; there is, of course, the condition of being 'un-American', as in the House of Un-American Activities Committee, which paved the way for the McCarthy witch trials of the fifties, but that shameful episode dealt with the notion of 'activities' – namely consorting with communists, real or imagined – rather than any general set of characteristics one is or is not born with.

(I hop off this ladder of thought for lunch, purchased at a nearby Seven-Eleven, which consists of yogurt, a shared Dunkin' Donut, and bottles of Singha beer. Then I climb back up, munching and thinking simultaneously, still in my hat.)

America, of course, is too plural to pin down to a specific national identity, and too powerful to worry much about it; Wales, on the other hand, is not only tiny but ever-defining itself so it won't wake up one day as England. Nonetheless, I have a suspicion that language lies at the root of the problem. And this is a problem.

If you start with the Welsh language, with the integrity of its grammar, the suffixes and prefixes that are the building blocks of its words – think of a charmer like *glaswellt*: *glas* means green, *gwallt* means hair, together they mean 'grass' – then there's no getting around the fact that there are qualitative degrees of the spoken tongue: from 'pure' Welsh, to everyday Welsh (marbled with occasional English words), to Wenglish. On this scale English ranks as a national kind of birth defect. Historically, because of North Wales's fortress-like geography, it's managed to withstand the invasion of English better than the South – with the exception of the extreme south-western seaboard – resulting in an inferiority complex that cripples half the nation's Welsh-speakers. Think of Mairwen and company and their self-proclaimed 'loose Welsh'. Think of R. S. Thomas, born into an English-speaking household, who asks in his poem, 'Welsh',

> Why must I write so?
> I'm Welsh, see:
> A real Cymro,
> Peat in my veins.
>
> She claimed me,
> Brought me up nice,
> No hardship;
> Only the one loss,
>
> I can't speak my own
> Language – Iesu,
> All those good words;
> And I outside them . . .

Living with a linguistic sliding scale for the past century or more has created what I can only call an atmosphere, or a mindset, of comparison in Wales. The very idea of some people being more Welsh than others comes from the fact that the bellwether of the country's fate, the Welsh language, was fractured long ago on the hard rocks of English into an emotionally charged hierarchy of subsets. Had English never infiltrated the national tongue, the whole concept of qualitative disparities within such a small nation might never have occurred to anyone.

If the quality of one's Welsh, and later the mere fact that one spoke it at all, was once a marker to others of one's nationality, what happened when almost all the residents of Wales came to speak English? Easy: new markers had to be found to define this elusive sense of *Cymreictod*, or what it means to be 'very Welsh' – lest, heaven forbid, one be mistaken for English. John Davies writes in *A History of Wales* about the various attempts to pin down Welsh identity over the years, and how around 1900 'Welshness' came to be associated with Wales's highest profile – and most thoroughly Anglicized – region, the South Wales coalfield. Attributes culled from the miners, he writes, included 'their political radicalism, their communal solidarity, their love of singing, their enthusiasm for rugby, their voluble and welcoming temperament and their lack of obsession with class division'.

It's a sad irony that the 'classless' or what Davies calls 'one-class' *Cymry* (fellow countrymen) should have come to find other means than economics of ranking one another: when everyone's poor, decide who's got more Welshness rather than who's got more money.

This is not to say that language no longer plays a role in Wales's nationality games. When I was learning the rudiments of Welsh in Lampeter in the summer of '92, Rod (the Canadian with the waxed face, mysteriously known to Eleri's mom) loved to tell people that his grandmother was Welsh. Inevitably, the first question out of his hearers' mouths was not 'Where did she come from?' but 'Did she speak it?'

Among Welsh-speakers like Eleri and Keith, language remains *the* litmus test of Welshness. It is, as one reviewer of Davies's book put it, 'our author's central message, that the historic continuity in Wales has been inseparable from the national tongue.' Yet the other night I didn't feel 'more Welsh' than the St David's Society of Bangkok because I can say *Mae'n boeth iawn ym Mangkok* – It's very hot in Bangkok – and they can't, or because none of them burst into song in the Churchill Pub. Remember, I can't sing either. And if we're tallying *Cymreictod* points here, it's only fair to admit that they're far more into rugby than I am (I've even lost the signal for my American football game, without finding out who won).

Truth is, there's no formula in the world for gauging Welshness, no recipe that calls for three stereotypes mixed with five pints of beer that will cook up a Welsh person. Except . . . except perhaps enthusiasm for the place, and a simple wanting to be there. The only reason I say I felt 'more Welsh' is that on the basis of an evening's talk (pretty paltry evidence, I admit), I seem to like Wales better. I miss the salty dampness and the bumpy landscape and fruity smell of life lived near big, manure-manufacturing animals. I miss Cardiff's Edwardian pretensions; I miss getting riled up at breakfast by the editorials in the *Western Mail*. I even miss those sparkly, evanescent trails the slugs leave on farm tracks in the night, which turn into ghostly threads at dawn and disappear by noon. My hosts, hospitable as they were, weren't so parochial about their nostalgia, which took more of a British than a Welsh cast. It wasn't what they said, or what language they said it in, it was what they didn't say.

'Are you in some kind of trance?'

'Huh? No, I'm thinking. Actually I'm finished thinking. How about going down to the bar and redeeming our coupon for those free drinks?' I'm adamant about not wasting this opportunity.

'In that hat?' asks Marguerite in a sceptical tone. I agree it's a bit much and take it off.

I was kind of hoping for Thai whisky, but we don't have a choice in the matter: moments after we render up the coupon (note that we're taking our parts as holidaymakers with Magister Tours very seriously), a perky cocktail waitress brings us two pink frothy things in shallow champagne glasses which bear an uncanny resemblance to liquid bubblegum. We do our best to linger, say, five minutes over them, and are back in Room 937 in under ten. I can't tell if they had any alcohol in them or not.

A fax has been slipped under the door in our absence. I feel so important. I've always wanted to get a fax in Bangkok. It's from Liz Shepherd, hoping we'd managed to find a taxi the other night. She adds, 'I did try Ambassador Morgan for you, but he's out of the country at the moment. Pity – he's a great character, and nationalistic in the nicest possible way.'

Cwympo ❧ to Fall

On our final day in Thailand Kittipat is two hours and fifteen minutes late for our appointed rendezvous. We sit on the edge of a box of philodendrons by the front door of the hotel and wait. Boredom drives me into one of the souvenir shops in the lobby, where I find holiday reading to rival the offerings of the Pangim Inn: *The Comfort Women: Japanese Sex Slaves in World War II*, *The 1995 Thailand Petroleum Report* and the *1993 Guide to Gay Thailand*. When Kittipat finally arrives he says just one word, 'Traffic,' which I'm beginning to think is Bangkok's all-purpose excuse – like smog in Los Angeles – for everything from being late to getting pregnant.

He wants to show us a rose garden but I take an unexpectedly firm stand on seeing Ayutthaya (pronounced Eye-u-TAY-a), the ruined former capital of Thailand, about two hours' drive from Bangkok. Kittipat graciously concedes. On the way we pass Thailand's biggest mall, then an indecisive stretch of modern, whitewashed buildings with red tile roofs. These gradually dwindle, leaving only an empty, agricultural plain swathed in the shimmering, traffic-light green of young rice paddies. Our entire journey is accompanied by a twangy-voiced English DJ counting down South-east Asia's top forty hits, all of which have a diabolical, house-music backbeat.

Ayutthaya was sacked twenty-three times by the Burmese before it finally fell in 1767. Before that it had been the capital of Siam for four hundred and seventeen years. Kittipat tells us that the city's destruction is still considered the greatest tragedy in Thai history. (Later I find a listing in my guide book which notes that the Thais annually re-enact the final sack, staged with elephants, swords, real explosions, and a cast of thousands.)

Ayutthaya is a World Heritage site, but you'd never know it. At the temple of Wat Phra Si Samphet, originally built as a palace in 1350, no one inspects our shoes. Only stray dogs roam the well-clipped grass corridors between truncated foundation walls, now crumbling into herringbone piles of red and blackened brick. The air breathes like unseen velvet, heady and hot, scented with the strong perfume of frangipani blossoms. Marguerite, Kittipat and I clamber among fantastically leaning pillars and dismembered buddhas while hundreds of whirring dragonflies make helicopter patterns around us, flecking the sunlight like an iridescent dust storm. All the signs say, wake up, Pamela, this is a dream sequence, but the sweat running down my back tells me it's real. At the centre of the ruins are three great stone *chedis*, huge bell-shaped monuments that once housed the remains of kings. Their exteriors are still charred after all these years from the fires used by Burmese troops to melt the gold off their outer skins.

The site is at once more casual and more intact that the European ruins I'm used to. There are no 'Do Not Climb the Walls' signs, no guards. The relative completeness of the place still commands my attention, demands my respect and even a little awe; but it's the small, sad details that get to me. In a corner, overlooked and unattended, half buried in rotting frangipani flowers, is a stone hand. I check the crippled buddhas but so many have amputated limbs I can't find its owner. The hand appears to be lying exactly where it fell two hundred years earlier, on the night of the Burmese attack. The rare combination of grandeur and tragic happenstance does a phenomenal job of stripping time from this spot; in a rush of shivers I'm yanked into a sense of immediacy, even fear. Local people are fond of claiming that the ghosts of soldiers and massacred townsfolk still roam these brick paths by night.

In its heyday, Wat Phra Si Samphet would have glittered as

much or more than the Grand Palace in Bangkok; yet my Western eyes, used to the grey ruins of Wales, find Ayutthaya's remains more accessible than all that razzle-dazzle. Just before we leave, the site is taken again, this time by hundreds of very young schoolchildren in lavender shirts and matching baseball caps.

'The attack of the purple ants,' says Marguerite.

Kittipat ignores them and tells us that in Thailand Buddhist monks shave their eyebrows, and in Tibet they don't. That's all, he says, he knows about their religious differences.

Ffonio 🐜 to Telephone

My last ration of bacon is digesting. Our luggage is packed. I've just called Ursula Imadegawa in Tokyo from an outdoor card phone, and she says she's still willing to put us up for a few days. 'Where've you been?' she'd shouted over the background traffic coming from my end. 'I've been waiting months to hear from you!' All this time I thought I'd written her from India with our arrival and departure dates, when it turns out it was Argentinians I'd written. Sigh. The superstructure that supports this Trip, all made of paper and held together by postage stamps, just gets away from me sometimes.

Last night we'd shed the remaining wistfulness of Ayutthaya on Pat Pong Street, Bangkok's infamous red light district. 'Don't go to Pat Pong Street,' John had warned us at the Stage Club in Singapore, which naturally put it at the top of my list. Just one block long, the street was mobbed by sweaty Westerners dickering in the nightly, outdoor market for T-shirts and fake Rolex watches. Inside open doorways girls in thigh-length stockings and no panties danced on bar counters, Bruce Springsteen's 'Born in the USA' throbbed from somewhere, and clear, carefully lettered English signs begged us to 'Drink Beer!', 'Smoke Cigarettes!', 'See Men Make Love!' The highschool-level attempt at titillation undercut the AIDS-tainted threat of the place. It had none of the smelly, gritty urgency of the sex joints on Eighth Avenue in New York, only an adolescent silliness that got into Kittipat, who brazenly lied in order to validate his parking ticket.

In response to our incredulity that he'd do such a wicked, wicked thing, he'd replied with evident glee and in perfect English, 'Hey, I'm baaad.'

I have one last thing to do now before he comes to take us to the airport for our overnight flight to Tokyo, and that is to call the Gibbon Lady. In her fax Liz mentioned a Welshwoman named Leonie Vejjajiva who's well known in Thailand for her work with the World Wildlife Fund in setting up an animal sanctuary here. 'Adopt a Gibbon' is her rallying cry.

I get Leonie's maid: sorry, madam is not home, but she takes my number. Well, that's that, I'm thinking, when Leonie calls back five minutes later. I'm impressed.

We talk for a long time. She's not Welsh-speaking, she doesn't have a Welsh accent, but she needn't explain that 'out of loyalty to mother', as she puts it, she feels very Welsh, even in Bangkok where she's lived since she moved here as a teenage bride in 1958. Leonie tells me stories of uncles who spent their whole lives in England but never lost their pile-driving, vowel-splitting Welsh accents (there are no diphthongs in Welsh, every sound is voiced); of how her mother had begged her never to return to the family home in Bridgend. Why, she'd asked her cousins after her mother died, had she been so adamant? They'd responded that the family had been poor, to the very edge of starvation, and had left Wales in the night owing a hundred pounds at a local market. Half a century later one of her uncles returned from England to pay the bill, but the clerk – who'd remembered the debt – refused to accept his money.

Almost on cue Leonie tells me I really should've met Gwyn Morgan. 'He's very Welsh,' she says. (Based on this Trip alone, if I were to deduce what set of characteristics the state of being 'very Welsh' describes, I'd have to say it refers to male diplomats who are perpetually out of the country: Gwyn Morgan is my third example of such. Aneurin Rhys Hughes in Norway and Hywel Kerry Jones in Belgium were the others.)

'Okay,' I challenge Leonie, 'so what does it mean to you to be "very Welsh"?'

She responds without missing a beat. 'It means someone who's been poor. Someone who's lived in Wales and is working class and not ashamed of it.' Later she adds, 'Being musical helps too. Music is very, very Welsh.'

Marguerite motions wildly that it's time to meet Kittipat near the philodendron box. As a parting question I ask Leonie if she's very active in the Welsh society here. For the first time in our conversation she hesitates. No, she replies, not really. Her husband is Thai, she says, and there's been trouble. At a Christmas party in the British Embassy once three young expatriate boys who were sitting at their table had gone up to her and said, 'Tell your driver to wait outside.'

I see. But Leonie is quick to cloud the issue. The Thais, she says, are just as arrogant, they don't like to mix with foreigners any more than foreigners like to mix with them. Still, I think to myself, you've managed to deal not only with racial integration but species integration. I'm pleased that my last conversation in Thailand is with the Welsh Gibbon Lady.

SIAPAN (JAPAN)

Croeso ✿ to Welcome

The subway car lurches toward Nishi-Magome in a fleet horse-trot motion. Marguerite and I have been sitting in a corner with our packs between our legs since Narita Airport; I have my head on my computer case, she has hers on a pouch she always carries. As we approach the centre of the city more people than seems remotely conceivable cram into the car, and it gets hot. Marguerite starts to chuckle.

'I can't believe you thought someone's hand luggage was a bomb in the Bangkok airport,' she whispers.

'That guy left it there. What was I supposed to think? I went with the smart terrorist theory over the stupid tourist theory. I was wrong.' My laryngitis has all but vanished.

I once saw a photo of a woman on the Tokyo subway wearing a little cap that had a suction cap attached. The idea was to affix the sucker to the wall so that when you fell asleep – as the perpetually exhausted Japanese always do – your head wouldn't loll on to the shoulder of the stranger sitting next to you. I could really use one of those right now.

Trit-trot, trit-trot, trit-trot.

When I wake, two hours later, the car is empty. It seems we've gone clear through Tokyo and out the other side. Nishi-Magome is the next and final stop.

Ursula had told me to come up out of the subway, walk to the main road and get a cab to Ebara Hospital, then to call her and she'd come meet us. I quote all this mechanically from my notes, and flag down a series of taxis. 'Ebara Hospital?' I ask the drivers

with desperate hopefulness. Genuine concern flickers over each
of their faces, but no comprehension. Damn. We walk what
seems like miles back to the subway station. 'Hospital?' I ask the
guard, hoping he knows some English. No. Finally I have to
call Ursula back and request the word for hospital in Japanese.
'*Beyoin*,' she says. 'You haven't been askin' for "hospital", have
you?'

Beyoin does the trick. We stumble out of the taxi and turn down
a compact side street, about the width of a farm track in-grown
with hedgerows. Concise, concrete houses in neutral colours, grey
mostly, line the roadway. Some have exuberant gardens but none
has flowers, only greenery. I feel like I've wandered into an archi-
tectural rendering of a neighbourhood sketched all in pencil and
not quite to scale. We're still in Tokyo, but in a residential neigh-
bourhood near the city's south-western hem.

Suddenly, bounding into the picture at the foot of the street,
strides Ursula. Bright green blouse. Blonde hair. Tall, robust, out
of breath. Smiling. She's like a great, fair, female Gulliver in an
Asian Lilliput.

'Welcome, welcome. Hope you didn't have any trouble.'

Trouble already seems a distant memory. Five minutes in
Ursula's company and I'm ready to sub-contract my life out to
her. She's competent, benevolent, she offers food and tea, she
doesn't always have time for the 'g's on the ends of her words
but she has time for us. Ten minutes, actually. Must pick up
her four-year-old daughter, Rhyannon. Meanwhile Jovita, her
freelance Filipino maid, will look after us. Then lunch.

Ursula doesn't speak Welsh, but I've been awake all night on
a plane, so what the hell. Besides, she seems to have committed
considerable energy before our arrival to lining up an infantry of
Welsh-speakers, both expatriate and native, for us to meet over
the next week. In the meantime, her tatami room is our tatami
room.

Ursula's tall, modernist oblong of a house is decorated with

Western-style furniture in pale, cool Japanese greys and seafoam greens, with the exception of the tatami room, which is entirely in the traditional Japanese style. She explains that the woven rice-grass tatami mats traditionally marked out a man's length, and are still used as units of measurement; people take stock of one another by the number of mats in their tatami rooms. A ten-mat room implies greater wealth than an eight-mat room, and so on.

'But now,' she says, 'they make three different sizes of tatamis. The littlest ones are called *danshi* mats, sort of the home furnishin' equivalent to public housin'. This way people with small houses don't have to lose face.'

I indelicately roll my eyes. Ursula continues.

'Four-tatami rooms are considered extremely bad luck. They're reserved for committin' suicide,' she explains, as if houses in Japan routinely came equipped with suicide rooms instead of more benign features like porches or basements. 'Four-tatami rooms only have doorknobs on the outside,' she tells us, clearly enjoying the drama.

I make a quick count of Ursula's mats: six. That's a relief. Her tatami room is lined with rice-paper screens and is empty but for two rolled-up futons in the corner and a small carved chest. Curiously, it smells like Wales. It never occurred to me that Japan would be damp and sweetly musty, but of course it, too, is surrounded by water.

We haven't even begun to unpack by the time Ursula returns with Rhyannon, a quiet little girl so neatly outfitted in a school uniform and Easter bonnet-style straw hat that she looks like a toy human. I just have time to take in a light brown shock of hair, a deep frown, and her eyes – underlined knife-straight, Asian fashion, along the bottom lid, with a wide, brown arch above – before she runs off to play with her Sailor Moon dolls in the living room. (Sailor Moon is a Japanese cartoon adventure heroine with immense hair the colour of carrot core, whose eyes, incidentally, look just like Rhyannon's.)

'I hope she's not upset that we're staying here?' I ask Ursula, wondering about the frown.

Ursula smiles. 'Don't get her wrong; she's a happy little girl but she frowns constantly. We call it her "So *this* is the world?" look. Don't worry.'

I do, but not about that. Ursula whisks us to a neighbourhood restaurant for lunch where we all climb on to a tatami-covered shelf and do our best to fold our legs under us without jamming our knees into the table. I curl one foot beneath me like a flamingo, as I always do, which Ursula pronounces the kiss of death to one's circulation. 'Lots of Western women in Japan have circulatory problems for that very reason,' she claims, wagging a finger at me, whereupon I reluctantly jiggle myself into a haphazard buddha pose.

It's an intense lunch. Given Ursula's sheer vitality and breadth of interests, her broad South Walian accent, and the knotty challenge of Japanese food protocol – chopstick manipulation, how to cup one's seaweed and tofu soup in the palm of one's left hand and tilt it with the fingertips of the right, which foodstuff to eat first, where to sprinkle the *fish shavings* one has been brought, how to shift one's weight without exposing one's panties – I'd almost be better off speaking Welsh. Actually, the hierarchy of Japanese table manners, which stresses ritual over personal satiation, is not unlike the structure of a standard Welsh sentence: verb first, noun second, incidentals last. My energy expenditure for both seems pretty much equal.

While we fret about food Ursula tells us half the story of her life and many other things besides. She'd come to Tokyo in the mid seventies to study Japanese wood-block printing. Friends at home had thought she was going to Torquay, in Devon, and had told her there'd be palm trees. Once in Japan she'd met a handsome law student named Yukihiro. They'd had too good a time and she'd left to study in Munich so he'd have a fighting chance of passing the bar exam. She'd gotten into German opera and art, but he'd passed, and in 1978 she'd come back to Tokyo as his wife. Their two children are bilingual; both she and Yukihiro speak only English in the house. Japanese seeps in from outside. Her own mother is Austrian, her father Welsh. A doctor had told her mom not to speak German to her children, it would confuse them and stunt their mental growth. Her mother had cried all night and after that had never uttered another word of her native tongue. Ursula felt she'd been cheated out of two of her three birthright languages. When she'd left for university in London all the signs in Cardiff had been in English; when she'd returned they were in Welsh. From Queen Street to *Heol Brenhines* in three years. Her friends in Wales have since learned the new old language; she supposes had she stayed home she would have, too. Instead she'd learned Japanese.

'Can't accuse her of taking easy road,' I scribble in my notes. Welsh may have its enigmatic moments, but Japanese is downright mind-bending.

A waitress arrives with hot rags precisely at the right time. I use mine to wrap my writing hand instead of wiping my fingers and face, recalling to Ursula that in Singapore we'd learned that a knowledge of Welsh could be useful in the most unlikely places.

'Someone' – I can't remember who, Keith? John? – 'told us that British troops in Bosnia had communicated in Welsh to foil Serb interceptors about a plan for UN troop withdrawals. How about that?'

She has to admit that's something. I feel the underside of my legs and find the flesh imprinted in a tatami pattern. Ursula speaks of Kabuki theatre, Japan's once-plebeian form of entertainment that's a kind of stylized, seventeenth-century version of today's action films, complete with gore, lust and melodrama; she records English-language plot summaries for tourists. Ursula speaks of her husband's love of singing Welsh songs and drinking beer – she'd left Wales, she'd once joked to a friend, because she was afraid she'd marry a short, dark man. Fate's funny, isn't it? She talks about Eyemate, a seeing-eye dog organization in Japan supported by *Cymdeithas Dewi Sant Tocio*. Did we know that most of the seeing-eye dogs in Japan are Welsh labradors? A long story attends this, beginning with something about a Japanese friend of hers offering an umbrella to a blind woman at a bus stop in South Wales, and ending with Ursula's mom escorting a litter of Welsh puppies to Japan (the details of this story are sacrificed to a piece of shrimp tempura that I ill-advisedly pick up with both hands, thus missing out on the use of my pen). She tells us how she, Yukihiro and a Welsh friend founded the St David's Society of Tokyo in 1980; since there was no place to meet they'd founded a British Club as well. Handy having a lawyer as a husband. Now there are about seventy-five members, a core of around thirty: lots of Welsh women married to Japanese men, passers-through, more than a few Japanese who'd worked or lived in Wales. Ursula is the secretary. Next month is the annual Owain Glyndŵr Lunch at an Italian restaurant in the Zen Nikku Hotel.

There's more, but I give up. Ursula's like a typhoon. Like the floods we'd heard about on CNN news that finally hit Bangkok yesterday. Her enthusiasm bursts the banks of one culture and saturates another, blending both in a rising tide of excitement in which we're just sleepy bits of flotsam, buoyed on the twin currents of her love of two countries.

Five o'clock in the afternoon, prone on my futon in the tatami room. Six hours in Ursula's company and already I've taken eleven hand-cramping pages of notes. This breaks the old Trip record set by Eleri and her mom at their luncheon party in Singapore.

Cynllunio 🦋 to Plan

I discover this the hard way: the moment your bum touches the back seat of a Japanese taxi cab you owe the driver six hundred and fifty yen (about six dollars and fifty cents). The fare climbs mile by mile thereafter. What happened to the concept of starting from scratch, I'd like to know?

Tonight I've gotten myself into a state over plastic food. At Ursula's insistence – and after a nap – we joined her in a cab ride to the Jiyogaoka subway station: we're to prowl around and see what we see while she has dinner with a friend. It's a fine, warm, starless night in Tokyo. The sky is absorbent, the same macadam colour as the cotton ball I'd used earlier to wipe my face clear of overnight grime. As in Ursula's neighbourhood the streets are minuscule, but here there's colour, primary colour, flashing everywhere in neon and splashed on long, vertical signs that we can't begin to read. We come upon a clutch of restaurants, each with a display case in front or at least a display window, inside which are priced plates of plastic food.

Forget your average dog toy hamburger; forget rubber joke food, or even those fake fruit refrigerator magnets. I'm talking about exquisitely detailed plastic meals: breaded shrimp glittering with lemon juice, nestled against a luminous, half-moon wedge of citron; tiny, artful pucks of sushi; an omelette with cheese bubbling out the edges; crisp salads; bowls of rice in which I can count the individual grains (and do); even a sweaty beer with foam slipping down the outside of the glass. All plastic. All perfect.

'It's art!' I cry to Marguerite, shaking her arm up and down in excitement. 'It's not nourishment, it's bloody art. The Japanese are brilliant.' I'm beginning to get positively rhapsodic on the subject. This usually comes from lack of sleep.

Marguerite indulges me for a while, then gently returns me to reality. 'Okay, calm down and let's talk about your plan. Don't you have a ton of people to see here?'

I'm wondering how the Welsh can capitalize on this idea. Plastic rain? Plastic sheep? Plastic verbs, alas, don't cut it. Japan, I tell her, in language terms should be the second most challenging country of the Trip (Argentina, with its nest of Spanish-Welsh speakers, will be the toughest of all). Not since Catrin in Delft, the little girl who was fluent in Welsh and Czech, will I have had to communicate with people whose Welsh may be better than their English, and whose other language is beyond my wildest prayers. I have scores of potential Welsh-speaking contacts in this country: the members of the *Clwb Cymraeg* at the Shimizu Girls Junior High School; Professor Mizutani; Irene Williams's star pupil, Takeshi Koike (to whom I also wrote and received no response), plus several other Japanese students who've been on the intensive summer programme in Wales, and still more who've been to Lampeter from Obiriin University on an exchange.

Celtic studies are big business in Japan. More than a few Japanese academics have taken bardic names – remember Hiroshi Mizutani is also known as Hywel Glyndŵr. Unfortunately the annual Conference of Japanese Celticists is held in October, and by then I'll be conjugating verbs somewhere in the Patagonian desert. But the Japanese aren't just Wales-mad: earlier Ursula gave me a tartan-printed brochure advertising the Thirteenth Annual Japan-Scottish Highland Games. The country is evidently as Celt-crazed as Germany. I can't begin to speculate on the source of Japan's Celt-lust, but I imagine if Julius Caesar knew that posterity – *Asian* posterity, at that – would develop such a crush on the pesty Celts, two thousand years after his wars against them, he'd re-impale himself on one of his grave-goods.

'I also need to go to Hong Kong to hear that choir,' I tell Marguerite. 'Got to check into plane tickets.'

'And don't forget we have to apply for visas at the Brazilian Embassy,' she replies. Brazil is the carrot I've been dangling in front of Marguerite's nose all the way around the world. It's to be our last destination of the Trip. She'll visit some old friends, speak Portuguese, buy books. I'll hang up my mutations for a little while and drink *caipirinhas* on the beach.

We both sigh. There's plenty of Welsh to be spoken in Japan before the sun can shine on us in Rio.

Chwarae Pel-Droed ✿ to Play Football

It's a Japanese holiday and the kids are off school. I emerge from the tatami room in my Thai elephant hat, shorts and big orange T-shirt to find Yukihiro in a pinstriped suit, serving Rhyannon and her brother Yoshi steaming bowls of seaweed, rice and tofu breakfast soup. In a panic I survey the kitchen and spot two trays set with tea cups, grapefruit halves (sections neatly cut), a package of English muffins, and the English-language newspaper, the *Japan Times*. Ursula is so acutely hospitable that I start doing a stack of dishes. When someone you've just met is unfathomably nice to you, it helps to cut the guilt with a little housework.

This is my first glimpse of the elusive Yukihiro, who is indeed short and dark. He's also good-looking, tanned and trim, with hip aviator glasses and a serious-looking briefcase.

'I almost slept with you last night,' he announces by way of introduction.

Does Welsh-Japanese hospitality know no bounds? I raise my eyebrows, hoping that the elephants on my hat aren't bringing me more luck than I need. He explains that he'd come in around 2 a.m. and almost decided to sleep in the tatami room so as not to wake Ursula. I wonder if he knew that he had Welsh-foraging houseguests. Well, I tell him, scanning a dark, scary corner of my brain for a millisecond flashback to Agnelo's flat in Bombay, it wouldn't have been the first time on the Trip I'd have woken up with a strange man in my room.

'What kept you out so late?'

'Oh, work,' he says nebulously, 'nothing unusual.' Every night is late. He routinely gets home between ten and midnight – late office hours, business dinners, beers at the British Club – then puts in a few more hours in his third-floor study upstairs. Have I seen it yet? That's why they bought the house. You can see Mount Fuji on a clear day.

I stand open-mouthed at the sink with the water running. Why doesn't this man collapse? Even though it's a holiday he's got at least half a day's work planned.

'Say, want to play football? Computer football? It's upstairs. You can see my dad's study. I'm goin' to be Manchester United. I'm always Manchester United, but you can be any team you want.'

Owain Yoshihiro Imadegawa, age eight, has decided I may not be so bad. Yuki*hiro*. *Yoshi*hiro. Rhyannon *Hiro*: it's not the name, Ursula told us, but the *kanji* – the Japanese pictograph – that's important in naming a child. 'Hiro,' she said, has an especially elegant coincidence of brushstrokes. Imadegawa means 'Now Outgoing River'.

'So, huh, do you want to play?'

I consider his offer. Marguerite isn't out of the bathroom yet, so I acquiesce, only to subject Wrexham – my team of choice – to a string of lopsided defeats at the hands, or rather feet, of the wily Manchester United. Out the third-floor window there's a stubble of TV antennas, red and blue tile roofs, and milky cloud-cover. I'll have to take Mt Fuji on faith; Yoshi I can see for myself. He somehow manages to look a lot like his father and yet is rounded – eyes, face, high, thick waist – in a way that's at once very Welsh. Like Rhyannon, like Marguerite's nephew and nieces in Paris, like Eleri's children, Yoshi speaks with the careful precision born of bilingualism. Yet when he gets excited, when his goalie, or rather his '*keep*-ah', makes a great save, or when he scores, the 'g's fall off his words and his voice goes dancing down the broad avenue of a husky South Walian accent. Come to think of it, everyone in this family betrays excitement in a palpable way: Yoshi and Ursula suddenly sound like spectators at Cardiff Arms Park, Yukihiro goes red in the face, Rhyannon stomps her feet and runs around. You've got to like that in the Imadegawas.

Garddu 🗲 to Garden

> Amidst the raging storms of life
> Never flinch, o heart of man –
> No more than the wind-tossed pine
> Deep-rooted in the rock.

At Meiji Shrine, in the Shibuya district of Tokyo, Ursula pays for us to try our hand at what amounts to metaphysical pick-up-sticks. We each shake a slender stick out of a cylinder which has a tiny hole in the bottom: the number on the stick corresponds to that of a pithy little poem called an *Omikuji*, printed on green rice paper. My poem likens me, as the interpretation on the back suggests, to a huge old pine rooted in the mountainside. *Dim drwg*, I tell Ursula, not bad. I like pine trees. Marguerite's poem says:

> Though you should fall behind
> Your travelling companions,
> Never turn your steps aside
> From the rightful path.

I find this enormously amusing. She looks crushed. 'I haven't fallen behind, have I?'

'Of course not. Well, maybe just for a few minutes there in India. Remember Ganesh, the god of wisdom and travellers, whose name you kept taking in vain? He probably asked his Shinto pals to give you a message.'

She frowns and for a while looks like Rhyannon. Meiji Shrine is an elaborate shock of cinnabar red set deep within a cypress grove. There's calm in the grey gravel path that leads up to it, calm in the dark, deep-water green of the trees; the air smells of lived-in earth and sweet wood. You'd never know the whole place had been fire-bombed in the war.

Ursula breathes deeply and spreads her arms. 'I love the damp,' she announces, telling us that in winter Japan is clear but bone-crackingly dry. It's when she misses Wales the most. She thinks there must be rainwater in her blood. We arrive at the gatepost of the shrine and step over the ghost-guard, a ground-level beam running between the two gates. The theory (unproven, to my mind) is that ghosts can't get across because they don't have feet (I thought ghosts just floated wherever they damn well pleased). Ursula, who has by now revealed herself as an even greater source of arcane information than I, divulges that in Japanese and Chinese lore it's traditional to tell ghost stories in summer. Why? Because it makes you shiver, and shivering cools you off. Makes sense.

I take a better look at the gates and discover they're actually gatekeepers: two enormous, wooden, totem pole-size grotesques in wire cages. Whether the latter are to protect them from us or us from them is never made clear.

'Shintoism focuses on nature,' explains Ursula. 'There's no personality cult based on a Jesus or a Buddha figure. Just ancestral spirits and nature gods. It's a very peaceful religion.'

We watch as she and the kids scoop up holy water with a brass ladle, pour it over their hands, take a sip, then spit it out. We do the same.

'What does the spitting mean?' I ask her. 'Some kind of purification thing?'

'The opposite. It means the water's dirty.'

Ursula is equivocal about Japan's relationship to the natural world, or rather, to the lessons the Japanese draw from their innate mastery over the vegetable kingdom.

'Children in this country are treated like bonsai trees. They're sculpted and shaped from a young age to conform to their family's wishes, which means precisely one thing and one thing only: studyin' hard, gettin' into the right university, then studyin' harder. I've already noticed there are fewer kids around for Yoshi to play with – they're all at home doin' math problems.'

She tells us about a famous crash study programme in which parents clamour to enrol their children from the age of two and a half. The course lasts for six weeks over the summer; during that time mothers aren't allowed to see their kids at all, fathers only once. Family is considered distracting. 'All in order to get into the *right* university, to get the *right* job,' seethes Ursula. 'It makes me so angry.'

'I'd think the whole country would be poised on the edge of one really big, pubescent uprising. Whatever happened to sex and drugs and rock and roll?'

Ursula laughs a little tartly. By now she's clipping her consonants like they're rogue branches long overdue for a pruning. 'Lately some kids have started to rebel, but just so you know how unusual that is, the older generation has taken to calling them "The New Humans", because it's so unheard-of for anyone in this society to step out of line. I have a theory about that.'

Naturally I ask what it is.

Ursula's theory is based on the teaching of the *kanji*. There is a right way, she says, and a wrong way to make the pictographs. There are no alternatives: an upstroke of the pen where there should've been a downstroke changes the meaning. Children are taught not to question or to use their imagination, but to copy and follow instructions. She sees this played out in her own household. When Yoshi invites expatriate kids over they all just hang around the kitchen until some sort of pastime spontaneously generates; when Japanese kids come over he immediately gets out a board game. Japanese kids like rules. Makes me wonder how someone like Takeshi Koike feels about learning Welsh, a tongue that mutates all over the place and is easy-going to the point of having at least two ways to say everything. It's probably the equivalent of sniffing glue.

'You know what word I most despise in the entire Japanese language?' she asks.

I don't have a clue.

'*Ganbate*. It means "I will endure".' I let her silence explain its connotations, and she doesn't correct me.

Beyond the park-like shrine grounds, Shibuya seems pretty darn hip and cool. In fact it looks a little like the Boulevard St Michel in Paris, up near the Luxembourg Gardens. Wide avenues, trees, neon. When the lights change we cross the street with more people than probably have lived and died on the isle of Anglesey over the past millennium. Ursula buys a mood ring. She insists on paying a lot of money for us to see a collection of Japanese wood-block prints, some of which, in the delicacy of their two-hundred-year-old ink impressions, suggest Meiji Shrine in a fine mist. It's oddly comforting that we have to tour the museum in one-size-is-too-big-for-all slippers, leaving our shoes in lockers near the entrance: no one makes any noise.

The undergarments counter at the Seibu Department Store reminds Ursula to tell us about the time she got a call from BBC Wales asking if she'd research Japanese girdles. She took on the job and discovered to her horror that there are three types of girdle from which to choose in Japan, all figure-enhancing rather than figure-reducing. The first lifts and separates the cheeks; the second has padding in the rear; the third and ultimate model adds padding to both the rear and hips.

That women anywhere in the world would actually want to add girth to their hips and/or bum is the single biggest jolt of culture shock I've ever received.

Serio 🐾 to Sear

We know where we are in Tokyo by the name of the nearest subway station (provided it's noted in the Roman alphabet). From Shibuya we all travel to the vicinity of Ishikawa-dai, the only station that's a feasible walk from Ursula's house, to meet Yukihiro for dinner at a Korean barbecue restaurant.

There's a tiny grill pit sunk in the middle of our table. Beer arrives, then slices of raw meat, almost transparent, certainly no thicker than my fingernail, which we are to place casually on the grill with our chopsticks in much the same series of motions that actors use to flick cigarettes in nineteen-thirties movies. Ursula has this down. I drop my first piece of meat through the grate. Marguerite asks for a fork.

Half an hour later – the beer's been coming and going at a pretty slick rate – and I'm flipping my meat with something that approaches insouciance. It occurs to me to ask Ursula what the heck this is that we're eating.

'Tongue,' she says. Deep inside me, somewhere between my conscience and my gullet, I grimace. A mutation that is not at all grammatical has just finished transforming me from a would-be vegetarian back into an omnivore.

Ursula tells us she thinks she has the only Welsh Lady costume in all of Japan. This seems a good time to ask her what the state of being 'very Welsh' means to her.

She thinks about it hard, and her tongue almost burns. I feel a cold glass touch my arm; it's Yukihiro, who's sitting at an adjacent table with Yoshi and a business associate, passing me his half-finished glass of beer. He points to mine, indicating that it's empty. He is an attentive man, and does this several more times through-out the evening.

'It means being unpretentious. Being honest.' Ursula has gathered her thoughts. 'I met Glenys Kinnock last week and I'd say she's very Welsh. Someone who doesn't suffer fools, who's eloquent, who above all is enthusiastic.'

Marguerite and I smile at each other. Ursula seems not to realize she's just described herself. She gives another example of the Ystrad Mynach Male Voice Choir, who came to Japan on tour a few years ago. On their first night they started a sing-song in a local pub; on the second night a crowd gathered, hoping they'd sing again, which they did; on the third night the place was packed. Then one of them noticed the bartender had raised his drink prices. Every last man got up and left, protesting that it's wrong to capitalize on people havin' a sing-song. That, says Ursula, is being very Welsh.

Neither of the Imadegawas will take any money for the elaborate beer-and-tongue fest, so I repay them in the old Welsh way, as the bards used to, by telling them a tale. It's a warm night, not hot, just warm, so I give them a near-ghost story, a true one. I tell them about a train I was on a few years ago that crashed into the back of another train and then exploded in a telescoping incineration of metal and plastic and flesh. Lots of people died. I didn't, but I got pretty badly hurt. My head swelled up to twice its size, broken ribs ran amok in my chest. The whole thing happened in the snow, in sparse woods that looked like a forest set painted by Breughel.

What strikes me now, I tell them, is how the immediate experience of disaster is so much like language-learning. Everyone looks a little horrified at this unforeseen perversity, but I go on. I never got a grip on the visual grammar of the wreck; I never saw the mutilated bodies, never saw the aerial view of the long Amtrak train zig-zagged off its tracks like a broken back, which TV audiences were shown ad nauseam. Once a woman bandaged my eyes I even lost my command of adjectives. No images, no faces, no coherence. Thinking back to my last conversation in Welsh, with Keith and John in Singapore, I realize it had exactly the same kind of gaps. Imperfect comprehension is like being blindfolded, like participating in the evening news before it becomes news, while it's still merely deadly confusion. Both kinds of incompleteness – rather like Welsh history and expatriate memory, come to think of it – elevate guesswork way above objective reality. I *think* John went to university in Bangor; I *think* I saw a Mickey Mouse decal stuck to the roof of the ambulance. Whether they're true or not, these impressions are mine to tell. Welsh learning and railway disasters: who knew they'd be so similar?

🜲

Ursula listens to my tale in silence, ignoring the flippant coda at the end. When I finish she swallows hard and goes straight to bed, dabbing at her eyes. Had we been speaking Welsh tonight I wouldn't have had the vocabulary to make her cry.

Bwrw Glaw ✿ to Rain

There's a fine rain falling this morning. Today is a big day for me. I've lucked upon a rarish meeting of the *Cylch Siarad Cymraeg Tocio*, the St David's Society's Welsh Speaking Circle, members of which are gathering this afternoon at the home of another long-time expatriate, Catherine Nagashima, in the seaside town of Zushi. I feel a tremor of nervousness but also real pleasure at the prospect of speaking Welsh again.

Since my last encounter with a *cylch*, back in Paris, I've discovered that the word originally meant 'the journey of the king's warband', which I gather used to make a circle around Wales, mooching off the peasantry. Marguerite urges me not to share this information with anyone. I know, I know. It does sound oddly familiar, but at least our circle has a much bigger circumference.

Yukihiro sketches us a miniature paradigm of the train route, once in the Roman alphabet, then again in Japanese, the latter to show people in case we get lost. The trip takes about an hour and a half. Once in Zushi we meet an Englishwoman named Laura at a prearranged spot near McDonald's. Laura has a sweet habit of beginning sentences with her eyes closed and finishing them with her eyes open. She takes us to a restaurant for lunch where she orders broiled eel for herself and chicken for us. The fowl comes in nice lacquer boxes but is virtually raw. Since Laura's already insisted on paying what will be an exorbitant bill I choke some of it down so as not to seem ungrateful. Her parents, she says, recently retired to a place near Hay-on-Wye. Scant reason to begin learning Welsh in Tokyo, it seems to me, but hey, it's a free activity in a costly city. Anyway, who am I to talk?

Back outside we follow her hand-drawn map to Catherine's house. The rain has become steadier and harder. We walk parallel to the sea, one street away from it. At each crossroads, if I lift my umbrella, I spy a quick glimpse of white-headed, khaki breakers, pounding the beach like a gang of angry marines. An uneasy feeling roots in the pit of my stomach.

After a few false turns Laura finds Catherine's number on a gate cut into a high fence. Behind it are tall, creaking pines and what looks like a compound of rambling wooden buildings, dripping, dark and rather sinister in the rain. It's hard to piece together any kind of visual understanding of the place with my head inside an umbrella. No one seems to be around. Laura disappears and Marguerite gives me one of those 'What have you gotten us into now?' looks.

When Laura finally returns she's in the company of a young Japanese man in his early twenties. 'This is Takeshi,' she tells us.

'Takeshi! *The* Takeshi?' I'm momentarily stunned out of my Welsh. 'Wait a minute!' It's like an order: we all stand there getting wet until I untie my tongue. Finally I get it out. '*Takeshi Koike dych chi?*' Are you Takeshi Koike?

I can tell my enthusiasm confounds him, and explain that I'm the one who wrote to him from Paris. Now he's stunned. Funny, I'd understood from Ursula that the *cylch* people knew we'd be coming.

Takeshi leads us to the second floor of a small, neat structure that turns out to be Catherine's husband's architecture studio. Inside a blond Welshman called Lawrence, who looks a lot like David McCallum, and Catherine herself – matronly yet a touch bohemian, with soft brown eyes, a kind of slim Gertrude Stein for the Welsh-speaking set of Japan – are already speaking *Cymraeg*. We're welcomed with courtesy but without exclamation. None of those How did you get interested in Wales?, You must have Welsh ancestry!, Where has your trip taken you so far? kinds of questions. I assume Ursula has filled everyone in on our mission and leave it at that; besides, I can't speak Welsh fast enough to hold the floor for more than cursory introductions.

Marguerite takes a seat on the steps to be unobtrusive, and opens a book. I overhear Takeshi tell Lawrence – or Lorens, as he writes it in Welsh – *Mae'r taeffwn yn dod*, The something is coming. *Taeffwn, taeffwn* . . . Oh. Typhoon.

Typhoon? No one said anything about a typhoon. I repeat this for Laura and ask her if it's true.

'Oh yes,' she tells me enthusiastically, 'it's supposed to be the worst typhoon to hit Tokyo in fifty years.'

'No!'

'Yes!'

'The worst in fifty years?'

'Um, since the war, they say.'

'Why are we here then?'

'Here?'

'You know, flooding, death, destruction. We're one street away from the ocean.'

'Oh. I see your point. I guess the coast *is* the worst place to be . . .' Her brow wrinkles up as the realization dawns.

'*Dechreuon ni!*' cries Catherine, clapping her hands. Let's begin. She goes over to Marguerite and tells her that whenever she's ready, we can all start the lesson. This is when it dawns on me that these people just might not have a real good grasp on our identity. The most alarming thing about this is its implication: do they imagine we're just folks who wandered in off the street seeking shelter from the worst typhoon in fifty years, and lo! one of us happened to speak Welsh? Huh? I'm deeply confused.

By now the studio is actually quaking from the impact of great, back-handed slaps of rain. Cause for concern, apparently, to none but me. Not unlike Humphrey Bogart assuring Claude Rains he came to Casablanca for the waters, Marguerite explains to Catherine that she came to see the beach, and is cursorily packed off to a loft to read. Takeshi, meanwhile, assumes a position at a blackboard near the front of the room, where he's drawn a map.

We're to have a lesson in 'Getting Around Town' in Welsh. (Fat lot of good it'll do us if we all drown in a tidal wave, I reflect, but refrain from sharing this consideration with the others.) The idea is for one of us to ask another, 'Say, can you tell me how to get to the library?' Then using Takeshi's map the second person is to respond, 'Well, you go past the hotel, turn right at the school, walk by the station, blah blah blah, and there's the library.'

As soon as we begin two more myopic individuals show up: Chris, an Englishman interested in learning Welsh, and Alex, an American with retro-Victorian side-whiskers whose grandmother introduced Welsh ponies to the United States. They're both essentially beginners, and Laura is a thorough novice; Catherine is a native speaker and Lawrence a fluent learner; I'm in the middle somewhere. None of this explains why Takeshi, whose vocabulary seems extensive but whose cadence sounds a little like a faulty staple gun, is leading the lesson. My mystification deepens. He opens by haltingly asking Catherine to tell him how to get to the *swyddfa'r post*, the post office. She responds like a natural. But then of course she is a natural. When Laura's turn comes I cringe for her – this exercise is kind of brutal if you haven't had a year or two of Welsh. As a branch whiplashes the studio I realize with a start that the question of the trip is staring me in the face: *Pam*, Pam? When the roof flies off this place I don't want my last role on earth to have been that of bit player in a Kabuki farce I don't understand.

'*Esgusodwch fi, ond ble mae'r darfarn, Pamela?*' Catherine's question, Excuse me, Pamela, but where is the pub?, hauls me back into our little circle of erudite lunacy. I stare at the map on the blackboard and begin to answer, '*Wel, ewch i'r farchnad, trowch i'r chwith ar y cornel*' – Well, go to the market, turn left at the corner – when she interrupts me.

'"Chweeth",' she corrects my pronunciation, 'not "chwith".'

This is a bit vexing, since Catherine and I have already sparred over the word for grandmother (I use the South Walian *mamgu*; being from Anglesey she prefers the North Walian *nain*), but I let it slide. My eye-widened attention is instead directed to the map on the blackboard. I know that place. As the waves pound Zushi and saner people seek shelter, I'm conceivably spending my last hours in a kind of mad hatter's Welsh class, where the Japanese novice drills the native speakers, rehearsing how to get around a town nearly ten thousand miles away that I already know like the back of my hand.

'*Takeshi, esgusodwch fi, ond Llanbedr Pont Steffan ydy e?*' I ask, pointing to the map. Is that Lampeter? His face lights up.

'*Ydy. Rydyn ni'n yn Llambed y p'nawn 'ma.*' Yes, he responds brightly, we're in Lampeter this afternoon.

Yeah, right, honey. Maybe in our dreams.

When the lesson ends we all race between the studio and Catherine's house, getting thoroughly soaked en route. Her living room is saturated with the mossy, overpowering scent of rain. As Catherine sets herself to making a truckload of pancakes on an electric griddle, working on a massive, round wooden table in the centre of the room, the rest of us gather around the TV to see Chris's video of last month's Eisteddfod. After about ten minutes of watching Eleri's cohorts parade around in long blue robes, I'm bored to the point of panic. I lean over and ask Takeshi in a whisper if he can understand what to me is profoundly unintelligible Welsh.

'*Na,*' he whispers back, '*dim o gwbl.*' Not at all. That's a relief. Three members of Catherine's son's rock band, all monoglot Japanese-speakers, show up unexpectedly and join us around the television, watching with improbable interest. Lawrence mentions Professor Mizutani. My antennae shoot up: he's the guy I've been itching to put the *Pam?* question to ever since I found his name affixed to a door in the Welsh department at Lampeter, back in 1986. I know he's been in Wales but is due back soon: Lawrence thinks he'll be in Nagoya next Saturday, a week from today. That's cutting it close – Marguerite and I fly to New York the Thursday thereafter – but I should still be able to see him. Lawrence then asks if we'll be going to Argentina. I nod, and he dashes off a letter to a friend who's teaching Welsh in the little town of Gaiman, in Patagonia, half a world from here. He gives it to me to hand deliver – 'Gwilym Roberts, Gaiman, Chubut' – and I stick it in my notebook.

Over pancakes I tell Takeshi of Irene Williams's deep regard for him. He's surprised, and blushes. During the meal he and I skitter back and forth between English and Welsh like jittery waterbugs, but finally dive into the latter and stay there. He seems surer of himself in Welsh, asks more questions, elaborates his answers at greater length. I suspect that he, too, was happy in Lampeter, and that speaking Welsh is a surer route back to that state of mind than a chalk map on a blackboard. He says he originally went to Wales to study English, on the Obirin University exchange programme.

Why Wales?

Because of his interest in music and Christianity, he tells me, it seemed the perfect place. I wonder if going to Britain to learn English and coming home with a mastery of Welsh isn't considered an egregious sin against sensibility in Japan, where speaking Welsh surely must be *baragouiner* in a big way. What did his family think about his going to Wales? He says that when the bilingual course prospectus came from Lampeter his mother glanced at the Welsh text and said it looked like someone had pounded on the type-writer keys with their eyes closed.

But how had he gotten involved in Welsh language?

'*Hawdd*,' he replies. Easy. His English wasn't good enough to use as a medium of study for other subjects, so he decided to take First Year Welsh. '*Dechreuwyr i gyd oeddwn ni*,' he says triumphantly. We were all beginners.

And this, I think to myself with satisfaction, is how a little practicality spawns a whole lot of unnecessary delight.

Gwlychu ✿ to Get Wet

Nearly home from the *cylch* encounter, Marguerite and I get lost walking to Ursula's from the Ishikawa-dai station. The rain is nearly lateral now, and our umbrellas mere hiccups in the wind. We close them to prevent sudden lift-off. It's dark as Panjim, and all the miniature streets look alike. We hike a mile or more; no sign of the Imadegawa homestead. We retrace our steps all the way back to the station and try again. This time I cry a little, figuring no one can detect tears in a raging typhoon. Finally we discover we'd gone wrong just steps before we'd decided to turn back. Marguerite lets out a primal howl of despair. We're both sopping wet.

No one's home, but Ursula's left me an old memo about the *Cylch Siarad Cymraeg Tocio* on the kitchen counter. It's a statement of purpose by Takeshi:

THE PURPOSES:
  to know about the language
  to enjoy speaking it
  to cause the revival of the language?
  to think of that importance of each language in the world
  which is detached from its utility . . . (based on my own
  imagenation [*sic*] that people who speak a minor language may
  treasure it more than those whose language's future is rather
  more secure, though there is no proof for this idea)
  to have fun with a new, rare thing?

To have fun with a new, rare thing. I like that. He makes Welsh sound like an antique hoola-hoop. I find a smile for Takeshi despite the gruelling strangeness of the day. I hope he's found a heady kind of freedom in the lyric non-necessity of Welsh that other Japanese men his age get out of reading porno comics and clandestinely jerking off on the subway, or don't ever find at all.

We wrap ourselves in towels and stand shivering in front of the

TV, watching the CNN Weather Report and wolfing down bowls of Coco-Puffs. The typhoon is named Oscar, and it's due to wallop Tokyo tomorrow morning.

Cario ♣ to Carry

Hundreds of tiny battering rams. I wake up thinking about hundreds of tiny battering rams. It's still dark; outside it sounds like the hollow guts are being ripped out of the wind. The rain must've gotten into my dream. Slapping against the glass door above my head it really does sound like a gang of small, scrapy attackers.

Marguerite and I are hunkered down in the tatami room on our futons. I nearly fall back to sleep, only to awaken moments later to a new sound. Marguerite opens her eyes in puzzlement. Slowly I get it: Yoshi is singing the Manchester United fight song as loud as he dare, just outside our door. I think it's a kind of mating call.

Today was to have been the *Omikoshi* Festival, a big neighbourhood bash marking the end of summer and beginning of autumn, in which the children were to have sung and danced in fancy clothes and the adults carried a portable Shinto shrine through the streets. We write it off as a wash-out, get up late, I subject Wrexham to more merciless defeats; then Ursula's mood ring suddenly changes colour. The rain stops. Yukihiro insists we all go prowl the still-slick streets for signs of life. A few paltry game booths have been set up near the local shrine where a play is also in progress, though no one's watching. Yuki disappears, then emerges from a grocery with a six-pack of Heineken under his arm, which he dispenses to Ursula and me. Marguerite's stomach is out of sorts and she declines.

The six of us amble around the neat neighbourhood shops like metropolitan beachcombers, muttering, sipping beer, playing in the puddles. Above us strings of carnival-coloured banners and flags snap in the breeze and flick water on our heads; from below they look like haphazard clotheslines on washday at the circus. Without my really noticing it, the way a tide comes in on the sly, the streets begin to fill with people. Subtle smells blend at the crossroads as each block association sets up an ad hoc kitchen on the sidewalk, serving anyone who's hungry everything from *yakitori* – grilled chicken on bamboo skewers – to cocktail franks and hunks of rubbery squid. Three giggling young women point at us from across the street, catch Ursula's eye, then look away; finally one of them resolves to be bold. She walks directly up to me, bows and hands me a litre-size paper cup of beer. Having just finished my Heineken, I bow back in acceptance.

'Look! Look, everyone, there it is!' shouts Yukihiro, whose face has turned striated sunset shades of pink and red from multiple beers. We all turn to see the *Omikoshi* rounding a corner, borne atop the shoulders of about twenty men in identical *hapi* coats – abbreviated, utilitarian kimonos that identify them as members of one local club or another. They gently set the little shrine down in the middle of the street. It looks like a royal dog-house and is surmounted by a gilded bird that I could have sworn was a rooster, but Ursula assures me is a phoenix. The partying intensifies. Yuki's downing beer with gusto and sets Rhyannon on his shoulders. A neighbour whispers something to Ursula and she bursts out laughing, simultaneously shaking her head no.

'On the next round it's the women's turn to carry the shrine. They want us to join them.'

Marguerite looks stricken and wisely borrows Ursula's key so she can go home and lie down. I size up the shrine. My pack looks heavier than that thing. 'I'll do it if you do it,' I tell Ursula.

I can see that this challenge tugs at her sense of adventure. 'Maybe,' she says equivocally, and we both drink more beer.

Time passes and nothing happens. It's getting dark and the weather's beginning to turn again. Ursula and I are on the verge of heading home when a spontaneous groundswell of decision seizes the crowd. A man rushes up and wraps us both in grey *hapi* coats and assures us we look most becoming; someone else ties a *hachimaki* around my head, a kind of kerchief-style headband that's twisted into a long cord. The word literally means 'wrapping the bowl'.

'Looks like we're doin' this, Pam. You ready?' shouts Ursula.

I'm about to answer when thirty or so tipsy women engulf us and ram us up against the shrine. Someone claps three times and with a communal grunt we all grab hold of the cross bars – massive things the size of house beams – on which the *Omikoshi* sits, and hoist it up on our shoulders. It's desperately heavy. How could I have been so wrong? It gets heavier still when a young woman jumps atop two of the front beams and begins clapping sticks together, counting out a beat. A wave-like stagger ripples through the mass of bodies, then we start shuffling down the street, keeping time with urgent, overlapping chants of something that sounds like 'heave-some-soya, heave-some-soya'. Ursula and I do the *soya* parts, gasping for breath in between. We're packed together so tightly I can take only wobbly baby-steps on the balls of my feet, crunching the woman's heels in front of me as Ursula is crunching mine.

I can hear her panting hard behind me. The whole world smells of sweat and beer and Ursula's perfume. Men run alongside us snapping photos and rolling videotape, laughing with unreined glee. 'It's not every day two Western women are crazy enough to displace their shoulder-blades in public,' gasps Ursula. I yell to her not to make me laugh.

When we finally set the shrine down I'm soaked with sweat and there's a crimson patch from my neck to my arm, destined to turn purple by morning. Ursula looks appalled. 'You didn't actually carry that thing did you? I just pretended.'

'Now you bloody tell me,' I cry, snapping her with my *hachimaki*. 'Jeez.'

When we get home I realize that one of my gold orb-shaped earrings is missing, or rather one of Marguerite's, since I borrowed them from her this morning. She looks wretched from stomach cramps, and more so when I break the earring news.

'They were a graduation present,' she says forlornly, rolling over on her side.

I go back to look for it on the street where we carried the shrine, but by now it's dark and raining, and I don't find a thing. I return in defeat. Half an hour later there's a whoop at the front door: Yoshi and Yukihiro are drenched and Yoshi's knee is bloody, but he gallantly presents Marguerite her errant earring.

'We went lookin' for it,' he tells her breathlessly, 'and we couldn't find it *anywhere*.' Ursula beams; Yoshi dug into the first syllable of 'anywhere' with a fierceness most Welsh. 'Then on the way back I tripped and bashed my knee on something and it was your earring. Look!'

We end the day in a celebratory mood.

Dysgu ✿ to Teach

'*Moshi moshi*,' says Ursula whenever she answers the phone.

'*Moshi moshi*,' says the woman at American Express, when I call asking if there's mail for us − a question that apparently cannot under any circumstances be answered unless we show up in person and politely ask it again.

Moshi moshi means 'hello' in Japanese. *Mushi mushi* means insect. As soon as I discover this I shun both phrases for the duration of our visit. This afternoon Ursula's dining-room table looks like a strategic command headquarters. We're trying to plan our remaining time in Japan and wedge in the visit to Hong Kong on the side. During the Trip I've collected two pages worth of Welsh references for Hong Kong, and try phoning what seems to be the most promising of them. The woman I reach is pleasant but firm: she's dealt with the Welsh Society of Hong Kong for thirty years and that's enough for anyone. Call someone else. I try and get no answer. Still, I learn some things. The Male Voice Choir has a charter which stipulates that the membership must remain at least 51 per cent Welsh; the St David's Society of Hong Kong is English-speaking; the *Cymdeithas Yr Hen Iaith*, the Society of the Old Language, which has a whopping thirty members, is Welsh-speaking.

Next I ring three English-language travel agencies about flights to Hong Kong. Each one puts me on hold and plays exactly the same muzak while I wait, a grotesquely synthesized version of 'Greensleeves'. Tickets, I finally learn, are expensive and availability slim. Not good. I hand over the phone and Marguerite tries calling the Brazilian Embassy to ask about visas but they tell her to call the consulate, neglecting to mention that the consulate, like American Express, has a profound dislike of doing business on the telephone. Things are going nowhere fast, so I try to plug into my E-mail instead. A quick check of rates uncovers something I should've investigated earlier: our on-line time in Singapore cost around three hundred dollars instead of the $9.99 I was expecting. This rankles. When I try to connect to CompuServe a terse message comes up on the screen: 'Due to Japanese regulations your E-mail is blocked.' I bang my head on the table.

Ursula looks over my shoulder, impressed. 'I *thought* you were a spy. No one in her right mind would actually travel around the world just to practise Welsh.'

It's now clear that neither Hong Kong nor the Mizutani rendez-vous will happen until at least next weekend, if at all. We'd initially been invited to stay with the Imadegawas for two days and already we've stayed four. I mention this. Ursula invites us to remain as long as we wish. We demur. She says we can keep doing the dishes and help with a huge Welsh Society mailing that's coming up. Okay, we say, deal.

She then calls Mizutani's wife for me, anticipating a Japanese response, but no one's home. So she tries Mr T. Iyanagi, adviser to the Shimizu Girls Junior High School *Clwb Cymraeg*.

'My Japanese isn't perfect,' she whispers with her hand over the receiver, as she waits for him to be found. Better than my Welsh, I tell her, perking up considerably when he comes on the line. A long conversation ensues. Ursula smiles, frowns, pushes her hair out of her face, and finally hangs up.

'Forget it,' she says. I'm crushed.

'All the girls who were interested in Welsh graduated, and the club disbanded. He's still working on Welsh himself, through a course that comes over the World Wide Web from somewhere in New England, but he says he's not that good. I think I overwhelmed the poor man. I asked him if he'd want to meet with you on his own, but that seemed to panic him. He said if you wanted to meet to please write a letter first outlining your intentions, and he'll consider it. If you want my opinion, it's not worth a trip to Shimizu.'

'I wrote him six months ago, for god's sake!' This is a real setback. Worse yet, that's Mark Nodine's course he's following on the Web. I begin visibly to brood.

Earlier today we went to a Buddhist temple in the Asakusa neighbourhood of Tokyo. A monstrous red rice-paper lantern shuddered like a zeppelin from the centre of the temple's pagoda-style entrance gate, the gate of the thunder god. Ursula told us that such a lantern is traditionally donated by the local *geishas* or hookers. Just as we'd done at Meiji Shrine, we tossed coins into a slatted trough, clapped three times and made wishes, mine being that Professor Mizutani would get the heck out of Lampeter and come home. Ursula told us that at New Year priests have to wear crash helmets when they collect the money, because so many people come to hurl coins for luck. Most Japanese, she reported, get married in the Shinto religion and die Buddhist.

Why the switch? I asked.

'Shinto's got a better wedding ceremony, with two priestesses,' she said, 'and Buddhism does a nicer funeral.' Packaging is all in Japan. Even though you may not be wild about the product, from death to sushi everything looks good.

Talk of handsome burials brought to mind one of my favourite

Welsh slurs, which I quoted to Ursula: 'There are parts of Wales where the only concession to gaiety is a striped shroud.'

She agreed that this sounded very Japanese. By all means die, but make it look nice. There's a Kabuki play, she recalled, in which forty-seven samurai warriors avenge the death of their lord by killing a local tyrant, knowing all along they'll have to atone by committing ritual suicide afterwards. Tragic, she said, yet ever so attractively staged.

Ever since I've been in Japan I've been tripping over reminders of Wales in the unlikeliest of places. Language, for instance. Despite the trampolining bounce of Welsh and the undeviating linearity of Japanese – the latter glides out of people's mouths and into my ear with the steadiness of a stock ticker-tape – the two languages share many of the same sounds. Wherever I go I hear Welsh noises in Japanese sentences: *maes* (pronounced 'mice'), which means field in Welsh, *nos da*, which means good night, and *cwrw* ('coo-roo') – beer – pop up constantly.

'"Coo-roo" means "to order" in Japanese,' Ursula told us, appropriately in one of the tempura restaurants for which Asakusa is aptly famous (I based the aptness of this judgement upon the exact resemblance of my lunch to its Platonic counterpart in the display case out front). 'I have a good language story,' she continued. 'When Rhyannon was very young we took her to Wales to see my parents. I'd been telling her she was going to visit *bamgu* ["bam-gee"], meaning my dad, and when we got there she recognized him and shouted out, "It's Bambi, it's Bambi!" Can you believe it? My daughter thought her grandfather was a bloomin' deer.'

Species confusion aside, the really funny thing about this story, I told her, is that *tadcu* ('tad-key') is the word for grandfather in Welsh. *Bamgu* is a corruption of *mamgu* ('mam-gee'), grandmother. 'So it's all wrong anyway,' I said. 'Even wronger if you're Catherine Nagashima and you say *nain*.'

We recounted to Ursula our experience with the *Cylch Siarad Cymraeg Tocio*, and she reluctantly confessed that there have been disagreements between the Cylch and the Welsh Society over the years. 'We have a mission,' Ursula said of the St David's Society, 'and that's to let the Japanese know we exist. Unfortunately it can't be done in Welsh. I want the Society to connect, to reach out, not to be exclusive. We're as much about bringin' Welsh culture to Japan as introducin' Japanese culture to Wales. I don't want us just to sit around and sing Welsh songs whenever we meet, but to go to Kabuki theatre and *learn* about this country. The more we learn about Japan the better we'll be able to share our love for Wales. Don't you see?'

Marguerite and I shook our heads up and down in unison.

'Some members of the Cylch think that the Welsh language is the important thing and that's that. And they're willing to be elitist to preserve it. I mean it is important and we need them too, but . . .'

Ursula mercifully trailed off, giving me the opportunity to finish transcribing her oration into my journal. Later I scrawl a question alongside: 'In the big world, whose mutation lessons are more meaningful, Ursula's or Takeshi's?'

Did I travel to Japan so I could say to Mizutani in Nagoya, *Des i o Docio* – 'I came from Tokyo,' correctly mutating my 'T' to a 'D' – or to learn to drink seaweed soup, spit out holy water and hoist a Shinto shrine with a woman who grew up speaking English in Cardiff? Having the opportunity to do both through the funnel of the same culture – Welsh culture – has kindled in me today a revolutionary new notion: that beyond Wales's borders, at least, the possession of two languages may not be an entirely bad thing, especially when one of them is English. It makes sharing a whole lot easier.

Ymdrochi ❀ to Bathe

Five p.m. The insistent ring of church bells in the air. Not the sweet, far-off sound of Sunday mornings, but a stern peal that's just begging me to ask for whom they're intended. Ursula reads my mind.

'The five o'clock alarm. The bells are telling children to go home and do their homework.'

What a concept. Sure enough, moments later Yoshihiro rushes in, grabs one of the little bottles of sweetened, fermented milk that he and Rhyannon perpetually suck on, and asks me to play football. Ursula tells him not to bug me and goes over to the wall by the kitchen door and pushes a button.

'You do that every night at this time,' observes Marguerite. 'What does it do?'

'I'm filling the *ofúro*.' We look bewildered. 'The bath.'

'You have a remote-controlled bath?' Marguerite is incredulous; I'm not quite so surprised because I happen to know they also have a heated toilet seat in one of the bathrooms, the one with the Welsh Lady dolls. It's not such a big step from a heated toilet seat to a remote-controlled bath.

'Oh yes,' says Ursula. 'The Japanese take their baths very seriously. An *ofúro* must always be forty-two degrees centigrade, and children are supposed to take one every day. It's not for cleaning – they take a shower beforehand to get the dirt off – but for soothing and calming. I like to keep the bathtub filled all the time anyway, in case there's an earthquake and we run out of water.'

Breuddwydio ❀ to Dream

Ursula doesn't speak a word of Welsh, but she's confident in her Welshness. It's not in the Welsh Lady dolls nor the lovespoons in her living room, not even in her voice, except when she gets excited. But still it's clear, because she'll tell anyone who'll listen that she's Welsh. Not British, not generically Western, but Welsh. Even taxi drivers, who tend to assume that all Westerners who aren't American must be English. In a conversation that lasts as long as the meter ticks, most passengers are content to communicate a relative sense of their nationality, if that. But not Ursula. She explains in her rather anxious Japanese that she is not English but *Welsh*.

(I must qualify this: it's not that Ursula is anxious speaking Japanese, but that she makes me anxious. Her words chase each other a little too fast, as if running to safety in the ear of the hearer where once behind the goal line of comprehension they won't be examined for flaws. Actually, the Japanese have a term for foreigners who learn to speak Japanese too well: *Hen'na Gaijin*, which literally means 'strange foreigner'. The rationale is that anyone who tries too hard to become something he or she is not must lack pride in his or her own nationality and tongue, and that's a kind of loss of face. No one will ever accuse Ursula of this violation, on empirical evidence or otherwise.)

Tonight the three of us share a taxi to yet another British Club – our third of the Trip – where we're meeting Alex, he of the shrubby side-whiskers from the *Cylch*, and Ruth Davies, a friend of Ursula's from Pontarddulais, near Swansea, who speaks Welsh but missed the Cylch gathering because she had the flu.

Two bottles of wine into the evening and we still haven't ordered dinner. Alex, who's American and has never been to Wales, but took up the language in Tokyo on account of his Welsh ancestry, tells us he once wrote a book called *Demon Lover* about talking dogs. But it's Ruth who holds the floor. She's about my age, perhaps younger, with frizzy red hair, freckles and a Welsh accent that I could only reproduce – maybe – by speaking multi-syllable words on horseback while impersonating a Swede. Two of her springiest phrases are:

'BEen To CANTerBE . . . Rry?' And,
'OOoo, TE . . . RibBle Place.'

Stories flow from her in English, though a host of other languages muscle into her conversation. I finally ask for a hierarchy, best spoken to barely spoken. The result is:

ENGLISH

WELSH

DANISH

PORTUGUESE

NORWEGIAN

SWEDISH

JAPANESE

By god. Marguerite and I raise our eyebrows at each other: did we hear right? We did. Ruth is the second Welsh-Portuguese speaker of the Trip. Third, if you count Roland, from the Stage Club in Singapore, Ganesh must've forgiven Marguerite. I ask Ruth about her Welsh.

'Oh, other languages creep into it now,' she says. 'I studied Welsh in primary school until I was eleven' – I love the way she says this, *elEV . . . un* – 'you know, high-falutin' Welsh, not the *Cymraeg y gegin* [kitchen Welsh] that my grandparents used. Nowadays I speak it to myself around the house so I won't lose it. Once it starts getting into my dreams I know I've refreshed it, so to speak, and can work on something else for a while. But keeping hold of Welsh takes care, you know.'

'Go on, Pamela, speak to her in Welsh,' urges Ursula, whom I could dismember right about now.

Ruth's close-set, shining eyes and red hair give her the look of an expectant robin, but I'm suddenly shy about speaking. I was ballsy at the *Cylch*, but that mood has gone utterly.

'*Dim ar hyn o bryd*,' is all I manage, Not right now. I'm such a disappointment to myself. People in one of my dreams spoke Welsh once, but I couldn't understand them.

'Where did you learn Portuguese?' asks Marguerite.

'Angola.' She says she ran a school for orphans there for six months, until the political situation got too dodgy. Before that she taught at a private school in Denmark for two and a half years.

'That was great,' she tells us. Ruth talks in an understated deadpan no matter how novel her subject matter. 'I took the kids on a lot of trips. We went to Turkey, Russia, Spain, even the US. We smuggled sneakers and jeans into Lithuania and traded them for musical instruments for the school. That was fun. But I really liked driving a big van around America. Intercourse, Pennsylvania, you been there?'

Both Marguerite and I nod. Amish country.

'We broke down once outside a pizza parlour in Brooklyn, and a gang of black lesbians surrounded us. I told them the problem and they very nicely pushed us to a repair shop. "Can't leave the fuckin' thing here," they said, "someone'll steal it. Maybe us."'

I order a plate of bangers and chips and excuse myself for a moment to check in with my new Hong Kong connection from a pay phone in the hallway. My phone card shows an earnest young woman in a cross-legged position; I shove her into the slot and dial. Mair, who'd been eager to help the night before, and was going to check into choir rehearsal dates and places for us to stay, is now subdued to the point of forgetfulness. I remind her that I'm the somewhat Welsh-speaking American who rang yesterday. Silence.

'My husband just left me,' she finally whispers. 'This isn't a good time.'

I stumble all over my apologies and put the phone down as if it were a viper. Hong Kong is a trouble spot.

When I return to the bivouac of black leather sofas we've commandeered in the Club's bar, Ursula and Alex are arguing about whether the word for suit in Japanese – *sebiro* – is a corruption of Savile Row or simply Japanese for back-to-front.

Alex dismisses the subject and tells me about a fluent Welsh-speaker at the Women's University in Nagoya named Kioshi Hara, who's a good friend of Lawrence and Takeshi's. This cheers me up.

'Get Takeshi to introduce you,' says Alex. 'He's your *sempi*.'

'My what?'

'Your *sempi*, the younger member of any relationship. He's at your mercy, he's got to do whatever you ask. Of course you'll be responsible for him after that.'

I don't like the sound of this on a number of levels, and try the Very Welsh question on Ruth, who pounces on it with gusto.

'Someone who's very Welsh, in my view, is someone who maintains a strong sense of identity, wherever he or she may be.'

I mention that this jives with the Japanese notion of maintaining face through identity. She nods and continues. 'I'll give you an example. I ran into a Western guy in a grocery store the other day, and said hello. He ignored me, but I wouldn't have it. I said to myself, I'm not going to let him act like he's Japanese, so I ran after him and told him I was Welsh and asked where he was from. He was German. He said he didn't speak to me at first because he thought I was American.'

'That's terrible!' I'm indignant.

'Hospitality,' adds Ursula, examining her shepherd's pie, which appears to have survived a brush fire. 'Hospitality is also very Welsh. You know, I can't eat this.' She marches off to speak to the chef.

Ruth points after her. 'That's very Welsh. Not letting people get away with things. Bugging people. My father's like that, very bolshy. He found a Japanese guy on his ham radio and now he won't let the poor man alone.'

Women often cite their fathers as being very Welsh. Ursula has said the same thing. The strong adjectives and verbs that define this elusive state of being – manfully shouldering one's identity, bolshiness, hospitality, taking pride in one's humble origins – are all traditionally masculine qualities. Salt of the earth stuff. Deirdre Beddoe, a Welsh feminist, once wrote that there's a male trinity of Welsh national icons: rugby player, male voice choir, coal miner. Women, she said, are culturally invisible in Wales.

It's not so much that they're invisible, it now strikes me, as simply not home. The women who most embody these 'very Welsh' traits, and I've met a lot of them since we crossed the Severn Bridge, eastbound, four months ago, have left the Land of Their Fathers. Japan may not be the world's most nourishing environment for independently minded women, but I'll warrant that given the freedom of distance and anonymity, it's probably easier for Ruth to be 'very Welsh' here than back home in Wales. For Welsh women like Ruth and Ursula, Rhiannon Delft, Eleri, Bethan and Rosemary, *hiraeth* and a string of foreign languages may be the price they have to pay for living up to a national ideal that was meant for their fathers and brothers.

I'm desperately tired even though I've mainly been speaking English. Just as we get up to go, around eleven o'clock, Yukihiro unexpectedly saunters in with six young trainee lawyers in his wake, ostensibly here for English practice. I watch with envy as Ruth and Alex slip away. Yuki orders a flood-tide of beer, and more wine for us. The infant attorneys, all about Takeshi's age, sit in a row on the edge of their seats like young rabbits about to be skinned. One of them asks Ursula what advice she has to offer as the wife of a lawyer. She responds that they should protect their health from too much work and booze, then gives Yukihiro a pointed look. He laughs.

An hour later one of the trainees has fallen asleep with his beer

clutched chest-level, in mid air. Marguerite's eyes have glazed
and Ursula's mood ring has changed colour. With the Welsh
crowd it was pink, after talking to these Japanese lads in slow,
meticulous English it's vivid blue-green. I'm not sure what this
means.

Dewis ✿ to Choose

Japan has cornered the market on roadside vending machines.
They're everywhere and you can buy anything from them: bat-
teries, film, cameras, beer. I even saw one stocked with bottles of
Scotch. The vogue in Ursula's neighbourhood, however, is to
line the kerb in front of your house with clear bottles of mineral
water, labels removed. I thought this practice had some religious
significance until Ursula told me it was to keep cats off the prop-
erty. They supposedly see their reflection magnified in the water
bottles and run away. I don't know: Japan does some great things
with folded paper, but I reserve judgement on the cat-protection
and ghost-guard schemes.

We've just done battle at the Brazilian Consulate, housed amid
a den of neon signage outside the Gotanda subway station. I'd
expected the office to be full of Brazilians, and it was, but not at
first glance. These Brazilians looked Japanese though they spoke
like the girl from Ipanema. Their Portuguese was perfect, their
Japanese heavily accented. What gave the game away, however,
was the curious air of good-natured inefficiency that hung over
the place: most un-Japanese. Marguerite explained that there's an
enormous population of Japanese-Brazilians living in São Paulo,
over one million. At least twelve of them are staffers at the Tokyo
consulate.

Bottom line: we don't see our visas until we produce copies of
airline tickets showing our arrival and departure dates in and out
of South America. These, of course, are in Rhode Island which,

of course, is thirteen hours behind Tokyo. We'll have to come back tomorrow with faxed copies.

When the faxes arrive the prices on the tickets are almost twice what I'd agreed upon with the travel agent. If this is true, neither of us can afford to go to Hong Kong. I put in an emergency call to the agency, which, of course, is closed.

A profound change has come over me this week. I no longer feel like a traveller, or even a Welsh-speaking fortune hunter, but a statistician in charge of troop movements. Hong Kong, Brazil, Mizutani, it's all making me crazy. Life has become less about exploring the moment than beading the next forty-eight hours of moments on to the string of my good intentions. No wonder I froze up the other night in front of Ruth: there's no room left in my head for Welsh.

In the middle of a Thursday afternoon we find a park off the Ginza, Tokyo's swank shopping district, its Fifth Avenue, and drop on to a bench. Ginza has block-long buildings and glamorous shop windows filled with pouty mannequins, but also, surprisingly, sky. By contrast midtown Manhattan is like a hall of mirrors for the human species: uptown, downtown, underfoot and, for all practical purposes, up above, the view is man-made, a reflection of what we can do with stone and steel. Our own image once removed. I was shocked to look across the street in Ginza and see the *back* of a building one block over, and clouds beyond. The boast is more fragile here, less complete (and bombed but half a century ago). Materialism Shinto style.

It's a between hour. The park is quiet, the air thick with dragon-flies whose wings catch the ripening sunlight as it disappears behind an office tower. For the first time on the Trip there's a tease of autumn in the dampness of the dusk. I get out my notebook and make a list updating our strategy:

1. Hong Kong. Go Mon. night, return Thurs. – same day we fly to NYC. PROS: hear choir, meet Welsh. CONS: too expensive? Return ticket, 51,000 yen (about $510).

Availability? Can't book till hear about South America tickets.

2. Nagoya. Go Sun., return Tues. PROS: meet Mizutani, Kioshi Hara, see more of Japan. Cheap (tickets 500 yen, or about $50). CONS: Lawrence now says Mizutani 'possibly back Sun.' Could be another Effie Wiltens fiasco. Kioshi Hara doesn't answer.

It looks like an either/or deal: Hong Kong and the choir, or Nagoya by train and Mizutani. As I'm fretting a young Japanese woman approaches and asks to pray for me. I didn't realize the situation was so manifestly dire. I say why not?, and she holds first her right hand above my head, then her left. Once I sneak a look and she corrects me sharply, 'Head down, please.'

As she leaves she gives me a card that reads, 'You Cannot Be Happy Yourself Unless You First Make Others Happy.' I'd thought conventional wisdom put that the other way around, but never mind.

I've required so much prayer that now we have to scramble to meet Ursula and a friend at a supermarket, of all places. She wants us to see Japanese fruit. When we arrive Ursula's already fondling a melon in what look likes an operating room with aisles and a frozen food section, everything is so antiseptically clean. It's a nice melon. Plump, firm, with a little leaf like a golf hole marker. Then she turns over the price tag and I understand why we've come. This is a sport, like trying on clothes you can't afford or going to open houses you have no intention of buying. The tag says one thousand yen, about a hundred bucks.

Ursula tells us that the Japanese attitude toward fruit is much like the Japanese perspective on children and bonsai trees. 'Strawberries are grown in tiny harnesses,' she explains, 'so they'll conform to a perfect shape. Apple trees are examined and every apple but the roundest one with the best colour is removed from each branch, so it will grow to be perfect.'

My god. The Japanese have fallen in love with their own plastic food. What unnerves me, though, is that a plurality of perfect apples pretty much implies that all perfect apples will be identical, or nearly so. I remember a Japanese proverb that Ursula mentioned to us: the nail that sticks up out of the wood must be beaten down. Japanese Welsh-speakers like Takeshi, Mizutani, Kioshi Hara and the old man with emphysema who wrote me from his hospital bed – are they all high nails just begging for a good hammering, or in a society that reveres ancient traditions, in which a contemporary wood-block print is barely discernible from one made three hundred years ago, is learning Welsh simply not considered the extreme eccentricity it is in the West?

None of the people to whom I dare put this question has been able to answer it for me.

Coginio ✿ to Cook

There's a restaurant in downtown Tokyo called 1066, run by a Welshwoman named Jane Best Cooke. Really. She was Jane Cooke and she married a guy named Best. I swear. We go there for fish and chips and mushy peas; I'm so tired I can barely chew. Jane is tired too, but at Ursula's urging she tells me the etymology of Welsh Rarebit or, more correctly, Welsh Rabbit.

'There were a lot of Welsh servants in nineteenth-century England,' she explains. 'When the masters had rabbit for dinner, upstairs in the dining room, the servants would eat toasted cheese downstairs in the kitchen. It was their rabbit, so to speak. Get it? Welsh rabbit.'

Got it. I have only one question for Jane: why did she name her restaurant 1066? She looks at me like I should know better. 'It's a very Welsh thing,' she says, 'to commemorate a defeat.'

After dinner, back at the Imadegawas: we're listening to a CNN report about Marguerite's favourite Hindi god, Ganesh, statues of whom apparently have been swigging milk from the tips of their elephant trunks all over India, prompting not only a miracle but a dire milk shortage as devotees race to slake his thirst. The phone rings. It's yet another Welsh friend of Ursula's named Gaynor, returning my call. (Ursula has prepared a three-page list of people with whom it would behove me to get in touch; I fear the woman never tires.)

'I'm not very good on the phone,' Gaynor declares at the outset of our conversation, 'most Welsh people aren't.'

Yeah yeah yeah. Forty-five minutes and six dense notebook pages later, I beg to differ. Gaynor is a thoughtful woman and an English-speaker of unmuddied opinions. The kernel of her argument is that the Welsh are essentially clannish, much like the Japanese. They're hospitable but they don't like outsiders becoming too enamoured of their bit of damp, rocky turf – very like the Japanese suspicion that anyone who takes too much to their language is wantonly perverse (I wonder uneasily if this is true of the Welsh; so far I don't speak *Cymraeg* well enough to have found out). Recently Welsh clannishness has taken an especially repulsive turn inward, pitting Welsh against Welsh.

'The language is the divisive point,' she tells me. 'There's a power elite of Welsh-speakers who've virtually taken over the country . . . But you can't have a multicultural society and keep all the best positions for a tiny minority of Welsh-speakers. That's like internal colonialism.'

Now there's a thought: the Welsh colonizing their own country in their own language. I secretly ponder what would happen if I locked Gaynor in the same small room with Boyd, of the Paris Welsh Society. He'd used the phrase 'internal colonialism' too, but not in reference to the same parties.

She's not much of a nationalist, she continues, though she acknowledges the Welsh do have a dinosaur-size bone to pick with England. 'I may go back there to live some day, but first I have to figure out why I left. It's a very small place.'

I'm making hanging-up noises when Gaynor reminds me that the husbands of women like Ursula in *Cymdeithas Dewi Sant Tocio* are a breed apart: generally upper class, sophisticated, well travelled. Not as tribal as most Japanese men, or Welshmen, for that matter.

'Remember, Pamela, you've been among very unusual people.'

'It's supposedly the granite,' says Marguerite when I get off the phone.

'Huh?'

'The granite absorbs the milk and makes it seem like Ganesh has drunk it.'

Marguerite has this god on the brain.

'You mean you don't believe in miracles?' I inquire, straight-faced.

Priodi 🌸 to Marry

A crowd erupts through the turnstiles moments after the subway train pulls into Gotanda station. It's easy to spot the unusual people: a middle-aged couple, she blonde and taller than he, a lot like Ursula and Yukihiro, though instead of Yuki's crop of dark hair I spy a gleaming, near-bald pate atop a lager-yellow shirt. To think I worried about not recognizing them.

Rose and Masa Iwata have been married thirty-two years, over the course of which they've acquired the timing of a crack comedy team. Rose, who's wearing a watch with two faces, is the straight-man; Masa, who has a pair of sweet, cavernous dimples, is the jester. She fusses and he pulls faces and we're drawn into their orbit of good-nature, within which they indulge in exasperated banter on the subject of how and where to go to lunch. We're their guests, we say, it's up to them.

They settle on a cab and we learn en route that Rose grew up in Wales but came to Japan years ago to teach English. Now she leads expeditions of Japanese high school students to England.

One student, she remembers, considered British bathrooms too beautiful to use. Masa, for his part, imports English-language teachers into Japan.

'We've got an import—export business,' says Masa, beaming.

The taxi drops us off in front of one of the bastards of ferro-concrete modernism and traditional Japanese architecture that seem to have populated Japan in the sixties, a banquet hall and convention centre called Happo-En – 'beautiful from all angles'. I wouldn't quite say that. I'd say it's what Frank Lloyd Wright and a strip mall speculator might have produced had they been locked together in a small room overnight.

We're shown to an elegant dining room with Western-style tables and chairs, looking out on to exquisitely primped gardens. We order fancy food – it's time, I've decided, for *sukiyaki* – plus warm *sake* for Marguerite, Rose and me, and a big bottle of beer for Masa. Back at the turnstiles he'd had the look of a coerced husband, but now he's cheering up considerably.

'Thought you'd be two old biddies,' he confesses, giggling.

We chat about the Trip and their lives. Rose has a stumper of an accent, the pucker-up vowels of Welsh-inflected English muzzled somewhat by the bared-teeth precision of Japanese.

'In London people ask about my accent and I say it's Welsh. They consider that a reasonable explanation. In Wales people ask about my accent and get upset when I say it's Welsh. So I tell them it's Japanese and they think I'm being facetious.'

'And here?'

'Here I'm just British.'

For the first ten years of Rose's life she woke, lived, learned and slept in the Welsh language. Then her parents moved to Kidwelly, an English-speaking area, and a line was drawn at the front door: Welsh inside, English outside. Her father was from England but learned Welsh and used it at home.

'There are different levels of the language,' Rose comments tactfully.

In the early years of their marriage the Iwatas spoke English together, but because Masa uses it all day at work, they switched to Japanese.

I find it ironic that the Welsh have a reputation for cultural insularity yet possess the hardware for easy-going bilingualism. When Rose was growing up she could shuffle languages without shuffling cultures. Inside and outside, public and private, were two sides of the same coin. Her children, like Yoshi and Rhyannon, are richer by a coin, but they've had to reconcile the two mindsets that come with their fraternal twin vocabularies.

'They decided to be Japanese,' Rose says of her own son and daughter. 'I spoke to them in English until they went to kindergarten, but it's been Japanese ever since. They didn't want to be different.'

I take a sip of *sake*. Lukewarm it's like drinking dishwater after washing up from dessert. A few days ago Ursula showed us a video called *The Dragon and the Rising Sun* about growing Japanese investment in South Wales, balanced by interviews with her, Catherine Nagashima and other Welsh expats living in Japan. Someone mentioned how similar the two countries were because people in both were short and liked to eat seaweed. The most interesting comment, however, was from Catherine, who said, 'A child has to be one thing or another first.' Only after she'd decided to be Welsh – her mother was English – did she 'get on with it'. So when she had children she decided they would be Japanese first. 'That was something I would do for them,' she'd said. Rose's kids chose to be Japanese and she'd accepted it with grace. Back in Norway, at the far end of this ragged kite-tail of lives and languages, Lynn Edwards was wistfully reconciled to his daughters' Norwegian identity. Ursula's children are still very young, but she's waging a heroic struggle to braid two cultures into them. Owain Yoshi and Rhyannon Hiro. I give her credit.

Wedding photos are being orchestrated outside in the gardens. At the centre of a semi-circle of attendants is a doll-like bride in a Western dress so vast and stiff it appears to have been constructed by an on-site carpentry crew. The photographer fusses. Rose says the Japanese demand perfection to the point of obsession. 'Maybe that's not so bad,' she ponders. 'The Welsh don't demand anything.'

I repeat something Ursula said about the Japanese, like the French, respecting Wales for its (once) near-perfect rugby team. 'That's something, demanding perfection in sport.' Rose raises her eyebrows.

Masa orders another beer and tells stories about his teachers, a high percentage of whom are Welsh, including Ruth and Lawrence. Over the years only one has died and another has had a nervous breakdown.

Not a bad record, I congratulate him. He drinks to that.

Rose says that when she told her family she was marrying a Japanese man they were shocked. 'They saw me bowing to him whenever he walked in a room.'

'And why do you not do this?' demands Masa, winking at us. She makes a noise that sounds like 'piffle'.

'The hardest thing to get used to here,' continues Rose, 'is not knowing what people think. We Welsh are blunt, but here it took ten years for me to find out that he only likes chocolate icecream. I'd buy different flavours and he'd eat them and smile and say "very good". But then he finally admitted he really only likes chocolate.'

'Yes, only chocolate,' reasserts Masa. They argue in front of the waitress about the wisdom of his having a third beer. It's his day off, he claims, and wins. The beer arrives.

Wedding photos are still going on. No, it's a different wedding. This woman is in a white kimono. Her hair looks like an elaborate dried flower arrangement. It has become clear that we are in Wedding Land.

Masa disappears and returns seconds later with a woman in a bright silk kimono holding a polaroid camera. 'We must have our own photograph,' he declares, and we do. The image that creeps out of that little rectangle of white mist shows that my hair has grown and my clothes need ironing, that Masa still has some beer left, that he's having a good time, that Rose is weary, that Marguerite can appear alert after consuming a mound of shrimp tempura.

🔱

Happo-En. A name that conjures up legends. Like Hikozae-mon Okubo, the fabled samurai who spent his closing years enjoying this picturesque garden. And no wonder.

No wonder indeed. Happo-En was an estate before it became Wedding Land, and the gardens still bear the touch of aristocratic care. Shrubs, trees, grasses, bamboos, ferns, all play their notes in a tight green composition of such density that it's almost a mental burden to appreciate it.

'There's a wedding here every hour,' says Rose, and I believe her. There are more bridal parties in this place than weeds. The brochure I picked up lists among facilities and services a beauty parlour, two Shinto wedding rooms and one Christian chapel, a grand Japanese-style ballroom (a '144 tatami mat room') and a class in table manners. I remark on this last and Rose tells us that such classes are popular. Her son recently joined a tea ceremony group at his university.

'You learn how to bow on tatami and walk in a kimono,' she says. 'The funny thing is that he looks like a big Welsh rugby player.'

Earlier we'd toured the reception-planning area so I could take pictures of plastic meals under glass. There was a choice of Japanese Dinner, Western Dinner or Mixed Dinner. Marguerite saw the price per head for the Mixed Dinner: one hundred and eighty dollars. I ask Rose if this can be true.

'Oh yes. In both Japan and Wales the two most important events in life are weddings and funerals. There's a sense of proportion in Wales, though; here couples routinely spend ten million yen [a hundred thousand dollars] on a wedding ceremony, then afterwards live in a tiny, cramped apartment. Life is so harsh here that when the Japanese celebrate they go overboard.'

Wedding guests are expected to shell out as well. 'A typical gift would be about thirty thousand yen,' says Rose. 'My son is twenty-nine and all his friends are getting married, so he's broke.'

We stop by a pond clotted with fancy Japanese carp the size of baguettes. Their mouths are as big as chicken eggs, and they come begging for food like dogs when you step near the edge. Rose and I watch their fishbreath blow the Welsh vowel 'w' underwater. *Cwrw, cwrw* (beer, beer).

Once again, as in song, the Welsh and the Japanese are united by beer. I like that.

Deall ✿ to Understand

Command station zero: Ursula's kitchen. I manage a plucky sort of smile when I learn Yukihiro has been inspired to make *sukiyaki* for dinner and is chopping vegetables like a man possessed. I don't tell him I had *sukiyaki* for lunch.

While he hews onions and fells giant, gleaming peppers, I call Lawrence for one final Mizutani update. Alas 'Lorens' answers the phone, and insists on speaking Welsh. Phone Welsh is, of course, anathema to me. It's an altogether different, rather ominous and much harder language. I take it this is celestial punishment for speaking to Rose predominantly in English. But hey, *Nid eir i annwn ond unwaith*, One only goes to hell once. I might as well do it with Welsh in my ear. *Clust doeth a lwnc wybodaeth*, A wise ear swallows information. (I found a list of Welsh proverbs today that I'd stuck in an obscure pocket of my luggage back in June.)

Unfortunately I understand Lorens all too clearly. Now Mizutani may be back Tuesday, or even Wednesday, he's really never been sure. I start a slow burn. How about Kioshi Hara, I ask; if I went to Nagoya might I be able to find him at the university?

Oh no, he says, Kioshi Hara moved to Tokyo long ago, didn't I know that? If I weren't so angry I'd find it very funny that all the misinformation has come through English. It's taken Welsh to clear up the mess.

When I ring off Ursula is clapping. 'You did it, you bloody did it!' she shouts. 'You were great! An American speakin' my ancestor's language in my house in Tokyo. Now I can put up a plaque that says "Welsh was spoken here." Bravo!'

'Yeah, well, Nagoya's dead. Hong Kong is our last hope.' As it turned out, our South America tickets hadn't cost twice the original amount after all, but by the time I learned this a rogue Japanese holiday – Remember the Dead Day – had snuck on to the calendar and all travel agencies were closed. Tomorrow morning is our last chance to book a flight. If we do, this will be our final evening with the Imadegawas. Should we or shouldn't we?

'You know,' says Ursula, leaning across her kitchen counter to pass me a glass of Johnnie Walker Black with pink and purple plastic ice cubes floating in it, 'you only regret what you don't do.'

Yoshi and Rhyannon are taking diabolical joy in bathing pieces of meat in viscous pools of raw egg, then dawdling them to their mouths with sticky chopsticks. Both of their placemats are mined with saffron-coloured puddles.

'Yuk,' says Marguerite.

'Gross,' I say. The more we grimace the more they bathe.

Raw egg is one of the pleasures of sukiyaki, though I'm concentrating exclusively on its other components: rice, thin ribbons of beef, stir-fried vegetables, a handful of chrysanthemum stems. I'd passed up the egg at lunch, too. For dessert we have Welsh spice cake made from Ursula's grandmother's recipe.

After dinner a recklessness gets into the Imadegawa family.

The kids are finding everything so funny their noses are running. Ursula asks me if I knew that Yukihiro's a druid.

'He didn't mention it. That pinstriped suit he wears kind of says "lawyer" to me, not "druid".' Yuki grins.

'Last year at the St David's Day Dinner he sang with a trio who called themselves *Y Druidau*. They did '*Ar Hyd y Nos*' and '*Myfanwy*', you know, all the old songs. He's even translated '*Myfanwy*' into Japanese. Do you know the story? It's true.'

I shake my head. This seems to call for more wine.

As Ursula gets into Myfanwy's sad tale I understand why it's a favourite of hers: it sounds like act fourteen of a Kabuki play (Kabuki productions can be interminable, which is why tickets are sold by the act). Myfanwy's father was a great singer who was disfigured in a mining explosion; after the tragedy he sang one last time in chapel with a hood over his head before committing suicide. Then Myfanwy's mother went mad. Time passed. Myfanwy became a famous opera singer. Her childhood flame wrote a song professing his enduring love for her, but before they could meet again she died of consumption. Afterwards he used the money she'd left him to apply to Oxford for a degree in music. He was supposedly the first person to use his voice as an instrument in the audition. He brought along a miners' choir as back-up.

'Give me your hand my fair Myfanwy,/"Goodbye" is all that can be said,' sings Yukihiro in a clear, soaring tenor.

'*Te wo tori tada, Myfanwy,/Iwou "sayonara" to,*' sings Ursula.

'*A dyro'th law, Myfanwy, dirion,/I ddim ond dweud gair – "Ffarwel!"*' I read in Welsh on Yuki's songsheet.

Ursula puts her head on Yukihiro's shoulder and softly croons,

> 'And we were singing hymns and arias,
> "Land of My Fathers", "*Ar Hyd y Nos*".'

She begins another verse and Yuki joins her, harmonizing with ease. They know the words by heart. This is not the first time these two have sung this song.

'Max Boyce wrote "Hymns and Arias" on a bus,' she tells us when they finish, 'on the way to see Wales play England at Twickenham. "*Ar Hyd y Nos*", as you know, Welsh scholar, means "All Through the Night", not "Harry's Got a Horse".'

Yuki unearths an old Boyce songbook called *I Was There*. He's bright red in the face. I remember something Ursula told me soon after we'd arrived. 'There's hardly much difference between the Welsh and the Japanese. They're both short, dark and welcoming, they play rugby, they get drunk on beer and then they sing. The only thing is, the Welsh sing in choirs and the Japanese sing into karaoke machines.'

'Here,' he passes the book to me, 'this is a good one.' It's called '*Asso Asso Yogoshi*', inspired by the Japanese rugby team's visit to Cardiff Arms Park. The song is from the point of view of a Japanese player, touched that the crowd is singing a special song for his team about a little valley in Japan where they make motorbikes. *Cwm Honda*.

Marguerite looks mystified. 'The crowd was singing a Welsh song named "*Cwm Rhondda*",' I tell her, laughing till my nose runs. 'The Rhondda Valley.'

It's a very Welsh evening that ends in an *ofúro* for the kids and *sake* for the rest of us. I may never hear the Hong Kong Men's Choir, but I'll leave Asia with the music of Ursula and Eleri in my head – two Welshwomen, an English-speaker and a Welsh-speaker, who for my money are about as 'very Welsh' as you can get. I'd like to lock them together in a room overnight; I'd bet money that Eleri would teach Ursula to say *Cymraes dw i*, I am a Welshwoman, and the entire mutation system besides, and Ursula would recount the great Kabuki dramas to Eleri.

Japan's language and its quirks and its culture are the cornerstone of Ursula's Welshness, they're what fire her up, get her pumped. She herself said enthusiasm was what being very Welsh was all about, and I agree. Her achievement – Yukihiro's achievement too – is the domestic mutation system, the wonderful Welsh-Japanese terra incognita, they've created in this household from the raw material of enthusiasm and respect for each other's cultures. By sheer willpower Eleri may have shapeshifted her bit of Singapore into a rendition of Wales, but she got little of Singapore in return; Ursula doesn't have Eleri's fluency in Welsh or her crisp grasp of

Eisteddfod tradition, but what Wales couldn't give her she's dug for herself out of Japanese soil and married to old-fashioned Welsh excitement. Perhaps the difference in these women's lives is less a reflection of temperament or language than of place. Maybe Singapore just doesn't have as much to give as Japan.

What Ursula has shown us of her husband's country has been her way of speaking Welsh to me. That we communicated in English is beside the point.

Gwingo ♣ to Writhe

They say that chronic indecision is the first sign of mental breakdown. Tonight we go to our futons with songs in our ears but excruciating uncertainty on the brain.

Dweud Ffarwel ♣ to Say Goodbye

Monday morning, still no reckoning on Hong Kong. To be safe, in case we've left by the time he comes home, we get up to say goodbye to Yoshi before he goes to school. I pull up a chair at the dining-room table and vow revenge for what he's done to Wrexham. One after another tears slip down his cheeks into his grapefruit but he doggedly keeps eating, panting a little between bites, resolutely silent. *Gambate*. I will endure.

We'll meet in Wales, I tell him, feeling strangled myself. *Gwnawn ni*. We will.

The travel agent tells me there are exactly two seats on this afternoon's flight to Hong Kong. Okay, it's fate. I start to give my credit card number but she stops me. 'No, no. You pay in cash. Must. Within hour or lose seats!'

Ursula tells me no way in heaven or hell could I get to American Express – my only source of cash in Japan – and the travel agency within the hour. Okay, it's fate. Thanks, I say, forget it. This is when I realize what's been bugging me. Japan has been one long conversation, and it's given me mental laryngitis.

My head and my notebook are crammed with voices, mostly in English, mostly Ursula's, but some in Welsh too. I should be happy, that's what this book is about, mapping the Otherworld of speech and memory, but my eyes are getting weary of waiting their turn. Japan hasn't jelled for them and they crave a good landscape. Green parades around my brain: the shimmering neon of Thailand's rice fields, the ripe lime of India's agricultural coast, the tender, neophyte green of this year's growth on Greek pine trees, the calm, moist, marine tones of the Belgian countryside at dusk, the first, the anchor green, of Wales.

A week from now we'll be in the desert.

I calmly go to my pack, get out our round-the-world tickets, call Delta, change our flight for New York to tomorrow afternoon, then call my parents in New Jersey and ask them to pick us up at the airport. I suppose if this were Kabuki theatre I'd have to head for the four-tatami room because I've failed in both my missions of hearing the Hong Kong Choir and meeting Professor Mizutani. But I count again: I'm still in Ursula's six-tatami room, and I feel like I've set us free.

INTERLUDE II

YR UNOL DALEITHIAU
(THE UNITED STATES OF AMERICA)

Gwybod ✿ to Know

Nothing trips up the weary traveller more than familiarity. The stern insipidity of Japan's grey rock gardens and the bafflement of its neon graffiti didn't faze me; the scent of my parents' living room in New Jersey on a warm September evening sends me for a loop. The mingled smells of heat, night and thick carpeting are so fused in my memory with the voice of the New York Mets baseball announcer that echoes of strike-outs past ring in my ears, even though the television set isn't on. For nearly half a year I've been programmed exclusively for forward motion, always in one direction – our airline tickets would have it no other way – always nipping at the heels of the future (except yesterday-squared, when we crossed the international date line). But the familiar smell of the house I grew up in puts a stop to all that. It winds me backwards, to a time when I was stationary, to my first eighteen years on this earth that I've just finished circumnavigating.

The bathroom window that sticks when you shower, the toe-treacherous metal tips on the basement stairs, the gurgle of my father's fishpond fountain, the faint kerosene odour of the dining room from my mother's oil lamps: I've left them time and again, to go to Paris years ago, when I first met Marguerite at Mme 'The Terror' Peneau's, to go to Wales the first and countless subsequent times. Long lived-in homes are a category of square-ones unto themselves, places in which to luxuriate in the art of taking things for granted, where you've always known how to get to the bathroom in the middle of the night and how to open the refrigerator door without being heard. It's a pleasure to be here, though jet-lag bleeds us of sleep each night with the unrelenting persistence of leeches.

My parents and Aunt Jane and Uncle Mort listen to our stories and laugh in the right places. I tie my cellophane fish from Singapore to the pewter chandelier in my mother's formal dining room. People speak English everywhere. This is perhaps the strangest thing. A couple of times, at the bank and the pharmacy, I have to stop myself from tapping Marguerite and whispering, 'Hey, there are other Americans here!'

But the familiarity fix is just a blink, a mirage in the Patagonian desert we'll soon be crossing by bus. Just like John the Baptist and St Anthony the Hermit, I'll find my proving ground in the desert. In some ways the whole world has been nothing more than a rehearsal for Welsh Patagonia, a limbering up of the language skills I'll need there more than anywhere else, more than Wales even. The Welsh-speakers of Argentina are bilingual, but the net that catches their imperfections is Spanish, not English, and I'll slip right through it. For me, not sharing in the majority language will effectively nullify the minority status of Welsh. I'll have to speak it. The Trip itself is on the line.

As we're restuffing our packs with warmer clothes I hear an item on the radio that catches my attention. It seems an American man was in a car accident in Vermont; he wasn't seriously injured, but afterwards he could only speak French.

No one believes me. You must've heard wrong, they all say. No, I swear, the guy could only speak French. It's a condition – it's rare, but there's a name for it. I can't remember it, but it has a name.

I've seen this look in people's eyes before, she's been travelling too much, they think. But hey, this opens up a whole new avenue of possibilities. Perhaps I don't have to spend a month traversing the Argentinian outback. Perhaps a discreet bash on the head is all I really need to become the world's only thirty-five-year-old monoglot Welsh-speaker . . .

Sad to say, I remain healthy and intact throughout our three-day stay in New Jersey. Over Danish pastry and bagels in the Kennedy airport cafeteria my parents heroically agree to pick us up in a month's time at the excruciating hour of 6 a.m. They'll have to get up at three. I point this out.

'It's an adventure!' shouts my dad, whacking the table. He's said that about everything from being in the navy to going to the town dump, ever since I can remember.

PART III

De Amerig (South America)

YR ARIANNIN (ARGENTINA)

Syddo ❁ to Dive

'Wait here,' I tell Marguerite. 'I'll call some people. Maybe someone'll invite us to stay.'

We're at a pay telephone centre in the Buenos Aires airport. Neither of us speaks Spanish. Marguerite's Portuguese helps her to read the signs, but that's about it. Now I regret stopping for more than a layover in New Jersey. Three days there was time enough for familiarity to erode my resistance to confusion. I can feel crankiness setting in.

I'm given a number and find the corresponding phone booth. First I try Arturo Lowndes, a television producer I met at the Aberystwyth Eisteddfod several years ago. His daughter tells me he's not home but gives me the number of his car phone. I catch him on the highway en route to the airport. Not, I learn, this airport. Buenos Aires's *other* airport.

'Pam! Where hav . . . wait . . . ving.'

'Arturo! I keep losing you.'

'. . . didn't know . . . oming. I'm on . . . evelin.'

I imagine our conversation is the vocal equivalent of reading by the light of a firefly. Finally I piece together some facts: he didn't get my postcard from India saying I'd be arriving today, and he's on his way to his *other* house in the Welsh village of Trevelin in the Andean foothills. We tentatively agree to meet there over the weekend of the annual Eisteddfod.

I'm covered in prickly sweat by the time we ring off. Next I try a woman named Valeri James de Irianni, my contact for the *Cymdeithas y Cymry Buenos Aires*, the Welsh Society of BA, whom

I'd also written from Panjim. My hand is dialling though my Welsh and my heart, both skipping a few beats, register a protest. When a female voice answers I dive in.

'*Sut mae? Valeri? Fi sy Pamela.*'

That does it. A torrent of Welsh spills out of the receiver. Her words sound like they have ruffles on them, soft, trilling sounds that I can understand but can't seem to respond to. An unmoored sensation, cousin to overnight flight exhaustion, rocks the booth and I have to put out a hand to steady myself. I ask her if I can respond in English if I have to.

She reluctantly agrees, and recommends that we stay in the Hotel Orly, right around the corner from Rona Davies, another member of the *Cymdeithas*. There's a meeting this afternoon. I should call Rona from the hotel and she'll lead me there if I'm up to it.

A meeting this afternoon? Damn. '*Wrth gwrs!*' I respond – Of course! – hoping I sound thrilled by the news.

By now I'm speaking Welsh. The problem is, I'm really speaking Wenglish. '*Mae taith* long *iawn,*' I tell her, '*dw i wedi blino,*' It was a long trip, I'm tired. The word for long – *hir* – slips my mind. Unfortunately my substitution isn't of much help to Valeri, who misses the foreign word in the familiar context. On the other hand, whenever I don't understand something she breaks into 'Welish' – Welsh and Spanish – which of course deepens the quagmire for me. Time and again we fall through the holes in each other's sentences straight out of comprehension. By the end of the conversation I've managed to approximate something of a gist, but it's rough going. This may be a very long month.

Dylwn ✣ to Ought To

Both Marguerite and I are loath to abandon the sanctuary of the airport bus when it reaches our stop in downtown Buenos Aires.

The suspended state of transportation can be such a blessing sometimes. It's early afternoon on Sunday and the streets are deserted, shop fronts dark or covered by protective grillework. No one's around, no one knows us. Anonymity can be pretty nice too.

'*PAM-eL-A? Pwy sy PAM-eL-A?*' (Pamela? Who's Pamela?)

Oh no.

A short square woman with copper hair and oversized glasses has been waiting for us. Rona Davies. I strap on my pack and fluster in monosyllabic Welsh. Rona isn't daunted; she claps her hands together and laughs and pats our backs and welcomes us to Argentina and tells us how tired we must be, poor things. Her Welsh has ruffles too, but she speaks slowly. Amazing: talking to her isn't difficult. In fact I'm doing okay. I turn around to Marguerite, who's trekking behind us like a dispirited donkey, and give her a thumbs up.

The dribbling toilet is not the most fiendish thing about our room in the Hotel Orly. The most fiendish thing is the fact that a symphonic version of 'Raindrops Keep Falling on My Head' is being broadcast from a hidden orifice that we can't find, and thus can't turn off. I give up, but after ten minutes Marguerite ruthlessly tracks the drivel to its source and disconnects it. She has announced her intentions of staying and sleeping while I 'do Welsh'.

Rona is picking me up in two hours to go to the meeting. '*Dylwn i fynd*,' I'd told her after she'd dropped us off at the hotel, I should go. The grammatical notes I've lugged around the world describe *dylwn* as follows: 'I ought to/should: This verb appears only with unreality endings, because actions that *ought* to be done are not a fact yet, and may never be.' *Duw, duw*, unreality endings, what a tantalizing thought. Linguistic slackers, they hold out a slender, perverse possibility that indolence will triumph over ought. Maybe I'll sleep through the alarm feebly produced by my ratty little travel clock and never get to this meeting. Unreality endings keep the door open, they're the suspense thrillers of grammatical tenses. Will I or won't I have a pretty good grasp of Welsh by the end of the Trip? I ought to, but this is not a fact yet and may never be.

The alarm works.

Two and a half hours later, Rona and I, arms linked, are careening down Avenida Florida, a hip pedestrian shopping street studded with Burger Kings and McDonald'ses. The bit of sleep I've had has freed me from the hangdog mood I was in earlier, brought on, I'm certain, by this blood-sucking Japanese jet-lag atop last night's sleepless flight. Rona steers me to the *subte*, Buenos Aires's underground, a rickety-clackity old system that nonetheless commands old-fashioned dignity from its stained tile stations and wooden tram cars, the seats of which were angled long ago for those who had better posture than we, today's riders.

Rona tells me that her father was Welsh – his parents came from Wales – and her mother Argentinian, but of Welsh background. She grew up in Chubut, the Argentinian state settled by the Welsh in the mid nineteenth century. She learned Spanish only when she went to school. We switch back and forth in a kind of polite tug of war between Welsh and English, but again Wenglish, the learner's crutch, is markedly absent from our conversation.

It doesn't take long to reach the meeting place, a large room in an undistinguished building that at once depresses me. It's painted a colour that's long since faded out of naming, and is lit by a lone fluorescent tube light. There's a small Welsh flag framed on the wall. Rona introduces me to Valeri, who asks if I can play an electric keyboard organ. The music person isn't able to come. I shake my head vigorously, no no, can't, not at all.

Valeri and Rona, in their fifties and sixties, respectively, are among the youngest of the twenty or so people in the room. The majority seem ancient beyond reckoning. I'm stricken with an irrational urge to save myself, to run to McDonald's and claim asylum from the past, from Welsh, from dinginess, but instead I stand by a row of metal folding chairs and smile vacantly. Several people shuffle over and introduce themselves in what I think is Welsh. I wouldn't have said so except for the occasional, isolated word that I recognize, and since I don't know any Spanish it must be Welsh that they're speaking. Steamrolling Castillian 'r's charge right through the soft, gooey centre of their Welsh vowels and plough them under furrows of consonants. I can't understand. This is awful, I can't understand *anything*. I feel like a fool.

Finally a tall, solemn-looking gentleman with a quiet manner and age spots kindly speaks to me in English. His name is Ioan Eilir Nichols, of Buenos Aires; he's worked forty years for the Bank of London and his English is perfect. As a boy, he tells me, he climbed to the top of *Yr Wyddfa* – Mt Snowdon – with his uncle. He still remembers it.

A woman in woollen knee-socks comes over and kisses me.

'Don't know who she is, someone's neighbour, I think,' says Ioan. People seem to accept my presence here as the Welsh pretty much have all around the world (except Bangkok), with the stoic understanding that things come on to them, like old age and illness, and now me. Or perhaps they're completely stupefied as to why I'm here, but I simply haven't understood any of their *Pam?* questions. I do grasp the fact that they thought I'd be advanced in years. Another old woman appears leading a still older woman, her mother, perhaps. The mother speaks to me slowly in Spanish.

'*DYDY HI DDIM YN DEALL CASTELLANO* [pronounced in Argentinian Spanish as "Cast-e-ZHAN-o"] *O GWBL. SIARA-DWCH CYMRAEG!*' She doesn't speak Spanish at all, shouts her daughter, speak Welsh!

The mother turns on an archaic amplifying machine she's carrying around and addresses me again, in even slower Spanish, as if she were addressing an idiot child. I give up.

'*NICE TO MEET YOU*,' I bellow in Welsh.

Mercifully the meeting starts. An aged woman takes the floor and inexplicably reads aloud from a children's colouring book of Welsh Lady figures in silly poses. Then faded songbooks are passed around, their covers printed with the words '*Eisteddfod*

Genedlaethol, Frenhinol Cymru, Maldwyn 1965' – The Royal Welsh National Eisteddfod of Maldwyn, 1965 – and we sing a hymn. The old voices are shaky, but they've known these notes longer than I've lived in my parents' house, and they harmonize with the confidence of youth. For me it's a nightmare. Now the words are clear, but the music eludes me. Instead of staffs and notes and bars there are only letters, or letter clusters, above the lyrics. I can't even fudge the melody.

When we've finished singing the president announces that *Radio Cymru* will be here on 14 October to interview the group, so be prepared (at least I get the date and the name, and surmise the intention). *Radio Cymru?* There's posh. Then we sing again. Afterwards a woman gets up and talks about her trip to Las Vegas. I'm following, I'm following, nope, lost it. My ears are working overtime like the old lady's amplifier, trying to gather every shred of evidence for my brain, when it hits me: she's speaking Spanish now. No wonder. Wait, she's back in Welsh again, something about slot machines. She continues to boomerang back and forth, me trailing about three beats behind each switch-over. I'm confounded as to why two such different languages sound so similar. Do these people have a Welsh accent in Spanish, the reversible match to their Spanish accent in Welsh? A sick feeling begins to creep up from my stomach: the exhaustion is back, feeling more than ever like a hangover I don't deserve.

We sing again.

Valeri rises and clears her throat. '*Nawr te, bydd Pamela yn trafod ei thaith hi o gwmpas y byd.*' Now Pamela will be discussing her trip around the world. Everyone claps.

No, no, no, no. No one told me about this. Oh, agony. I get up and smile vehemently and commence on a shaky rendering of our journey. Whenever I get stuck for a word Valeri or Rona instantly cries out, 'Say it in English,' which makes me suspect that the crowd is more eager to have its tea than hear my report. I stop abruptly. More clapping. One last hymn with the longest amen in the world, then we all sit down to buttered bread, tea cakes, and *maté*, a herbal brew reminiscent of tea that tastes like a fire put out with water, supposedly made from the leaves of a member of the holly family. Argentina's national drink. I ask if I can wrap up some food for Marguerite in my napkin. Yes, they say, but first tell us your nationality, your *real* nationality. American, I guess, won't do.

Hungarian and German, I say. Doesn't explain my Welsh quest, but *dyna ni*, there we are.

Oh yes it does, claims a Scottish gentleman along for the ride. That's where the Celts came from. That explains it.

No, says someone else in Welsh. No, the Celts came from Japan.

So did I, but much more recently. I ask Rona to take me home.

Morio ✤ to Voyage

The next morning I beg Marguerite to tell me the alarm never rang, that it was all a dream. She whips a butter-stained napkin out of the trash.

'Explain this, then.'

Sigh. Last Sunday was the two-*sukiyaki* day. We were with Ursula and Yukihiro in Tokyo, drinking wine and singing Valleys songs in English about rugby players and coal miners. Yesterday, exactly one week, eleven time zones and ten thousand miles later, I spent four hours singing hymns in Welsh and drinking herbal tea here in Buenos Aires. Different lunacies for different hemispheres, I suppose, but nicely congruent, yes?

Everywhere we've been so far, throughout Europe and Asia, Welshness has been a secular construction, consciously fashioned by English- and Welsh-speakers alike out of song, grit, expatriate salaries, pride in origins however humble, a profound respect for difference, and beer. Add to that a streak of wounded defiance – directed most frequently at implacable forces of human nature like history, injustice and fate, and less often but more practically at the English government – plus an unreined and unapologetic joy in anything the least bit interesting, and that about sums it up. We've seen a lot more gaiety on this trip than striped shrouds.

But yesterday was something new. Or rather something old. The meeting of the *Cymdeithas y Cymry Buenos Aires* introduced me to a different Welsh-speaking culture – I don't believe it has an English-language equivalent, at least not any more, which means it's virtually non-existent in contemporary Wales – one I recognized immediately from history books and daguerreotypes and hymnals but never expected to encounter myself, least of all in the swank city of Buenos Aires. This was the Wales of the chapels, of temptations forsaken, of temperance and tea parties, of musical harmonies baited to catch the ear of an austere, Welsh-speaking god. The Wales of the last century.

In 1865 one hundred and sixty-three Welsh emigrants left Britain aboard a ship called the *Mimosa* and sailed to Patagonia in southern Argentina. For the most part they were merchants and towns-people of the middle class. They didn't have to leave Wales, they elected to. As Glyn Williams points out in *The Welsh in Patagonia*, unlike Welsh emigrants who went to North America in search of economic liberation, the foremost goal of the people who settled the Chubut Valley in Patagonia – known in Welsh as *Cwm Camwy* – was cultural liberation. 'The entire history of the early attempts to establish the settlement,' writes Williams, 'points to the cen-trality of language and religion in its formation.'

The Patagonia venture came during a rare intersection of strengths and weaknesses in Welsh history. Up until 1914, when the Church of England was disestablished in Wales, if you were not Anglican you were Nonconformist, and, it was reasoned, if you didn't support the state religion the state didn't need to support you (Nonconformists were denied full citizenship under British law). By the midpoint of the nineteenth century Wales was over-whelmingly Nonconformist, with the Calvinist Methodists – believers in predestination, the stern doctrine that only a portion of humankind is elected by god – leading the pack. In 1851 there were two thousand, eight hundred and thirteen Nonconformist chapels in Wales. John Davies estimates that during the first half of the century a new Welsh chapel was completed every eight days. Based on the census of 1851, the Welsh, in percentages and numbers anyway, were the most religious people in Europe.

Compared to the Anglican Church, the chapels were a bastion of Welshness, principally because of Nonconformity's willingness to support the Welsh language. It was, after all, the tongue people spoke: how else to get the message across? (This is how Welsh got its reputation for severity. Remember Hywel Harris? For a while there it was not a language in which folks did much laughing.) But strength in religion did not prevent paranoia in other areas. In 1847 three government commissioners produced a report on education in Wales commonly known as the 'Blue Books'. Better known as 'The Treachery of the Blue Books'.

Education throughout Britain at the time was abysmal – the United Kingdom was the most economically powerful nation in Europe, yet its populace received the least provision for basic education – but the commissioners singled out Wales as a moral and educational horror story. The crux of the problem stemmed from the fact that students who were enrolled in state schools were taught in a foreign language they didn't comprehend (English), while those who were educated in Welsh weren't able to communicate with the commissioners. It was further implied – some say by jealous Anglican clergymen – that a singular laxity in Welsh sexual morals, which probably had something to do with what was taught in chapel, lay at the root of Welsh ignorance.

The Welsh were naturally outraged, and set out to do what any insecure nation of uncertain means criticized by its bigger, stronger, English-speaking neighbour would do: they began to educate themselves in English. They martyred the Welsh language and one-up'd the Victorian English at their own game, putting a lock on those petticoats for the next seventy years. While the Nonconformists still employed Welsh in chapel and Sunday school, they essentially supported whatever scheme would keep their schools Nonconformist: language was a lesser issue. If it was of greater utility to teach in English, so be it.

Michael D. Jones and his followers did not share this view. Jones argued, in John Davies's words, 'that the chief weakness of the Welsh was their servility – the result of English control of their land, their industries and their commerce, and the dominance of the English language over their courts and schools'. It's no surprise that Jones became the chief backer of the Patagonian settlers, who, like him, sought to establish a progressive colony of Welsh-speaking, chapel-going citizens in the Argentinian desert. In *Y Wladfa*, for a while anyway, the old language did indeed become the medium of chapel, school, economy and government, and every man and woman over eighteen received the right to vote (*gwlad* is country in Welsh; *wladfa*, which has lost its 'g' in a mutation, means something like 'countryette' or colony).

Reports based on a preliminary exploration in 1863 by Lewis Jones and Love Jones-Parry – of whom I will say what I've yet to read elsewhere in print, that they were either blind, self-deluded or compulsive liars – asserted that the Lower Chubut Valley, which is about eight to ten miles wide and seventy miles long, was a paragon of fertility and offered good pastureland. Simply put, it wasn't and didn't. Chubut was a nightmare. Here's what Glyn Williams has to say on its natural environment:

> The Lower Chubut Valley is a misfit valley entrenched in the Patagonian Plateau, the valley floor lying some 300–500 feet below the level of the plateau . . . Several strongly marked characteristics distinguish Patagonia from the rest of the South American continent, the series of flat-topped plateaus rising in steps from east to west . . . the arid, rigorous windswept climate; and the unusual poverty of the flora . . . The prevailing winds are from the west or southwest . . . and they blow with unusual violence and great frequency.

Why Lewis and Love weren't made to eat Patagonian dust I don't know. Despite the terrain the settlers managed to irrigate the valley and found towns like Trelew, Gaiman, Rawson and Porth – later Puerto – Madryn; a year later they established a twin colony, *Cwm Hyfryd* (Lovely Valley), about three hundred and fifty miles due west in the Andean foothills. In between was, and still is, a vacuum of all but wind and desert.

Today there are over ten thousand Welsh-Argentinians in Patagonia and Buenos Aires, most of whom are monoglot Spanish-speakers, though from what I hear Welsh is enjoying something of a revival. This is the extent of what I've learned in books about the Welsh in Argentina. Plus the fact that there's a 'Miss Mimosa' competition in the town of Trelew (pronounced Tra-LAY-ew) every year, in which, according to the North American Welsh newspaper *Ninnau*, 'twelve beautiful young women of Welsh descent parade in different styles of apparel (sport, formal, lingerie)'.

I don't know what I'll find in Chubut. Everywhere else we've visited I've met expatriates from contemporary Wales, not simply the children of a Wales that's moved on – a Wales in which most of those two thousand, eight hundred and thirteen chapels now sit like skin shed from the soul, locked and empty on the backroads – but renegades who left home in order to move on themselves. To move on economically, to learn about Kabuki theatre, to see the world. The Welsh who sailed on the *Mimosa* a hundred and thirty years ago left home to move on spiritually and patriotically. Their descendants inherited a Welsh-speaking version of Utopia and became Argentinian citizens, but they, to judge from the members of *Cymdeithas y Cymry Buenos Aires* at least, haven't moved on at all. I feel like I travelled further yesterday with Rona Davies, backwards by a century, than I have with Marguerite over the past four months. Time travel is fine for the desert, where natural eccentricity must breed something similar in humans, but damn scary in the *capital federal* of Argentina.

Wylo ❧ to Weep

A travel-writing friend of mine once called me after a trip to South America. He'd spent some time in Paraguay, where he'd been the only man in glasses, then a weekend in Buenos Aires before returning to the States. He told me he'd almost cried because the city had been nearly as beautiful as Paris. He felt, he said, plugged back into all that was fine and delicious and gifted in the world.

We don't have time to fall in love with Buenos Aires, and the weather doesn't cooperate, but under a gush of rainwater we earmark a host of latent digressions:

The window of a gourmet food shop dominated by a precarious pyramid of cobalt-blue springwater bottles. 'Look, Tŷ Nant,' cries Marguerite, who knows as well as I do that the stuff is bottled in Lampeter. We look closer and find around the blue dome boxes of Brazilian chocolates, a tinned fruitcake made in Chubut called *La Galesa* – Spanish for 'The Welshwoman' – and Macedonian halva. Our journey past and future recapped in designer food.

Chic professional dog-walkers, four leashes to each hand.

The Art Deco jewellery of the city streets: a corner balcony curved like a tiara; massive entry lamps, acorn-shaped and spiralling at the top and bottom into wrought-iron tendrils like the acanthus leaf doodles of Aubrey Beardsley; entrances starched stiff in half-moon awnings of glass fretwork, reminding Marguerite of the rigid collars shackling Dutch burghers in seventeenth-century portraits; cupolas whenever I look up, getting rain in my eyes, the mammary glands of the city cast in bronze and concrete. Everything here reminds us of something else.

A Yom Kippur service blaring from a car radio.

Recoleta Cemetery, the Père-Lachaise of Buenos Aires, where Eva Peron is buried (much to the distaste of the Argentinian hoi polloi). Avenues of elaborate mausoleums the size of generous bathrooms, many with barred windows through which those attracted to death, can stare down wooden caskets draped in lace. More desolate, less carnivalesque than Père-Lachaise; riddled with feral cats.

Women weeping without restraint in the balcony at the matinee performance of *The Bridges of Madison County*, carefully re-applying their eye make-up in the ladies' room after the film.

A blue-clad maid snapping a sheet through french doors swung wide open on a hotel balcony.

Jesus's legs in the Catedral Metropolitana, stroked tree-trunk brown on an otherwise pale frame by the frequent need and vast numbers of the faithful.

The only guide book we could find to Argentina was *Lonely Planet*, usually reserved for somewhat scruffier destinations. Though it's a little out of date – 1992 – Argentina's last military dictatorship fell eight years before its publication. Still the authors found it prudent to include the warning, 'In event of a military coup or other emergency, state-of-siege regulations suspend all civil rights; carry identification at all times, and make sure someone knows your whereabouts.' Jesus's dirty knees make more sense to me now.

Gwneud Camgymeriad ✽ to Make a Mistake

I call Rona from a pay phone. Well-dressed men, more men with long hair, I mean really long hair, than I've ever seen in my life, mostly wearing suits, and women in business-meaning high heels, brush noisily past. Despite her frequent encouragements to 'Say it in English, Pamela,' we speak Welsh. For some reason we discuss unemployment. *Heb waith*, she keeps saying, many people are *heb waith*. I hear this as *hebwaith* and have to ask her what it means. 'Without work,' she says in a thick accent. What's the MATTER with me? Of course, *heb*, without; *gwaith*, work. One little mutated 'g' and I go all stupid.

The good news is that the woman she recommends we seek out in Trelew is Elena Arnold, the same Elena Arnold who is cousin to Eirlys of the Singapore Welsh, who runs a bed and breakfast. We have a plan.

The Buenos Aires bus station is an ant colony of confusion. Actually ant colonies are far less chaotic. Construction, people with luggage, bus fumes. We buy a generous stash of food, four *empanadas* and two enormous fried beef sandwiches, for the twenty-hour, overnight ride to Trelew – Chubut's Big City of about seventy-nine thousand people. Again, transportation is my friend: twenty hours in a quiet, rolling sanctuary to reflect, to daydream, to watch the scenery, to jointly recall the past four months. (As we've travelled, our conversations have become increasingly cryptic: 'Remember that little town in Greece?' 'Which one?' 'The one with the ferry.' 'Oh, you mean the one with the big wind.')

Our first mistake, obvious fairly quickly, is that there is no scenery. A brief stretch of cattle pastures soon gives way to table-land flat as it is empty, the only deviation being cast-offs from the sky, cloud shadows that give the dun-coloured earth an illusion of depth and texture. A few scrub bushes pock my field of vision, but that's about it.

Marguerite's just begun an interesting comparison of Buenos Aires and Rio de Janeiro – her theory is that Rio embraces the New World, more like Los Angeles, while BA, like New York, strives to overcome it – when one of our two bus drivers gets up and pulls a video cassette out of an overhead bin. Our second mistake dawns: this is not a quiet sanctuary, this is a movie bus. Worse yet, the films are in English with Spanish subtitles. Consequently we are the only two people on the entire bus who cannot escape the immortal dialogue of *Death Train*, about a team of attractive people who save Europe from a nuclear bomb aboard a hijacked railway car.

Soon after *Death Train* ends the bus pulls off the highway. It's about 9 p.m.; we've been travelling almost seven hours. Everyone else gets off and marches unencumbered into a restaurant, as if they do this every day. Who knows, maybe they do this every day. I grab my computer and Marguerite our obscenely big bag of food, and we sit outside on a chilly bench to eat our sandwiches. The bus driver looks upset, but disappears into the restaurant. Moments later he returns with a Spanish-speaking German who explains that dinner is included in the price of our ticket. We docilely follow them inside and everyone looks at us, smiles kindly, then returns to his or her food, relieved: the imbecile Americans have been fetched. We down big plates of spaghetti at a breakneck pace to catch up with the others.

Patagonia is not a state of Argentina but a territory, referring to all land south of the Rio Colorado, which roughly amounts to half the country. When the sun rises we're there. Notice I didn't say 'When I wake'. That would imply having slept, which I haven't.

If possible, there is even less to see here than up north. The world is reduced to brown blank space and a horizon line. Night rain has left puddles alongside the road the colour of instant coffee thinned with skim milk. When we begin to see blown trash in the form of tattered shreds of plastic, wrapped around the thorny scrub growth, my heart sinks: Trelew can't be far, and that means Welsh verbs conjugated with a tired brain on an empty stomach. In Welsh it's not simply a matter of remembering the verb form for whatever tense you happen to be in, and plugging it into your basic, one-size-fits-all sentence. You have to remember the verb form all right, but then you have to consider your sentence selection too: maybe you'd like a nice normal sentence, or perhaps an emphatic sentence, or, if you're feeling a bit frisky, an abnormal sentence. Different occasions require different sentences, and different sentences require different verb constructions. Then, of course, there are always the mutations to consider.

Rhywbryd, dw i eisiau 'sgrechain. Sometimes, I want to scream.

Welsh is an unwieldy language, top-heavy with grammatical gingerbread. The reason for this is that it's infuriatingly unstable, and over time its instability has been codified into a glut of rules. The building blocks of English are immutable; learn 'em, figure out how to put 'em together, and that's it. English words are the atoms of spoken physics. Unless they're split – which takes a whole lot of force and wreaks havoc when you do it – they remain unchanged, true to their intrinsic nature. Welsh words, on the other hand, are like molecules: they can be broken down and recreated, they perpetually change and adapt according to the linguistic environment. No single unit in a Welsh sentence is ever immune to outside influences. Prepositions grow tails depending on the pronouns they serve; adjectives change sexes; mutations alter words instantaneously, on contact; plurals, of which there are vast varieties, disguise familiar sounds. All this creates a lovely ripple effect on the tongue and to the ear. Codified in grammar texts for learners like me, it's a pain in the neck.

'The only way to do it is to do it,' says Marguerite with the infuriating wisdom of someone who doesn't have to do it. I've got to call Elena Arnold so I can free us from the Trelew bus terminal, where there's a giant photo-op cardboard cut-out of a penguin and a baby seal, with holes for our faces.

'You want to be the seal or the penguin?'

'Just stop procrastinating and call her. That's what you're here for, isn't it, to speak Welsh?'

I know, I know. I can fret over grammar till the cows come home, but that sweet rippling incantation that is a well-spoken Welsh sentence will never come from my mouth unless I keep practising. I walk very slowly over to a pay phone. Maybe she won't be home.

'*Bore da!*' Good morning!, she answers.

I immediately tell Elena I'm a learner, as if that's necessary. *Dysgwr dw i.* That buys me a few long gaps while I search for words. *Dych chi'n siarad Saesneg?* I can't help myself, I need to know if she speaks English. No, not a word. Then I play the Eirlys-in-Singapore card. At first she hasn't a clue what I'm talking about, then something clicks, whether in my language or her memory, I'm not sure. I quickly take advantage of the connection to ask, *Oes gwely a brecwast gyda chi?*, Do you have a bed and breakfast (literally, Is there a bed and breakfast with you)? She immediately gives me directions. We're in. I'm so proud of myself I don't care that Trelew looks like (or so I imagine) a mining town on the Alaskan tundra.

Gofalu ✿ to Care

When we wake up, several hours later, it's cold outside the bed-covers. Elena's gone and the kitchen smells of fresh-baked oatmeal cookies. Her house is blank and uninviting on the exterior without much to distinguish it from a big cardboard box, just like the rest of Trelew. Inside, however, it's filled with handsome antique furniture and Welsh paraphernalia: a tea towel from Wales, several love spoons, a blown-glass red dragon, even the poster we'd seen at Keith's, with the words to T. H. Parry-Williams's poem, '*Hon*'.

Beth yw'r ots gennyf i am Gymru? Damwain a hap
Yw fy mod yn ei libart yn byw. Nid yw hon ar fap

Yn ddim byd ond cilcyn o ddaear mewn cilfach gefn,
Ac yn dipyn o boendod i'r rhai sy'n credu mewn trefn.

A phwy sy'n trigo'n y fangre, dwedwch i mi,
Pwy ond gwehilion o boblach? Peidiwch, da chwi,

Â chlegar am uned a chenedl a gwlad o hyd:
Mae digon o'r rhain, heb Gymru, i'w cael yn y byd.

'Rwyf wedi alaru ers talm ar glywed grŵn
Y Cymry, bondigrybwyll, yn cadw sŵn.

Mi af am dro, i osgoi eu lleferydd a'u llên,
Yn ôl i'm cynefin gynt, a'm dychymyg yn drên.

A dyma fi yno. Diolch am fod ar goll
Ymhell o gyffro geiriau'r eighafwyr oll.

Dyma'r Wyddfa a'i chriw; dyma lymder a moelni'r tir;
Dyma'r llyn a'r afon a'r clogwyn; ac, ar fy ngwir,

Dacw'r tŷ lle'm ganed. Ond wele, rhwng llawr a ne'
Mae lleisiau a drychiolaethau ar hyd y lle.

'R wy'n dechrau simsanu braidd; ac meddaf i chwi,
Mae rhyw ysictod fel petai'n dod drosof i;

Ac mi glywaf granfangau Cymru'n dirdynnu fy mron.
Duw a'm gwaredo, ni allaf ddianc rhag hon.

Aberystwyth, 1949

What do I care about Wales? It's just an odd chance
That I live on her land. All she is on a map

Is a sliver of earth in an off-beat corner,
Just a nuisance to those who believe in order.

And who lives in this backwater, just tell me that?
The refuse of humanity; for God's sake, don't

Cackle about entities, nations and countries;
Plenty of those, leave out Wales, around in the world.

I'm fed up long since with the strange caterwauling
Of these Welshmen, Lord, keeping up their complaining.

I'll be off, away from their speeches and writings,
Back to my childhood haunts; my fancy will take me.

And here I am. Thank goodness I'm finally lost,
Far from the clamouring words of all extremists.

There's Snowdon and its crew; here's the bare, naked land;
Here's the lake and the river and crag; to be sure,

Here's where I was born. But see, between earth and sky,
There are voices and phantoms in all these places.

I'm uncertain, and now, I don't mind telling you,
I feel a kind of weakness creeping over me,

And the claws of Wales clutching, torturing my breast,
God preserve me, I cannot escape from this one.

'Leave out Wales, around in the world.' That must be why this poster is so popular with expatriates and the descendants of expatriates: no one can. Not Parry-Williams, not Keith, not Elena, not even I. If we all share one thing it must be our respect for irony. Such a small nation, such a large world; and yet, here in another bare, naked place, the same poem about forgetting that reminds us. Reminds me that our travels don't describe a long thin line so much as a fugue, arranged for a world's worth of images and voices. We didn't leave Wales to travel to fourteen countries around the globe, we've merely used geography as a tool to mark her different moods and phases, essentially travelling no further than Parry-Williams on his way home.

When Elena returns she offers us tea and cookies. Elena Arnold has an oblong face and grey hair; she's a shorter version of the Welsh travel writer Jan Morris. Her manner is polite yet distant, as if the desert has taught her it's a good idea to keep space between all things. Without any of us realizing what we're getting into, we embark on a strange, triangular conversation at her kitchen table. I speak to Elena in Welsh; Elena speaks to Marguerite in Spanish; Marguerite speaks to me in English; I respond to Marguerite in English; she responds to Elena in Portuguese; Elena responds to me in Welsh. Not necessarily in that order.

The benefit of this scheme is that it's equally tortuous to all parties. Whenever I take more than five seconds to respond, Elena translates her question into Spanish, and between us, Marguerite and I usually figure it out. By my second cup of tea I've relaxed a bit. In contrast to the wholly alien Romance languages, Welsh seems like an old buddy. All goes well until Elena asks a seemingly innocuous question about the different foods we've eaten on our Trip. For some reason I miss the easy (but mutated) phrase *wledydd wahanol*, different countries. Instead of resorting to Spanish Elena takes a shot in English: 'places', she repeats. I hear this as 'pies', and launch into a long story in Welsh about how as a child I used to bake pies with my mother. Elena stares at me as if I've eaten my tongue, then says a few words to Marguerite in Spanish.

'She says she asked you what foods we've eaten in different places.'

I decide it's time for a stroll around Trelew.

Ffynnu ✤ to Thrive

Trelew is a town on a grid under a kind sky. The crystalline air, sharp and bracingly clean, gives its one-storey homes an emphatic, hyper-realist presence that their architecture doesn't deserve. The very pragmatism of the place, its sturdy, graceless commitment against the desert, is a testament to nothing so much as the word Ursula passionately hates in Japanese, *ganbate*. I will endure. In the air, though, there's romance: sunlight the colour and sheen of clarified butter, clouds of every variety. Towering white ones stack precariously overhead, low streaky ones prowl the horizon like sharks.

It's 5 October; the lilacs in the town square are just about to bud. Marguerite grew up in Brazil, so to her this is small change, but to me it's the far side of the looking glass. Lilacs in October in an Argentinian town named for Lewis Jones (*Tre* means town; Lew is short for Lewis) – apart from the look of the place, it's the essence of what it means to me to be FAR AWAY.

The town is thoroughly Argentinian but for a few street names like Avenida Abraham Matthews, and the San David information centre and tea shop. We wander into the *Museo Regional*. There's a stuffed penguin and a moth-eaten condor, a few arrowheads and a starfish. There's a lot of old Welsh stuff, too, with faded labels in Spanish: an organ, a gargantuan family *Beibl*, hand-coloured photos of women with names like Ellen Jones de Williams (meaning that Ellen Jones married a man called Williams, and curiously used a touch of Spanish to link their names), trophy chairs from the local *Eisteddfodau* of 1960 and 1942, and a correspondence course diploma in horsemanship from the Beery School of Pleasant Hill, Ohio, made out to one John Finch Davies. Inexplicably, there's also a bust of Voltaire.

On the way out I stop to sign the visitors' book and see that someone named Takashi Matsuka from Yokohama was here last year. I grunt and show Marguerite.

'At least it's not Effie Wiltens,' she says, smiling. Then she asks me what I think of Elena Arnold.

'She's okay, not exactly overflowing with warmth, but certainly pleasant.'

'You know, from what you've said about the group in Buenos Aires and what I've seen of Elena, these people seem more like the Welsh of Wales – you know, a little reserved, a little suspicious, though kind enough – than anybody we met on the Trip. I feel like I'm back in Lampeter.'

When we leave the museum the sky is vein-blue and a perfect rainbow is arched over Trelew, one end seeming to emerge directly from the head of a statue of Lewis Jones. I take it as a sign that we will thrive here in *Y Wladfa*.

Gwasgu ✽ to Press

Elena Arnold has seen fit to charge us forty dollars for our bed and breakfast. Money is tight, and the going low rate in town is half that.

'But you know her cousin,' fumes Marguerite, outraged at the audacity. 'You speak Welsh! You gave her a red dragon pin! Why couldn't she give us a break?'

I'm a little miffed too, but I have a secret fondness in my heart for Elena because last night she told me I spoke Welsh well. What's more, for the first time in my life, I believed it.

We now face an eight-hour, east-to-west bus ride across the Patagonian desert. I'm determined to attend the Eisteddfod tomorrow in Trevelin, and so hopefully to meet Arturo Lowndes and see a bit of *Cwm Hyfryd* as well. This time we knowingly don't buy food for the trip.

For seven of the eight hours, but for some crazy, Martian-looking rock formations, the dry earth – now chalky brown, now deep, rosy rust – is stretched taut across the bedrock and empty of all but pale scrub and a few wild ponies. After a while I realize what I miss out here; there are no verticals in this world. Only telephone poles and some scrawny poplars planted around a hand-ful of oasis-style farms challenge the insistence of the horizon. The sky is still the richest thing in sight, full of formal, level-bottomed clouds skirted by distant squalls. They seem unimaginably heavy, squashing the desert flatter still. When we do come to a few hills the land doesn't roll up to meet them but rudely coughs them straight up, their tops pressed by the sky's weight into even ledges that look like bastard children of the horizon line.

Out of the middle of nowhere a flock of screaming yellow parrots flies past our window, eye level. In all this drabness it's like electric shock by colour. Marguerite says they remind her of tropical fish.

About an hour into the trip the curlier-headed of our two bus drivers passes around a box of *alfahores*, excruciatingly sweet little sandwiches filled with a sinful substance called *dulce de leche*, a kind of caramel. We get ours first because we're sitting directly behind the driver; my foot, when crossed over my opposite knee, bobs about three inches from his head. Despite the potential for disaster it's a good spot from which to study the Argentinian *maté* ritual. Five or six times throughout the trip the non-driving partner fills a hollowed-out gourd – nicely embellished on the outside in rings of silver plate – with dried herbs, then pours in hot water from a thermos and inserts a silver-plated straw with a filter on the end. The stuff bubbles ominously from the bottom like green sludge, but smells of freshly-mowed grass. They pass it around between themselves and some friends, then repeat the whole ordeal an hour later.

We stop near the halfway point for lunch in a paltry exception to the emptiness that has a name (which I've since forgotten), and therefore must be a town. Marguerite and I wait expectantly for a meal ticket but none comes. This bus-food thing just seems to elude us. I write in my journal, 'Teeth crunch on windblown grit. Two-by-two grid of dirt streets, tiny box houses. Rationality a meagre thing in the desert.'

My hand jags as I write this, catching on certain letters like a misfiring engine. The more Welsh I speak the harder it is to write in English. Put up a monument for me in this god-forsaken place: I actually switch to Welsh in my own notebook.

After lunch what I've feared most comes to pass, and the drivers start showing movies. Again they're low-budget American imports, one about a murderous motorcycle gang, another about a murderous male stripper. By the beginning of the second film bumps have begun to appear on the horizon; by the end they've grown into big brutes of mountains, their snow-tipped peaks interlaced for all eternity in my mind's eye with prodigious male genitalia bulging out of a black leather bikini.

Finally I understand why the Welsh pioneers bothered. As we approach Esquel, the Big City of western Chubut, population twenty thousand, the earth grows curly. It also grows *glaswellt*, green hair. *Cwm Hyfryd* is no dirty trick of naming, it's for real. There are sheep here and meadows lustrous with alpine run-off, wild daffodils and, in the distance, the lavender flanks of the Andes. We both keep saying the name, the Andes, to remind ourselves we're in South America. But for that name and a kind of raw grandeur, a New World scale in which small-country cosiness has no place, we could be in North Wales.

As we pull into Esquel the driver turns on the radio and 'Unchained Melody' by the Righteous Brothers fills the bus.

Llesteirio 🐜 to Frustrate

Trevelin, population fifty-five hundred. Getting here last night – wedged into the back of a half-century-old bus with our packs shoved on top of us while *Sound of Music* scenery rolled past – was not what I'd call a good time had by all.

This morning the gas heater in our room at the *Residencial Trevelin* has tried to kill us with its efficiency. I had to wake the owner and mime death by extreme heat to get him to come turn it down. Outside, though, the air is cool and has the same scrubbed clarity as that of Trelew and, some dim memory tells me, Norway.

At 10 a.m. the streets are scrupulously deserted. Trevelin has the look of a tidy frontier post with cedar-log buildings, the smell of woodsmoke in the air, sharp, vegetable greens and maroons of new-born intensity and, this morning, low clouds curtaining the mountains. The houses are of utilitarian ugliness, many with corrugated iron roofs. As soon as we get accustomed to the place, wee, cultural idiosyncrasies begin to sprout. The trees lining the town's few streets are severely bobbed, European crew-cut style; you'd never see that in backwoods Maine, which until now is what this place has called to mind. A sign in Spanish points the way to 'The Grave of the Horse that Saved Daniel Evans'. There are street signs for Avenida Guillermo Brown and Calle Ap Ieuan (the latter translates to Son of Ieuan Street, *calle* being Spanish for 'street', *ap* Welsh for 'son of'). Local tea houses are called *Casa de té Nain Maggie* – Grandma Maggie's Tea House (Catherine Nagashima would be so pleased) – and, the Welsh idea hijacked entirely by Spanish, *Casa de té El Adobe*. Road signs point the way to Chile, but the town's seal shows the red dragon of Wales atop a rising sun.

Locals, when they finally emerge, seem careless of the exotic hybridity that gives travel writers like me such a natural buzz. Two old men stop to have a chat in front of a house called Troed yr Orsedd, which in Welsh means Foot of the Throne, as if they weren't cultural icons but two old men jawing the morning away. One is in a tweed cap and jacket with a proper necktie, looking for all the world as though he'd been beamed here from the Lampeter Post Office, the other in full gaucho gear including snappy black cowboy hat and baggy trousers tucked into low, accordion-pleated boots. I'm enthralled.

I'm also frustrated beyond belief. Here in a place where shops advertise T-shirts claiming *Rwyn Falch o Fod yn Gymro*, I'm Proud to be a Welshman, I can't communicate in *either* of the two languages of Wales. It steams me that Marguerite is far better off dickering in 'Spanuese'. On a tour of Trevelin's Museum of Old Welsh Stuff she chats amiably with the elderly, Spanish-speaking curator while I follow behind muttering to myself about linguistic injustice. My only consolation is a Spanish label that identifies the island of Anglesey as *Isla de Môn*, the Isle of Môn. The translator has bypassed the better-known English word in preference for the old Welsh name of the Druids' island. I'm glad to see that Welsh doesn't always need English to broker for it in the big world.

Toward the end of their tour I finally blurt out, '*Dych chi'n siarad Cymraeg?*' Do you speak Welsh?, which flusters the poor woman no end.

'*O ydych, ydych. Ond dweud y gwir, dim ond tipyn bach.*' Yes, yes, Well, to tell the truth, just a little bit.

I feel like I'm in the right film with the wrong soundtrack.

Canmol 🏵 to Praise

No answer at Arturo Lowndes's house. Just as I'm blasting Trevelin and Arturo and the fact that there's not a shred of evidence that an Eisteddfod will be held here today, we turn an obscure corner and come upon four young women, arms linked around each other's waists, striding down the middle of the street singing one of my favourite hymns. Marguerite and I stand frozen as 'For the Beauty of the Earth' reverberates in high, clear, shivering four-part harmony. Though they sing in Spanish I know the words to the English refrain:

> Lord of all to thee we raise,
> This our hymn of grateful praise.

Strange to say I haven't heard this hymn in a church – or chapel – in years, yet it's been echoing in my head all around the world. I'd wanted a sign that the Eisteddfod was happening today, and here it is: if these women aren't practising for one of the upcoming singing competitions then I can't say 'Aberystwyth' three times fast.

(Aberystwyth, Aberystwyth, Aberystwyth.)

The Trevelin Eisteddfod

Here in the middle of nowhere it comes as a shock to have to pay ten bucks each to get into the *salon central*, Trevelin's town hall, where the Eisteddfod is about to begin. Once inside we assess value for money. The *salon* is overflowing with metal folding chairs; up front is a stage decorated with bundles of branches (read: forest), and a crudely painted backdrop of the sun setting over the mountains. In the middle are two large, empty chairs to be occupied by the winning bards-to-be. Marguerite pointedly recalls that we paid less to see *The Bridges of Madison County*.

The crowd is dauntingly well-dressed in funeral and/or wedding gear. Men wear suits and woollen waistcoats with ties tucked in at the neck – more memories of Lampeter on market day – older women, especially, hats and their best dresses (the last time I saw a pillbox hat covered in blue silk flowers was when I got stuck in wedding traffic in Pontrhydfendigaid in 1988). As the hall fills and people take their seats faces become more prominent than clothes. Looking over the Argentinian audience I see the old men of Wales blowing their noses with crisply starched handkerchiefs. They have shiny weathered features with ruddy patches on their cheeks and swimming eyes. Their wives are solid and pasty with big glasses and sensible permanent waves. Kids tug at stiff holiday outfits as they run up and down the aisles. Everyone in Trevelin, young, old, middle-aged, is here except the curator of the town museum. She never gets to come, she told Marguerite, because you never know when a stray tourist may want to see the collection.

'How the hell am I going to find Arturo Lowndes in this crowd?' I whisper to Marguerite in a panic, as a man with a take-charge attitude approaches the microphone and clears his throat.

'*Spanishspanishspanishspanish*Arturo Lowndes*spanishspanishspanishspanishspanish*.'

I grab Marguerite – my only communicative link to this seven-hundred-year-old Welsh extravaganza, imported here to the foothills of the Andes – and yell, 'What what what? What's happening with Arturo?'

She begins to answer but Arturo is already striding up to the stage where he conducts the crowd in an oompa version of Argentina's national anthem. The omens are with me today. I snag him afterwards and we agree to meet tomorrow morning in chapel for the *Gymanfa Ganu* – the hymn-singing festival – after which we'll join him for a barbecue at his house.

A little girl takes the stage and the hall instantly falls silent. After a team of experts finally manages to lower the mike to her level she sings a song in Spanish which Marguerite tells me concerns the lifecycle of a lobster. We clap vigorously. She returns to the audience. A little boy repeats the song. Then another little boy. Then a little girl. Then another boy. Repetition threatens to turn the lobster ditty into another '*Milgi Milgi*'. I flip through my programme: this is the first of forty-nine competitions, all of which have numerous contestants and will entail lengthy evaluations by a panel of judges. The metal seats are already beginning to get a little hard.

All of the announcements and most of the singing and poetry recitation contests are in Spanish, though about a quarter of the competitions are noted as being *en gales*, in Welsh. The first of these – recitation for the under-seven crowd – has only one entrant, a blonde child who narrates a poem about a *Tedi Ber*. All I can make out is, Teddy Bear, teddy bear, your ears are clean, your eyes are . . . some darn thing I can't understand. I'm impressed by these kids' lack of inhibition. Once again, I feel like I'm missing the Welsh singing gene. Even the littlest ones seem to know their way around a microphone, and those who can't sing show no fear of belting it out anyway. This is all the more remarkable when Marguerite begins translating some of the judges' comments.

'Man, they're brutal,' she tells me. Everybody gets a long, con-sidered evaluation before prizes are awarded. Poor posture. Bad timing. Fidgeted. Sloppy diction. Forgot the words. In one case the judges refuse to award any prize at all even though there was only one entrant in the category – Welsh recitation again – because the woman just wasn't good enough. Still, I'm glad to see that the *Tedi Ber* kid gets a Barbie doll for her troubles, and that the judges value craft over kindness. It enraged me as a kid to be tossed sugar-coated platitudes instead of considered criticism: the message being that whatever I was doing wasn't important enough to merit improvement. That's evidently not a problem this afternoon.

The day wears on. There's an annoying child of about ten in a pinafore-style blue dress who's entered every competition in sight, including the Welsh ones. I'll bet the other kids hate her. The organizers have cleverly put the children first, then teenagers, followed by the adult events, with the real crowd-pleasers – competing choirs from all over Chubut – at the very end. Just before intermission three young tenors take on the hymn '*Mae' Deisiau Di Bob Awr*', I Need You Every Hour. The first two have decent voices but their Spanish accents rumble right over the Welsh lyrics and leave them for dead; the last one, however, sings in soaring, pristine Welsh. An elderly man with veins in his cheeks, two rows ahead of me, listens with eyes closed, mouthing the words as tenderly as if he were fitting them with wings. When the young man finishes the crowd goes wild, clapping and stomping and patting each other on the back. This is the rugby of Chubut.

Intermission

Boom time for *Casa de té Nain Maggie*, apparently *the* place in town to down a few brews during the break. It's jammed. A black and white photo of a toothless Grandma Maggie, withered and bundled up like a baby on her hundredth birthday, hangs on the wall. No one here has ever heard of decaffeinated anything.

We order one *té galesa* to split between us. The spread that soon arrives stuns me into silence: one magisterial pot of brewed tea, two slabs of bread with butter, cheeses, jams, and ten varieties of cakes cut into four-bite squares, including the dark fruitcake called *Torta Galesa*, the region's speciality that we'd seen in Buenos Aires, plus apple pie, raspberry cream torte, and another pie with a cream filling so rich it must've killed the cow that made it.

'*Buwch*,' says Marguerite, shivering in a sweet spasm, 'way too much sugar.'

'How appropriate. That means cow.'

'Huh?'

'Cow. *Buwch* is cow in Welsh.'

She rolls her eyes. 'Now you know why Maggie was toothless.'

Everyone around us is hashing over the competitions with respectful earnestness. I have to keep reminding myself that these people are technically no more Welsh than I am Hungarian or German. The fact that they're speaking in Spanish helps.

'There seems to be real compatibility between Welsh and Spanish,' muses Marguerite. 'It avoids all that ugliness between Welsh and English.'

This is true. When a Welsh person speaks English fifteen hundred years of historical baggage come spilling out of the closet; Spanish is relatively free of such weight, though around the turn of the century the Argentinian government did think it best to quash the aloofness of the Welsh settlers by enacting a law that all public school teaching would henceforth be in Spanish. The Welsh made the Argentinians nervous. They didn't want to assimilate, they put Wales above Argentina. Some newspapers in Buenos Aires contented themselves with merely pointing this out:

> [I have] met Argentine citizens native to the place that do not speak a single word of the Spanish language due to the exclusive teaching of Welsh ... It is undoubtable that such men ... will grow up as Welshmen, think as Welshmen, act as Welshmen and their family will always be an exotic plant among the other Argentine families.

Others bashed the Welsh outright:

> These colonies [the Welsh settlements in Chubut] are ... concentrations of inertia and vice. It is better that they have not adapted to the milieu. The congenital vices of their race have remained shut off like themselves in their colonies.

Bashed or lamented, Welsh Patagonians never entirely gave up their ancestors' goal of safeguarding the old language, though the threat of piracy now came from Spanish instead of English (ironically, some responded to the Spanish Only campaign by retreating into English, of all things, as a 'non-partisan' third language). Since the beginning of the century, however, linguistic erosion has taken its toll. Of the ten thousand Argentinians of Welsh descent, fewer than a thousand souls speak the language any more, and these are mostly old people. Our waiter, who looks like the twin of an old boyfriend of mine in Wales, can only talk to Marguerite in Spanish.

The Trevelin Eisteddfod, II

We've lost our seats, which is fine since I'm on a sugar-driven caffeine high, and probably couldn't sit still anyway. I feel like I'm sweating tea.

It's evening now, and the crowd has relaxed a little. Ties are still fiercely knotted, but there's more whispering during recitations and children-as-projectiles have begun ricocheting around the room. By nine or so I can't tell if the quartet and small choirs are singing in Welsh or Spanish. Marguerite tells me that Argentinian Spanish is different from that of other South American countries: the double 'l', so notorious in Welsh, is pronounced *zh* here, rather than *y*, and the stress on plurals and all words ending in vowels is on the penultimate syllable – same as in Welsh. This latter quirk gives *Castellano*, as Argentinian Spanish is known, a similar riding-the-train-tracks bumpiness, which I hope is why I can't tell it apart from Welsh tonight. The other option is that sugar has eaten away large parts of my brain.

Sure enough, 'For the Beauty of the Earth' is sung by five different quartets, which mercifully banishes the lobster song from my mind. Bards are crowned, both women. There were forty entries in the Best Poem in Spanish category, two in Best Poem in Welsh. Small children dance on stage in green outfits that make them look like Brussels sprouts.

We've been standing propped up against the wall next to a woman who comments on our English. Before I can mention Welsh she runs off and comes back with her mother, an elderly lady who has the same fleecy white hair and sweetly stale breath of my Hungarian grandmother. Her name is Melody Evans. She tells us her mother was the first white woman born in *Cwm Hyfryd*; her father was Scottish and English. She feels Welsh, she says – her husband speaks Welsh – but she speaks only English and Spanish. Hearing English reminds her of her childhood; it's obvious that *Saesneg*, so reviled by Welsh nationalists, is precious to her. Four years ago, she says, the BBC came and filmed her family because they were known to be typically 'Welsh'.

My conversation with Melody has drawn urgent shushing noises from the crowd, including a teenage boy in an AC/DC T-shirt. The onslaught of Methodist hymns shows no sign of abating when we finally leave at 11 p.m., overstuffed with nine hours of music and poetry. I find it endearingly perverse that just when I'm speaking and comprehending Welsh better than ever before, this Eisteddfod – the most traditional of all Welsh events I've attended in fifteen countries around the world – has been held in Spanish. Now I know how that Patagonian guy felt in the movie we saw in Paris; though he was able to speak Welsh in Wales, most people he encountered could only speak English. No wonder he had an affair with the miner's wife, it was probably stress relief.

Walking to the Residencial Trevelin under brittle stars, between vast patches of starless night that I hope are the mountains, the parochialism of the Welsh–English debate seems to shatter into so much useless energy. Down the street the people of Trevelin are staying up late practising Welshness through the medium of Spanish. Somewhere in Japan I'll bet someone is singing '*Myfanwy*' right now in Japanese.

I understand that Welsh struggles like a hothouse flower in the chill of its own soil, and I believe that is wrong, and that the old tongue is worth all the careful tending in the world. It's just that tonight the world is so big and Wales is so far away, and Spanish, for now, is enough. Too bad I don't speak it.

Cwafrio 🌺 to Quaver

'No more singing, please god, no more singing.' I hear the words in my head and try to quiet them lest anyone in chapel can read minds. My thoughts would reek of treachery. If there are mind readers here they'd also know that after last night's tea and this morning's breakfast I'm convinced I'm suffering from caffeine poisoning.

Arturo is at a portable keyboard up front; we're in a pew toward the back; a man with a TV camera is hovering in the aisle, waiting for us all to burst into glorious song. When this eventually happens inside the little Methodist chapel where the *Gymanfa Ganu* is being held, Marguerite and I don't join in, and the camera quickly pans away from us. No one told us we had to bring our own hymnals. I look over someone's shoulder and see that they wouldn't have done us much good anyway. Musical notation is again written in what I've learned is called the Welsh sol-fa system, a reputedly simple way of writing music without staves, devised last century, in which letters or shapes take the place of notes. Most of the big male voice choirs in Wales still use sol-fa as well.

For an hour and a half we sit and stand, sit and stand, like members of a religious aerobics class. At first the conductor, Melody's son, chooses the hymns, but then he opens up the choice to the congregation. Most selections are in Spanish, and these are attacked with vigour by young and old alike; but whenever someone requests a hymn in Welsh at least half the singers fall silent, and this wreaks havoc with the tune. It's a comment on the fortunes of *Y Wladfa* that the thin, quavering sopranos of old women, producing sounds that pierce a vulnerable spot in my forehead, meshing imperfectly with the uncertain, searching baritones of old men, are all that make up the Welsh choir of Trevelin. Yet when someone finally requests 'Calon Lan', literally Pure Heart, the most famous of famous Welsh hymns, there's an initial clap of hymnals shutting as one, and then every person in chapel except us opens his or her mouth and sings, in Welsh, from memory.

Ysbrydoli ✿ to Inspire

Arturo Lowndes's big old car smells of sunbaked vinyl and the nineteen sixties. We wind and climb out of Trevelin into the Andes, into high spring and pure air, where colours are honed by the sunshine to an almost surreal radiance. PINK cherry blossoms, YELLOW forsythia and daffodils, BLUE sky, PURPLE mountains, GREEN grass. It's as if Arturo, who seems to have some clout in these parts, had the place colourized for our benefit.

On the way he tells us that his wife's family is Welsh, and that she speaks it fluently.

'You mean you don't?' I'm stunned. We met, after all, at the National Eisteddfod of Wales.

'Nope,' he says in perfect, matter-of-fact English. 'Family's from Brittany originally, then Scotland. Branch in Devon that produces Presbyterian ministers. I speak a dialect of Malay, if you're interested.'

'The Bretons came from Wales,' remarks Marguerite, who gives me one of those 'See? I've paid attention' looks.

Malay? Here I've been bludgeoning my conscience over the fact that I've been speaking to Arturo in English. That was a waste of time.

We pass a winding earthen driveway that disappears into a copse of fir trees; Arturo says it's his neighbour's place. 'He's Japanese.

'Nother Japanese guy in Esquel who sings in fluent Welsh. Think he's away though.'

Arturo's house – a good ten minutes' drive from the Japanese neighbour's – is a many-gabled mansion of natural woods with a distinct Alpine atmosphere. It's set on a ledge in the hills, cushioned by a ring of evergreens above which snow-capped mountains ride into perfect clouds. Healthy-looking young men and women frolic on the front lawn – members of the Trelew choir, yesterday's big winners, who camped nearby overnight. When we arrive they break into sweet song, kiss us welcome, then, still singing, begin to dance around a patch of daffodils. Arturo's wife Rosa comes out of the house wearing a colourful apron and looks upon the dancers, beaming. Arturo runs and fetches an accordion, straps it to his chest and strides into the scenery, squeezing out a fast-paced jig. The choir members respond like maenads, whirling each other around in a spontaneous frenzy while Arturo plays on, a big, fair, jovial demi-god in a suit and tie.

Marguerite and I stand and stare. 'It's a bloody *twmpath*,' I whisper, a kind of impromptu Welsh country dance. The scene is so ferociously wholesome and picturesque that if Julie Andrews and the Von Trapp children came bounding out of the house right now, I wouldn't be surprised.

While they're making merry Rosa introduces us to one of her brothers, an old man with bright eyes who's been barbecuing a whole Patagonian lamb for our dinner. Fine, downy ashes are trapped in his ears and chin stubble, reminding me, improbably, of Ed back in Delft.

'He speaks no English,' Rosa slowly tells us, feeling for the words herself, 'but Welsh, fluently.'

'*Dychchinhrrrffchrrmmmmmmrrrch?*' he asks, reaching out to shake hands.

I nod uncertainly; I've been in this situation before. This is the dreaded Old Man Mumble, a chain of mucus-basted grumbling sounds that aspire to the Welsh language but never quite get there, in my ears anyway. The brother-in-law's posture, a little stiff and crick-backed, as if he just got off a horse, his weathered face, abrupt politeness and those throaty grunts are familiar to me – he has twins who hang out on the main street in Lampeter, leaning on canes and spitting – so I know in advance I don't have a prayer of ever understanding him. He has no trouble with my Welsh at all, but whenever I speak he has the unfortunate habit of responding, and that's got to be nipped in the bud. I smile at him, bow a little for good measure, and run away.

The choir members leave in another shower of kisses, and Arturo takes us on a tour of his mansion. It's called *Pelangi*, he tells us, which means Rainbow in Malay. Marguerite asks him how he wound up spending so much time in Indonesia.

'Oil business keeps you moving.'

'I thought you said he was a television producer,' she whispers to me, wagging her index finger back and forth to underscore my error. This is a strange, schoolmarmy habit she picked up some-where on the Trip.

'Yeah, well, don't listen to me. I thought he spoke Welsh, too.'

Lunch is a massive meal of three languages, the grilled lamb, assorted salads, wine and flan. One brother is silent; He Whom I Can't Understand is unintelligible; Rosa and her sisters-in-law speak perfectly comprehensible Welsh; Arturo addresses me in English and everyone else in Spanish; and Marguerite is stunned mute after watching one of the brothers-in-law mix Sprite into his red wine. Rosa says that when she was a child she and her eleven brothers and sisters spoke Welsh exclusively until they went to school. The local Mapuche Indians who lived near her parents' farm spoke Welsh too.

'*Ro'n nhw'n wedi bod gofyn am "fara",*' she recalls, They used to come and ask for bread. The Mapuches in Patagonia and Breton farmers looking for *bara* and *gwin* on their way to Paris: both found Welsh a poor language in which to beg. It certainly didn't help the Indians much, as they're almost extinct now in Chubut.

'Butch Cassidy used to live near here,' Arturo suddenly announces. 'Robbed a bunch of Welsh banks.'

After dinner Arturo takes us on a tour of his estate. 'Here is where my swimming pool will be,' he says with a grand sweep of his arm, 'and here, my tennis courts.' Arturo delivers all his English sentences in a curious take-it-or-leave-it tone, as if he's decided in advance that his listeners' reaction is of no concern to him. It occurs to me that this may be merely an expression of fluency rather than actual diffidence. I speak fast in Welsh when I want to show off (usually with disastrous results). He leads us to a flowering tree that's been blooming for seven years straight. I'm about to compliment him on it when, thank god, I see that the flowers are made of silk, carefully affixed to the branches with tiny wires.

'Ha! Bet my neighbour Roy Jenkins it would flower. "Na, it's junk," he said. Came out here one night and tied 'em on. Boy was he surprised.'

Arturo decides to take us all on a tour of Los Alerces National Park. Richard Llewellyn used to live up there, he declares, wrote a novel called *Up Into the Singing Mountain*. Wasn't as successful as *How Green Was My Valley*. People here didn't like him, too bohemian or sophisticated or something.

This doesn't surprise me. Llewellyn was an expat, and the Welsh Patagonians – but for the fact that they live nine thousand miles away – are essentially the people who stayed home.

Rosa begs off, saying she'll meet us later in Esquel, but He Whom I Can't Understand and his wife agree to go along for the ride. High speeds on gravel roads, I discover, create a buzzing in my head I'd thought could only be produced by alcohol or a dentist's drill.

Alerces are immense Patagonian cypresses that look like giant sequoias, or so my guide book tells me. They grow deep within the park in a grove that's only accessible in summer, and by boat. Since it's still spring we content ourselves with driving around Lake Futalaufquen – the big word means Big Water in Mapuche – and alongside the malachite-green River Arrayanes (named for a tree with red bark that feels like fur). It's almost too much beauty for one vista: spectacular lakeland cupped at the knees of close, immense mountains. Unfortunately the scenery inspires Arturo to get his camcorder out of the trunk. Marguerite ducks into the back seat.

He points it directly at me. 'Okay, Pamela, you're on!'

I mime a little tap dance and then give my vital statistics in Welsh. After that my mind goes blank.

Later the five of us stroll out on to the middle of a suspension footbridge, the kind that's always giving way in old cartoons. Directly below us is a geological event: the meeting of two rivers, one of which runs to the Pacific, the other to the Atlantic. The waters are clearly of different colours, which don't mingle, but swirl together like a tie-dyed T-shirt in blues and greens. The Grateful Dead pop to mind. Fish pop into the mind of He Whom I Can't Understand.

'*Maechrrrchchchhwyrrrrchwwwchmmmmmrch*,' he says, and embarks on a mysterious discourse that sounds like a kitchen sink disposal, accompanied by waves and gestures that make the bridge sway.

I nod my head and repeat '*Yn wir?*' a few times, which means Really?, but come away clueless. Later his wife calmly informs me in Welsh that there are trout and salmon in the lake, and that the fishing is great. Comprehension works in mysterious ways.

Pobi ✿ to Bake

To Marguerite's great surprise Arturo doesn't drop us off in downtown Esquel, but pulls into the driveway of a woman named Vicky Pritchard. The knowledge that we're going to someone's house for tea must've arrived in my brain through the medium of Welsh, and I forgot to translate it for her. Such prosaic trifles are the stuff confidence is made of. I understood in Welsh, and the fact that Marguerite has been in the dark means no one repeated the news in English. It hits me hard at the door of Vicky Pritchard's concrete bungalow on a modest sidestreet in Esquel: I Can Speak Welsh. Just about five months ago Tim and I'd had to retire from the commotion of sunny Lampeter into the back room of a pub in order to share 'something other than common-place conversation'. Welsh had only symbolic value for me back then. Today I've used it for regular workaday conversation and that is an extraordinary thing.

Inside we find that Rosa and the other family members are already here. First we're herded into a tiny front room to visit a bedridden woman who kisses us hello. She looks pretty spry to me, and tells me, '*Americanes dych chi sy'n teithio o gwmpas y byd yn siarad Cymraeg!*' You're the American woman who's travelling around the world speaking Welsh! This is what I was going to say. Nothing comes in its place, not a thing. Desperate, I smile and make kindly, pan-linguistic noises.

We arrive in the kitchen just as Vicky resolutely sets down a worn tin kettle on a Rayburn-style stove. This has to be one of the most welcoming gestures in the entire catalogue of domestic events. I feel instantly at home. Vicky has fair hair drawn back from her face, kind eyes, and the skill of a pastry chef. Cakes and pies, including another rendition of the killer-cream tart, crowd the table. I'm still feeling leaden from lunch, but we're encouraged to eat.

Vicky spoke Welsh as a girl but says she's rusty now because she doesn't use it much any more. Her husband speaks only Spanish, or so he claims. He stares at us, then comes up and pokes me and exclaims, 'Beautiful!' I go red.

'Tell him he's blind,' shouts Arturo, at whom I scowl.

Vicky sits next to me and takes out photos of her family. For the next hour she and I comment in comfortable, rudimentary

Welsh about the lives of people I don't know. We mostly toss around nouns and verbs, and the occasional adjective as an exclamation. Hardly any prepositions at all. It's fun. It's like playing with building blocks. Here in the kitchen of a stranger, with soft ripples of Spanish lapping around us, I'm finally having fun with what Takeshi called this rare, new thing.

And so is she. Vicky is clearly self-conscious about the quality of her Welsh, but it's the simple self-consciousness of someone who's out of practice, not the inferiority complex that troubles so many Welsh-speakers from contemporary Wales. The atmosphere of qualitative comparison that divides people there simply doesn't exist in Welsh Patagonia. Vicky's ancestors arrived in Chubut before English became the majority language in Wales, and she and her compatriots have never questioned the quality of their Welsh or their Welshness. If either has slipped, if they've become more Argentinian over the years, that's both a matter of personal choice and a natural progression. Though Chubut is a poor and unglamorous place in which to scrape a living, I've witnessed less cultural anxiety here than anywhere else on the Trip.

Vicky thinks she may have relatives in Cardigan, and asks if I've been there. I have. She wants to know where it is. *De Gorllewin Cymru*, I say, South West Wales. She shakes her head. No, that means nothing to her. Vicky has this language and some relatives and recipes for tea cakes, but Wales itself is a distant abstraction. I have the opposite, a little language, too, but mainly the feel and smell and look of the place that I hold in my head. As we're leaving – a friend of theirs has a B & B nearby – both Marguerite and I thank Vicky for her hospitality.

'*Na, na,*' she says emphatically, '*diolch i CHI am ddod.*' No, no, thank YOU for coming. She says that even though there are other Welsh-speakers in Esquel, they rarely use the language amongst themselves. Only the old people, she admits a little sadly, only the old.

Taro ✿ to Hit

We spend all day shivering on the streets of Esquel because I refuse to sit in the seedy bus terminal. In *The Old Patagonian Express*, a guy on a train tells Paul Theroux, 'Esquel is only a little bit pretty.' I fear he grossly overstated its appeal. We try to eat in a place called the Palace of the Chicken but they'll only give us a whole chicken. What would we do with a whole chicken?

We spend all night recrossing the desert on Mar y Valle, the Sea and Valley line. This time we're shown just one movie, an inspirational comedy about a down-and-out American baseball team that gets to the World Series. When we stop for a break at the halfway point and the driver flips on the overhead fluorescent lamps, it's like being hit by lightning. Marguerite and the other passengers look like cadavers. So do I when I see my reflection in the window.

Around 5 a.m. an ashen-pink sunrise defines the desert from the sky. At five fifty-five the bus rolls into its bay back at the Trelew station.

Chwerthin ✿ to Laugh

By 9 a.m. it's an old morning. I make my final 'Hello. This is Pamela Petro, I don't know if you got my postcard, but I'm visiting Welsh communities around the world . . .' telephone call of the Trip. Luned Roberts de Gonzalez of Gaiman, Chubut has been expecting me, though she thinks my name is Petra. From what I've been told, Gaiman, a settlement of around four thousand people about ten miles west of Trelew, is the 'most Welsh' town in Chubut, and Luned and her sisters are the 'most Welsh' folks in Gaiman. My source is her brother Arturo Roberts, who – by sheer coincidence – lives five minutes from my aunt and uncle in Basking Ridge, New Jersey. I'd tracked Arturo down through *Ninnau*, the English-language newspaper he publishes for the Welsh community in North America, and asked for an introduction to his family in Patagonia.

Luned is succinct. So succinct, in fact, that she doesn't wait for my halting Welsh but switches to excellent, slightly Spanish-inflected English. If we come tomorrow we can attend a high-school Welsh class, have lunch with her, go to an adult Welsh class, then a *Merched y Wawr* meeting (Women of the Dawn) and finally a choir rehearsal, all in one day. Her sister Moelona has a B & B.

Pay dirt. I leave her with a *Da iawn*, Very good, and we creep to an inexpressibly grim but cheap *residencial*. There's no heat, no hot water, and our room is the colour of plastic vomit. Welcome to the downside of all that plastic food in Japan. Visions of Ursula's tatami room taunt my memory.

Five months of movement and, more recently, three long-distance bus rides in less than a week have begun to tell on us. Marguerite has developed a deep, chest-wrenching cough that gets worse by the day. I've picked up a number of compulsive fears, principally of losing my notebooks, but more cosmically of having failed in my mission. In saner moments I realize I haven't, that failure is just an expression of exhaustion, but still I permit myself no peace. Whenever I have a free moment I drill my Welsh brain in the future tense, the conditional, colloquial phrases. In Argentina I haven't had the company of my four hundred-odd taggers-along, the members of the Welsh L, who've been my silent practice mates the breadth of this world. Argentina hasn't linked up to Compuserve yet, so I'm without an electronic mailbox. By comparison to their arcane chatter I always felt like a regular kind of gal; without it I'm left to define the cutting edge of oddball on my own.

On a sidewalk in Trelew: we know ten people in the entire seventy-five thousand square mile state of Chubut, and of those ten, it would have to be He Whom I Can't Understand now bearing down upon us. We left him two days ago in Vicky Pritchard's kitchen on the other side of South America. I had no idea he lived in Trelew.

'*Dychchchmmmmrrrwwgggg?rrrchmeddygmmmmychcychggg!*'

I must be getting better at this. I pluck the word *meddyg*, doctor, out of his friendly garble, and indeed we establish that he's on his way to the doctor's. Encouraged, he tells me more, but all I can do is helplessly shake my head and smile. We both laugh, grasp hands, and continue on in opposite directions.

Glynu ✿ to Cling

> I was in a new country, among people speaking the same language but of a hundred years before, with the manners of that time, and a wonder to me, as if the clock had slipped, and I had come from sleep.
>
> RICHARD LLEWELLYN, *Up Into the Singing Mountain*

A thin copse of poplars, vivid and vertical in a flat world, stakes Gaiman's claim against the Patagonian desert. As the bus bumps down the only road into town through this least green, least Welsh, of landscapes (god, how those first settlers must have missed the damp), we come upon a row of billboards. *Casa de Té Plas y Coed* advertises the first one, half in Spanish, half in Welsh. A word-for-word translation is Tea House House in the Woods, which is as impish as it is redundant, since trees are pretty scarce in these parts. Another, emblazoned with the Welsh dragon, reads *Casa de Té Ty Nain*, Grandma's House Tea House, and still another *Casa de Té Ty Newydd*, New House Tea House. Must be the place.

We get down from the bus on a wide street under a vacant

blue sky. Only the sun is out: no people, no dogs, even. Just wind, ever bloody blowing wind, pelting fine sand into our hair, our contacts, our ears (the *Lonely Planet* author rightly identifies Patagonia as 'purgatory for contact lens wearers'). The main drag seems too wide for this little town. Most side streets, I can tell at a glance, peter out after a few hundred yards in camel-coloured mounds of earth. This visible encroachment of the desert lends the unpretentious, brick and stucco homes a simple heroism. They cling resolutely to their tidiness and prominent geometry: an almost tangible statement of Welsh defiance in the face of this wretched, remorseless climate.

Gaiman means 'Stony Point' in the Tehuelche Indian language. Not an imaginative stretch.

It's easy to find the grandest building in town, the Instituto Camwy, where Luned (pronounced LIN-ed) is principal. Not surprisingly, the school looks just like what the Welsh built best in the nineteenth century: a chapel. Inside, in a room that smells of schooling, the varnish on its floors and walls and bookshelves ripened to a deep, tortoise-shell brown, we find Luned and her minions. Luned is a stocky, middle-aged woman with a square face, intent, dark eyebrows and long grey hair pulled back in a bun. If Frida Kahlo had painted a Welsh mam, Luned would have been the result. 'Petra!' she announces in welcome. No, Pam, I say.

A bell rings. Some responsive urge deep in my being tells me to change classes. High school. I haven't gotten over it yet.

Luned is brusque and busy as principals tend to be, and takes an organizational approach to us, as if we're out of place and need to be put back in it. For now, it seems, our place is in her sister Tegai's care. Tegai is tall and trim and soft-spoken, with a gentle manner and delicate freckles around her cheekbones. An elderly prettiness clings to her features, and she's dressed in a sensible woollen skirt and tights, the very image of an unmarried blue-stocking in her later years. Tegai has less of a facility in English than her powerhouse of a sister, and it is to her that I address my first Welsh words in Gaiman (Luned's English is so good and her time so stretched that a pressing sense of urgency tongue-ties me in her presence).

Tegai shows us around the school. She, too, thinks I'm Petra. When it opened in 1906, privately funded by the Welsh community, courses were taught in Welsh, English and Spanish. Then it closed for a short time in the fifties and reopened as a public school, with classes taught exclusively in Spanish; English and French were the foreign languages. Recently, however, Luned succeeded in badgering authorities into reinstating Welsh at *Coleg Camwy* after a forty-year hiatus. This term in fact marks the first time students have had the option to study Welsh or French as their 'foreign' language (English is required). Out of a class of forty, sixteen have opted for Welsh, many of whom have no Welsh ancestry at all.

Tegai tells us that she teaches art classes here and is also curator of Gaiman's museum. I remember someone in Buenos Aires saying, '*Dych chi ddim yn nabod Tegai, dych chi ddim yn nabod Chubut,*' If you don't know Tegai, you don't know Chubut. When she leads us outside to her car – we're to drop our gear off at her sister Moelona's B & B – I can see tiny pleats in the fine, fair skin around her eyes. They're less evidence of age than of the dry, dusty wind of Patagonia, which works on the flesh like a kind of invisible sandpaper, wearing it into crevices in exactly the same way it erodes the wrinkled earth formations in the desert.

Moelona is another whom Chubut has aged prematurely. She's seventy-two, two years younger than my mother, but looks a decade older. She is even taller than Tegai, also trim, with a sweet, shy smile and a habit of tilting her chin down like a little girl when she speaks, pronouncing both English and Welsh with slow, deliberate, somewhat quaking care. Her posture is a silent missionary for Calvinist doctrine. When Moelona shows us to our room the first thing I see is a bilingual copy of the *Nuevo Testamento* in Spanish and English, placed next to my bed. Marguerite has one too.

In the past hour, modern plumbing aside, we haven't encountered a shred of evidence that Gaiman has been included in the passage of time.

Atgyweirio ✿ to Mend

My heart is skipping beats with sickening regularity: I've finally lost my notebook. The minute Tegai's Renault pulls back up in front of the *Instituto Camwy* I race into Luned's office and there it is, on the windowsill. Thank god. I go to put it with my journal and find that it now is missing. I break out in a sweat, hoping I've left it at Moelona's. Marguerite pats me on the shoulder in a way that scares me. I think I'm visibly losing control.

It's 10.15 a.m. 'You have been invited for coffee,' announces Luned. 'Next door. Go. You have forty-five minutes before Welsh class. Go. Go on.'

We go. Next door is a flat-roofed brick bungalow with Welsh dragon decals in the windows. A man with captivating eyebrows answers my knock. They're thick and dark and seem to be the launching pads of a perpetual, inquisitive enthusiasm. Beneath them their owner is bustling and efficient in an unfussy, rather Welsh manner, with the taut look of someone who scrubs himself shiny each morning. He's Gwilym Roberts.

Gwilym Roberts, Gwilym Roberts . . .

'*Gwilym Roberts!*' I capture the thought. '*Duw, duw, mae llythyr 'da fi amdanoch chi!*' Well, well, I have a letter for you! From the depths of my notebook I produce the letter Lawrence John wrote to Gwilym at Catherine Nagashima's house in Zushi, in the advent of the great typhoon. Gwilym is tickled. Even more so that we know Catherine. He went to university with her in Aberystwyth thirty years ago. I can almost hear the thud in my ears as Welsh worlds collide yet again.

Gwilym and I speak in Welsh. Gwilym and Marguerite speak in English. ('All right for her,' he tells me, 'for you *Saesneg* is the language of the *bradwr*, the traitor.') No matter whom he's address-ing his cadence never changes, always rides the heavy chop of Welsh intonation. It's only when I hear Gwilym speak that I realize how different the ruffled Welsh of Patagonia has sounded these past couple of weeks; it's like the difference between British and American English.

Gwilym is from Cardiff, but he speaks North Walian Welsh as do the Argentinians. I wonder if I sound American or South Walian to them. This is the third year he's volunteered to teach Welsh in Patagonia, not at the school, but to adults throughout eastern Chubut, about seventy in all. His pronunciation has a teacher's careful emphasis and clarity; in fact his words are so clear that I can almost see them as he speaks, and they're transparent. I have no trouble looking straight through them to the meaning inside.

Gwilym tells me that Gaiman's one pub, which we saw on our way to the school – a whitewashed, vaguely Mexican-looking spot inexplicably called *Y Dafarn Las*, the Blue Pub – opens at eleven-thirty at night, half an hour after pubs in Wales officially close. Given my impending exhaustion this is not good news, but it doesn't matter. Listening to Gwilym is like getting drunk on hundred-proof language. I can hear my own Welsh soar by association.

Eleven a.m. The bell rings over at the school. I put down my coffee cup mid-sip: this time my impulse to dash is appropriate. We race back and are shepherded into a small classroom where Marguerite has a coughing fit. Twice a week sixteen teenagers – many wearing white uniforms over their jeans that make them look like butchers' assistants – sprawl all over the desks in here cracking gum and trying to wrap their tongues around a two-thousand-year-old language, born on a continent nine thousand miles away. Their teacher, Gabriel Restucha, isn't much more than a teenager himself. Last year he and two other students from Gaiman went to Lampeter on the same programme I attended; this year six young people managed to go. All nine won hefty scholarships paid for by local townspeople. These grants were no mere acts of kindness. Gwilym made it clear that there's real poverty in Chubut. Friends of his work three jobs and still earn under a hundred dollars a month. When money is this short you don't squander it, you buy only essentials. I wouldn't have guessed that the pragmatic folk of Gaiman consider language an essential, up there in the imperative category with food, clothing and shelter, but they must.

'The rot set in two generations ago,' Gwilym had said of the decline of Welsh in Chubut. These new Welsh-speakers are Gaiman's response to that decline, its verbal skin graft on to a withering heritage, and local pride in their success is palpable. In fact, their success is so bloody evident it makes me envious (the students' near-fluency is a comment on either my thickness, or the relative ease with which Welsh may be learned without the crippling crutch of English).

Like me, Gabriel has no Welsh ancestry. Unlike me, he's up in front of a classroom drilling kids in the days of the week.

'*Sut mae dweud "Domingo" yn Gymraeg?*' he asks them, How is *Domingo* said in Welsh? *Domingo*? Marguerite and I look at each other like people who've stolen key pieces to one another's jigsaw puzzles.

'Sunday,' she whispers.

Ah. '*Dydd Sul*,' I respond, two beats late.

As Gabriel is prone to frequent backsliding into Spanish, Marguerite actually gets more out of class than I do. It's bizarre to listen to Welsh being taught without English holding its hand, but liberating, too. The Spanish prompt-words pry Welsh out of its English orbit, and give it the respect due a *foreign* language, much more than a *lesser-used* language is usually afforded. After the vocabulary exercises Gabriel gives me a chance to ask the kids the *Pam?* question. Why have they chosen to study an esoteric language like Welsh when French has so much more currency in the world? They stare at me like I'm crazed. Where would we use French around here? they ask, shrugging and looking at each other as if to say, All right, now ask us a real question, lady. Gaiman may be one of the few places in the world – outside of Wales – where practical people learn Welsh.

The second half of class is held outside, conducted by Gabriel's assistant, Eluned Wigley (known between us as Little Luned), who organizes a vicious vocabulary game. The students sit in two rows on a concrete playground with their legs outstretched, and each student is given the name of an animal in Welsh. When Eluned calls out two animal names – *ci*, for instance (dog), and *pysgodyn* (fish) – one student from each row jumps up, hop-scotches at high speed through the others' legs, then flings himself or herself back into place. The game finally breaks up when a wounded girl runs off yelping into a corner, but before any permanent damage is done to the private parts of Gaiman's future leaders.

Class ends on a calmer note, with Eluned sitting cross-legged in bellbottom jeans on the concrete, playing a small Welsh harp – historically the instrument of choice in Wales – that she's unzipped from a state-of-the-art nylon carrying case. If only weather-proof nylon had been available in the Middle Ages, a notably cold, wet, snowy time, things might have turned out differently for the Welsh bards.

Cnoi ✠ to Chew

One p.m. I can't believe the day's not even half over. We race back to Moelona's to retrieve my journal, find it sitting on her kitchen table amidst the plates, condiments and silverware of the midday meal. I barge in and interrupt her prayer. Without much thought I'd pegged Moelona as the piously baffled, ascetic sort, but I'm proved wrong. 'I thought it might be yours,' she says, handing me my dog-eared notebook. 'I would've read it but I had to fix lunch.' She delivers this in aged slow-motion, just the way she moves. Wry humour is the last thing I suspected of her.

Moelona lives near a seaweed-processing plant on the other side of the River Chubut from the town centre. Every time we come or go we're treated to a deeply pungent odour of marine decay, which seems at odds with the dust-blown aridity of this place. All the more appropriate, I suppose, that we have fish for lunch at Luned's.

In a town of meagre, streetfront bungalows, Luned's house has the grandeur of a country manor, set off by itself behind a stand of trees. It's the last structure on a side street before the road ends in a rough dune pocked with litter – a bookend between the finite dream of Y Wladfa and the frontier. Luned, Tegai, Moelona and their brother Arturo are great-grandchildren of the colony's founder, Michael D. Jones – or 'Miguel D. Jones' as the street signs refer to him – which makes them the First Family of Welsh Patagonia. The language rot that Gwilym so energetically combats in his students never gained a foothold amongst the Roberts clan. They may use Spanish with lesser mortals, but the old tongue is their linguistic currency of choice. I now understand why Chris Rees, director of the language programme at Lampeter, referred to Luned as Gymraes drwyadl, a thorough Welshwoman. Would he say that, I wonder, about Ursula? One holds the citizenship, the other the language. Both are beacons of Welshness in places that hundreds of generations of Welsh people never knew existed.

Our meal is a breakneck affair, downed between school bells. We're served good, hearty stuff: fish, pumpkin, boiled potatoes. A sense of duty weighs heavily upon me as I chew. Whenever I say anything in English I feel like I'm taking the lord's name in vain at the first Thanksgiving (like the settlers of Chubut, the Pilgrims were another group who came to the New World at the behest of a Calvinist god to make a point here on earth). Welsh has symbolic value in this household; those who can, speak it, with the exception of Little Luned, who's temporarily lodging here. She's an immensely likeable young woman, a student at the University of Wales, Bangor, come to Gaiman to practise her Spanish. Eluned's mother is a professional harpist, her father, the head of *Plaid Cymru* (members of what the author of *The Xeno-phobe's Guide* would call 'The Taffia') – hence her Welsh is impeccable. Too good, in fact. I revel in the knowledge that she and Big Luned keep slipping into Welsh with one another when she's supposed to be speaking Spanish. Precisely my problem with English in Wales, and the reason for the Trip.

How often do you come across Welsh impeding the learning of Spanish, the world's eighth most-spoken language? I love it.

Two p.m. Time to meet Gwilym at the bus stop. Like a country doctor Gwilym travels near and far treating the Patagonians' ailing vowels. This afternoon he has a class in the tiny hamlet of Dolavon, about twenty minutes away, and we're going with him as show-and-tell.

Luned walks us down to the main street. A flowered babushka over her braided bun has transformed her from a Welsh mam into the image of one of those round, Russian nesting dolls that children get as gifts. She's at her most endearing telling us of her struggle to lose weight.

Ateb ✿ to Answer

If I didn't know better (and come to think of it, I don't, really), I'd swear Dolavon were a two-dimensional film set for a spaghetti western. All we see is a main street, one house deep, and a lot of airborne dust. It smells as if there's a great deal of horse manure somewhere close at hand.

Gwilym's class is composed entirely of middle-aged and elderly women, all of whom spoke Welsh as children and are struggling to do so again. Why is it always the old women of the world who take the task of remembering so to heart? The ancient communicant who stopped to share her grapes with us in Thessaloniki – like these women, she, too, was practising an ancient language (though Welsh predates Christianity). It's always the women who go to church (or chapel), women who speak the old tongues. Why? Because after a lifetime of chores they finally have time? Because the old men their age are dead? Or perhaps because women who've been unselfish all their lives have nothing left in old age as uniquely theirs as the first language they spoke as children.

Maybe. It is also possible they've got a serious crush on their teacher. In Gwilym's case it's not hard to see why. He's a veritable gushing fountain of Welsh words and phrases in an otherwise arid landscape, lavishing wit and energy upon his students in a decidedly flirty way.

'*Wel*,' he teases, '*ces i llythyr heddiw trwy Pamela*.' I got a letter today through Pamela.

He fans one of them with it. *Ooooo*, they say.

'*A dych chi'n gwybod o ble mae e'n dod?*' And do you know where it came from?

Long, pregnant pause of dancing eyebrows. They're into this. They really want to know.

'*Des y llythyr o Docio! Dych chi'n credu? Tocio!*' The letter came from Tokyo! Can you believe it? Tokyo!

Hearts seem to be pumping pretty fast. Boy, can this man teach.

The students ask us questions, most of which Gwilym has to translate for me from ruffled, Patagonian murk into Welsh. How old are we? Thirty-five sends shock waves through the room. I don't know if this is because the blush of youth is still upon us or because we've reached this advanced age without marrying. Why don't I have a family in Wales? How can I make a living writing books about the Welsh?

Gwilym mercifully interrupts the question and answer to give everyone a recipe for a potato tart. Then he points at Marguerite and teaches us the expression *troi fy modiau*, twiddling my thumbs.

I try to tell the class I'm from the *Gogledd-De* part of the United States. Everyone looks quizzical. Gwilym asks me if I want to rephrase that. No, I insist, I know where I'm from, the *Gogledd-De*. There's consensus that if that's the way I want it, so be it. Only later do I realize I've declared myself to be from the North-South.

After class many of the women come up and kiss us, and Gwilym invites us to share the apple tart one of the students makes for him as a snack each week. He has another class coming up, but we have to catch the bus back to town if we're to stick to Luned's schedule.

Six p.m. On the ride back from Dolavon, as before, we were the only people on the bus in sunglasses. This time, however, the route took us through outlying farms and pastureland marked by runs of poplars, the trapezoids of shade they cast staking ad hoc property claims beneath the big sky. Sheep at last. I knew they had to be here somewhere. It was the first truly attractive landscape I'd seen in eastern Chubut, made possible by irrigation canals dug by the settlers after a perceptive woman named Rachel Jenkins had suggested the idea. Gwilym told us the area is so isolated that children gather by the roadside once a week to watch their favourite entertainment – the bus – kick up dust as it passes by.

In our absence the magic of relativity has transformed Gaiman into a little gem of urbanity. I just have time to buy myself a key ring with a Welsh dragon on it that says 'Gaiman, Chubut' and scrawl the Welish name *Superkiosko Bryn Gwyn* – White Hill Superkiosk – in my notebook before we head to the *Merched y Wawr* meeting. Inappropriately, the Women of the Dawn are assembling at dusk.

All three Roberts sisters are in attendance. Not surprisingly Luned takes charge. Tonight's programme is a report by Gabriel's two cohorts about their experiences in Lampeter, plus 'a brief speech by Petra about her trip'. Lordy, not again. For the first half hour I listen to a young wunderkind who seems to have learned Welsh the way some people quit smoking, with the ease of applying a patch to the skin; then his friend takes over and tells a story about meeting a wonderful Japanese professor in Lampeter who speaks fluent Welsh. This kid's accent is so thick that a good three minutes go by before I realize he's switched to Spanish, but I refuse to let the matter drop.

'*Oedd ei enw e Professor Mizutani?*' I ask, smouldering. Was his name Professor Mizutani?

'*Oedd,*' he responds. Yes.

Something cosmic hates me, but I decide to let it pass.

When he finishes Luned introduces me and says in English, 'Ask her only simple questions. She attended the programme three years ago.' I'm at once relieved and a little miffed. I talk on and on and on, because, well, why not?

Marguerite tells me later that Luned leaned over and whispered to her in wonderment during my speech that she hadn't known I spoke so well.

This doesn't surprise me. 'How could she?' I cry in self-defence. 'I haven't even had time to conjugate in her presence, much less mutate.' No question, my Welsh has improved on this trip, but it still bears the vulnerability of newness. In other words, it's undependable.

Trosglwyddo ✤ to Hand Over

Back past the citadel of mouldering seaweed to Moelona's. We can look forward to two more whiffs before the night is over.

As I feared, my whisky flask is empty. We split a candy bar for dinner. It's said that some people have more than thirty-two teeth; surely this day has more than twenty-four hours.

Nine-thirty. Choir practice for the townspeople of Gaiman. It's a round-up of the usual Welsh suspects, ages fourteen to seventy, at least: Luned and Tegai, Gwilym, the wunderkind, even the young man who won the solo hymn-singing competition in Trevelin last weekend.

Gwilym tells us it's a crying shame that while half the choir members are Welsh-speakers and the other half are learners, the director – herself a fluent speaker – addresses the group only in Spanish.

'She's probably worried about offending somebody,' he says, with more accusation than empathy in his voice. 'I mean, we *sing* in Welsh, why can't we *speak* in Welsh?'

In Singapore Eleri'd had a keen, no-nonsense quality to her direction, but tonight's practice is the equivalent of musical boot camp. The director is a talented finger-snapper who's worn a track suit to practice, doubtless in anticipation of working up a sweat. She makes the group repeat Welsh phrases ad nauseam until they ring true in her ear. I'm beyond telling the difference.

It's funny how many male voice choir directors in Wales are women: lone female beacons in a sea of male voices, the musical mams responsible for making the boyos sing on key. It's a happy corollary of the Welsh diaspora, it occurs to me, that there aren't enough men out here to sing by themselves: women finally get to join in and have some of the fun.

I, however, identify with a bored toddler making gurgling noises as her parents sing up a storm. It's happening, I think to myself: this kid may be drooling, but she's *becoming Welsh* before my eyes. She's unconsciously absorbing her birthright of sounds and scales – an unbroken transmission of Welsh culture millennia old – as I only listen. Sheep, music and language. For reasons beyond guessing these things have thrived in the desert.

In the midst of a song, voices suspended in intricate harmony, I see Luned leave her seat and tortuously thread her way toward us from one end of the room to the other, until she reaches Marguerite. She whispers something into her ear. Then she embarks on the long journey back, the director scowling fiercely all the while.

'What did she say?'

'She said O. J. Simpson was acquitted. She said she thought we'd want to know.'

When practice ends a man comes over and starts chatting amiably to me in Welsh. Though his accent is slight he's one hundred per cent incomprehensible. I fear I've been given only so many words to speak and understand each day, and today I've run the well dry.

As we leave he makes a noble effort to speak in English. 'I must learn better English. And you,' he says, 'you must learn better Welsh.'

Moelona is waiting up for us. 'I just wanted to tell you,' she says carefully to me, 'how well you spoke today. So much better than those boys at the Merched y Wawr meeting.'

Llwyddo ✿ to Succeed

Morning in this great flat absence of all that is Wales.

No one is surprised we've come to write about the town. Reporters do it all the time, they say. Film crews, journalists, people with microphones. The Princess of Wales is coming next month. 'Not *our* princess,' the citizens of Gaiman politely imply, and it's clear they're speaking not as Argentinians but as Welsh patriots. Still, they maintain, they'll be polite.

Before I came to Patagonia I'd read in *Ninnau*, Luned's brother's newspaper, that some people in Chubut refer to themselves as '*Anglos*' to differentiate them from Argentinians of Spanish or Italian stock. These folks must be bound and gagged somewhere, because we haven't met any of them. Arturo Roberts once told me that his grandparents considered themselves Welsh – his grandfather, he insisted, was killed in a bank robbery by Butch Cassidy – and his parents called themselves Welsh Patagonians; he and his sisters are simply Argentinians, but their cultural markers, from language to manners, remain those of nineteenth-century Wales. I'd love to hear how their generation responds when Gaiman's children, sent to Lampeter to study language, start bringing Gorky's Zygotic Mynci CDs back home to the Chubut Valley.

Over breakfast of soft-boiled eggs and toast Moelona's husband David tells us that without a triad of interlocking motivations for building a life in the desert – spiritual, political (meaning linguistic) and economic – *Y Wladfa* would never have maintained its cultural identity. David chats while Moelona stands at the stove grilling toast above an open gas flame, an iconic image ready to be transferred forever to my memory: knees locked behind her, calves thrust backward making an S-curve of her lower profile. An oddly gymnastic musculature for so frail a woman.

David doesn't actually speak Welsh; he is the son of English missionaries, born in Patagonia but educated in England. I ask him why he came back here. Silently, in extreme slow motion, without looking at her, he aims his thumb at Moelona, who twitches as if a bug flew in her ear. David is even taller and frailer and slower than she. His eyes smile faster than his mouth.

I don't tell David, I don't tell anyone, that R. Bryn Williams, the historian of record of *Y Wladfa*, called it 'one of the Welsh nation's most magnificent failures'. Makes you wonder how many magnificent failures Wales has had (I'm afraid the answer is quite a few: Owain Glyndŵr's brief uprising and the unforeseen collapse of the coal industry rush immediately to mind). Williams was right. *Y Wladfa* has not succeeded in its goal of providing a secure home for the Welsh language, but then again, neither has Wales, where only recently, a century after the settlers sailed on the *Mimosa*, have such sentiments even been articulated as a national goal.

For now, then, let a small, personal success tide over those seeking a happy ending. We visit the bank. A problem with phone lines makes a cash advance impossible. (Did I say happy? How about bittersweet?) A helpful, youngish clerk who speaks a little English is summoned to explain the situation. This is clearly difficult for her, and in spontaneous frustration, more to herself than to us, she mutters something in Spanish that ends in *Cymraeg*.

'*Cymraeg?*' I cry in excitement. '*Dw i'n siarad Cymraeg!*' I speak Welsh!

'*Chi? Mae Americanes sy'n siarad Cymraeg?*' An American woman who speaks Welsh?

We both jump into the old language and chatter excitedly. Marguerite and I still don't get our money, but at least I know why. This is better than being complimented by a Roberts sister. When you can use Welsh at the bank, you know you've made it.

Tour buses are lined up today in front of *Casa de Té Plas y Coed*. We pass them by and walk out of town, a fierce, operatic wind at our backs. It's cold as we climb a flat-topped hill overlooking Gaiman, past clay hovels carved precariously into its crumbling flank. At the top the wind rams us so hard we actually stumble. From here the world is a barren brown void, a bowl of great distances with nothing in it. Beneath our feet, their grey slate headstones battling the wind as they themselves fought it in life, are the Welsh Patagonian dead.

Marguerite is unnerved, and kicks uneasily at a creeping plant that trails throughout the graves, a desert version of undersea coral. New life made from dead things. Her cough reminds her too much of her own mortality, she says, and huddles by a wall seeking shelter as I walk among the markers and photos and names, all borrowed out of context from a green land too far away. *Gwalia T. de Carbonelli, bu farw 1956*, 'Wales' Carbonelli, died 1956. The grave photo shows a woman who looks a lot like Judy Garland. Nearby lies Walter Caradog Jones, whose Welsh inscription says he was born in January 1863, in North Wales, and died in Gaiman, November 1926. He must've been two years old when his parents emigrated to this country.

The cemetery is an essay on bleakness: the dead and their view of nothing. Still, its tombstones stand straight and tall as Moelona, as the poplars and the courageous walls of Gaiman's compact houses. Resolute is a word I must learn in Welsh.

It's a little disturbing to go from the graveyard to Gaiman's Museo Gales, and see the things these people used in life, now on display as artefacts polished and dusted and labelled by Tegai Roberts. Rarely does one get the chance to feel the span of elapsed lifetimes encapsulated in ten minutes' imagining, but we get that chance today. Tegai greets us, though says she must run off to do her weekly radio show.

'It's about Wales,' she apologizes, 'but I speak in Spanish.'

Two cops patrol the museum's lovingly cared-for collection, investigating an overnight robbery of six pesos from the donation box. I hear the tick of a clock on the wall behind me; Gaiman is a member of the temporal world after all.

Treiglo ❦ to Mutate

At the end of Gaiman's main street, just after a bend in the road, is the Wonderland of trash. Rocketships made of soda cans. Gardens of plastic flower petals peeled from bottles of dishwashing liquid. It's a park cryptically called *El Desafío*, The Challenge, a bit of whimsical lunacy between the Welsh and either the desert or their worst landfill nightmares. My guidebook calls *El Desafío* 'Gaiman's answer to Disneyland'. I'd call it a secular, overwrought Christmas display made entirely from recyclables.

The man responsible for this lark is a retired folk artist who calls himself Herculito, Little Hercules. Herculito converses with visitors via hundreds of hand-painted messages in Spanish: 'This park is being created by a single man since April of 1980. Respect his effort, don't damage it.' 'Not the 12 works of Hercules, but the 50 works of Herculito.' 'Not something of this world nor another world, just something different.'

If Herculito doesn't mind, this is what I'll say the next time someone asks me why I've gone to so much trouble to learn Welsh. While it is very much a language of this world – at least of four of the seven continents, anyway – everywhere, even in its own country, Welsh is just something different. Something to be recycled, saved, re-membered from the detritus of the past into a language that people from different countries can use together at the bank. It's a lesson in the power of mutation, just like Herculito's.

It's a clear night, and chilly. I've left Marguerite home at Moelona's to write our one hundred and fifty-first, and hopefully final, post-card of the trip. She's clearly headed for a bad case of laryngitis. Tonight Gwilym is holding a late discussion group for three women in their early forties, all of whom have the kind of snug relationship with Welsh that comes from long association, a sort of complacency-by-inheritance. I'm still being polite with the language, and therefore muster a far clearer, more careful accent, but they have the better vocabularies.

I ask them about *El Desafio*. Neither Gwilym nor the women can give me any details. It's as if they've only heard of the place by rumour, and not often at that. The park is less than a two-minute walk from *Instituto Camwy*, where we're meeting tonight. I guess Herculito doesn't get out to choir practice much.

Gwilym changes the subject by asking me briefly to describe my trip for his students. When I come to Holland he stops me. 'I once met a Dutch woman who speaks Welsh like a native,' he enthuses. 'I think her name is Effie Wiltens.'

The last five months blow away like so much dust in the Patagonian wind.

After class I begin to walk home when one of the women calls after me, her voice rising at the end in what sounds like a question. I can't understand her accent, so I smile and nod, and keep walk-ing. She calls again, then finally runs after me and points to her car, a kind, expectant look on her face. She mimes opening a door, then holding a steering wheel. I accept her offer of a ride home.

In the three minutes it takes to drive over the River Chubut and past the seaweed plant, we hold the Welsh language as a newly spun web between us, each terrified of demolishing our thin thread of understanding. She speaks no English and I no Spanish. Throughout class her accent tortured the sweet Welsh sounds, while sleepiness stole words from my tongue just as I was about to speak them. Now we both improve a little to meet the other halfway, relieved to admit to another learner how hard it is to speak this old language, buoyed out here in the darkness by the absence of perfection.

Everywhere I've been people who speak Welsh too well have intimidated me. Rosemary, Eleri, Luned: all pirouette atop the competitive pyramid of the Welsh language, yet they have another trait in common as well. All of these women have placed an emphasis on knowing over speaking. On content above form. Luned and Eleri were organizers, Rosemary needed someone to talk to. Tim, Iori and Gwilym, by contrast, indulged form over content, and volleyed words to me as coaches do tennis balls, caring less about what was said than how I said it. If there are gender conclusions to be drawn from this, make them yourself.

The car pulls up in front of Moelona's and I get out. Over my head thousands of sharp stars tear small holes in the night. I smile to find the Southern Cross suspended directly above David and Moelona's house. That would make them happy. Atop it runs the Milky Way like a dim stripe down a skunk's back. It's called Caer Gwydion in Welsh – Gwydion's Fort – named for a mercurial shapeshifter in the Fourth Branch of 'The Mabinogi'. Mutation is the name of the game in Wales. Even more so in these outposts of Welshness that scatter this planet.

Waving goodbye, Gwilym's student calls something to me in Welsh, but I can't hear her. I've already shut the door.

EPILOGUE

Gorffen ✿ to Finish

Paid cheto ar Pam, Don't cheat on Pam
[because her voice is like a toy and every
time I'm near her I feel like a sandwich].

Gorky's Zygotic Mynci, '*Paid Cheto
Ar Pam*', from '*Bwyd Time*'

Listen to the band: don't cheat on me. But they'll cheat on you if you're not careful. *Cheto* is no more Welsh than I am. *Twyllo* is the word that means 'to cheat' in the old tongue.

I've been cheating on you too. Perceptive readers will have noticed something funny about this book, maybe by the third, fourth page. It's written in English.

A story about running away from English can only be told in English. That's a good one, isn't it? Another joke for that old Celtic comedian, the god of Irony. Every word I've written has carried me further away from my last Welsh conversation downwind of the Gaiman seaweed factory, further away from the language I travelled so far to learn. Telling my story has, to a degree, undone my Welsh. Such is the fate of a minority language. I will now and forever remember the Trip in English.

As for the other Trip – *Y Trip, Nofel Antur i Ddysgwyr*, my adventure novel for learners – Charles the drug lord got bashed on the head in the end by one of his own peons. We, however, made it home alive, though Marguerite did succumb to a fierce coughing sickness and a long period of speechlessness. It was another nicely symmetrical irony that she lost her voice the very night we crossed the border into Brazil. When she finally got the opportunity to speak Portuguese, nothing came out of her mouth. Exactly five months earlier I'd lost my voice in Wales.

Wales. *Cymru. Gymru.* Which one will it be?

Once on the bus, somewhere out in the vast negation of earth and sky called the Patagonian night, Marguerite commented that it felt odd, unfinished, to be heading home to the United States. Wales, she said, should be our final destination.

I've felt exactly the same way, but to return to Wales is to chase a phantom of sentiment, or perhaps tidiness, that evades the lesson I've learned by speaking my way into terra incognita: there can be no geographic endpoint to this Trip. There is only an unreality ending, something as perishable and invisible as an idea, because *Cymru* is my final destination, and *Cymru* – home of fellow countrymen and women – is a place that only comes into being through speech. I guess you could call it the consequence of language.

Wales, by contrast, is a beautiful, wet, green, rocky protrusion that keeps the Irish Sea from breaking upon the Cotswolds. It needs the Welsh language in order to survive, but the language doesn't need it (in the best of all possible worlds, that is; having been so beleaguered for so long, Welsh will require all the protection Wales can give it). Take the long view: the tongue called *Cymraeg* was once spoken in what are now parts of England and France as well as Wales. Boundaries and countries, however, are subject to mutation by politics and time. From this perspective Wales is no more than a vessel temporarily cupping the Welsh language – the few swallows that history hasn't evaporated nor invaders yet drunk.

Languages are not territorial creatures, but the people who speak them are, and we're the ones who try to bind speech and place together. In my own country there's a battle brewing over the pre-eminence of English. Many Americans believe that their national identity is inseparable from the English language, and have begun an 'English Only' campaign to combat the rise of other tongues, especially Spanish. By this argument the entity called the United States is dependent upon English, but English, since we all know it originally came from somewhere else (I hate to break this to my compatriots), is surely not dependent upon the United States.

Cymru is something that happens whenever people speak Welsh, and occasionally when they don't. It happens when Ursula explains in Japanese to a bewildered Tokyo taxi driver that she's *Welsh*, not American, not English, but *Welsh*; it happens when Pat and Eirlys speak Wenglish on the phone in Singapore; it happens when an Argentinian conductor nitpicks in Spanish, when choir members follow her lead and sing in Welsh, when a toddler unconsciously takes in both. *Cymru* is a place waiting to be spoken into life at any moment anywhere around the globe, a legion of terrae incognitae poised for exploration through speech, music, memory, enthusiasm and, certainly, beer.